QDA

_ A QUEER DISABILITY ANTHOLOGY _

_ A QUEER DISABILITY ANTHOLOGY _

RAYMOND LUCZAK
Editor

SQUARES & REBELS
MINNEAPOLIS, MN
USA

IN GRATITUDE

The editor wishes to thank David Cummer for his editorial insights as well as Jennifer Bartlett, Bryan Borland, Christopher Bram, John R. Killacky, and Adam Marsnik for their assistance with this project. He is also grateful for Lennard J. Davis and Scott Jordan Harris for their permission to be quoted at length in his introduction.

COPYRIGHT

Squares & Rebels
PO Box 3941
Minneapolis, MN 55403-0941
squaresandrebels@gmail.com

Printed in the United States of America.
ISBN: 978-1-941960-02-8
Library of Congress Control Number: 2015911322

A First Squares & Rebels Edition

CONTENTS

"Without deviation from the norm,
progress is not possible."
—Frank Zappa

RAYMOND LUCZAK

No More Inspiration Porn
Introduction

Half a lifetime ago, in the fall of 1988, when I first saw Cook Friedman in a large room at the Gay and Lesbian Community Center, I had no idea who he was. He was lanky with a head of thick curly hair and a sexy smile, and he sat with a wooden cane. I had just moved to New York City, and in those pre-Internet days, there wasn't an easy way of connecting with the Deaf LGBT community. I decided to try the next best option, which was EDGE (Education in a Disabled Gay Environment); it was listed among the groups that met at the GLCC.

Folding chairs were arranged in a circle. A tall older man with a thick mustache looked embarrassed by a young Deaf man with limited motor skills blatantly fixated on him. An older feminine lesbian sitting in a wheelchair gave me the nicest smile of anyone I saw. A clean-shaven man who didn't seem to be physically disabled joined us. There weren't many of us, but because there was no American Sign Language (ASL) interpreter, I wasn't sure how well I'd be able to lipread and follow the discussion. Luckily everyone was fairly easy to lipread. Cook turned out to be the person in charge. He was funny and kind.

Afterward we became friends. He lived in a tiny railroad flat a few blocks away from GLCC. I was agog at the size of his vinyl record collection. He loved music, and he knew where each album was. His record player seemed to have its own shrine where the walls of his cramped living room were graced with records squeezed into shelves. He was very proud of the fact that the author Christopher Bram, his neighbor and friend, modeled his character Jack Arcalli's home in his novel *In Memory of Angel Clare* on his apartment. Cook told me stories about the halcyon days of the 1960s and 1970s when he dated Judy Garland's last husband and partied in St. Mark's Baths and worked in a record store on West 8th Street where he met John Lennon and

Yoko Ono as customers and danced all night long in discos. He was working as a hairdresser during the 1980s when he started to notice that his body wasn't always cooperating with him. He felt strangely uncoordinated. Then he learned why: multiple sclerosis.

I had heard of MS before. My first sign language teacher had it. When my deafness was diagnosed at the age of two and half years, I was immediately outfitted with a bulky hearing aid in a chest harness and brought to an elementary school near my home for speech and lipreading lessons. Sign language was forbidden.

In my small hometown, there was an older Deaf man who was a high school dropout from the Michigan School of the Deaf and he worked as a dishwasher for the Holiday Inn, although I wouldn't know these two facts for a number of years. I did notice an incontestable fact about him: on summer days, while sitting in front of a bar on Aurora Street, he always seemed to be teaching someone how to fingerspell and sign. I remember a few occasions while in the car my mother turned my head away not to look at him. This made me doubly curious about his hands. I sensed they were capable of saying something more than just directional gestures, but I didn't understand that it was a fully-realized *language* on a par with English.

Then I was mainstreamed full-time in a Catholic school for five years. I felt increasingly suicidal. My hearing classmates treated me as the runt of their class, and I cried a great deal. Then one day I turned off my faucet of emotion completely; it would take me years to allow myself to feel unfettered emotion in front of a stranger. My face revealed nothing for fear of being bullied again. It didn't help that my own hearing family—I had eight siblings—never slowed down their dinner conversations enough to enable me to follow them. First I had to figure who was speaking and then *what* they were talking about, and if the subject was changed in mid-course, I had to figure *that* out all over again. I grew up feeling orphaned *and* a second-class citizen in my own home.

One day I came across my older brother David's *Boy Scout Handbook*. In it were the two most life-altering pages of any book I'd ever seen: it showed the manual alphabet, mistakenly called "Indian Sign Language." I took a flashlight and the book, and hid inside a closet where I learned each handshape. I fell in love with the concept of being able to say *something* with my hands. Then I realized I needed to save myself from those increasingly dark feelings. I had to tell my speech therapist that I needed to learn Sign. My oddly assertive request surprised her. That summer of 1980, when I was 14 years old, I met Mary Hoffman, who was hearing. She came to my house one morning and we sat outside under the apple tree in the backyard. She was an extremely skinny woman with long hair, and her fingers were like sticks with fingernails. She brought along a binder in which she'd mimeographed a number of pages from a sign language dictionary. She said that she would teach me approximately 20 signs per session.

It turned out that wasn't enough for me. I ended up learning the entire book in our first meeting, so she tested my reception skills. I immediately—and correctly—said, "Home. School. Church." She was pleased yet nonplussed. She didn't know any more signs. She didn't talk about grammar or syntax of ASL; I had learned only vocabulary. We signed to each other in the English word order. I began to feel a sense of hope. My hands were my future, but I wasn't sure how or what.

Then came the days when she unexpectedly couldn't show up. My mother told me that Ms. Hoffman had MS. I couldn't imagine what it was like not to be able to move much suddenly one day, and being able to get around the next. I thought that was so weird. Yet I've never forgotten the fact that a disabled person taught me the beginnings of Sign. Four years later I ended up attending Gallaudet University in Washington, D.C. I blossomed at last in ASL and came out as a gay man.

So when Cook said, "I have MS," I mentioned my first sign language teacher. I didn't know much about MS, though. He then laid bare the reality of living with the disease. Some days it got so bad that it'd take him two hours to get out of bed. It didn't matter how badly he needed to pee, and the bathroom door was right next to the head of his bed. Sometimes he had to plan ahead the use of his daily energy allotment so he could do only essential tasks; he had an overweight dog named Fred who needed walking up and down Perry Street. Diet was key to controlling his symptoms. But what really got me was his honesty about his love life. He said that he couldn't always control his erections so if he were to have sex with a hot guy, he couldn't count on his penis to get hard; sometimes he became unexpectedly erect ten minutes after the guy left. That, for me, was a revelation. I began to wonder what it really meant to be queer and disabled, and I haven't stopped wondering ever since. Through his example, Cook taught me the value of compassion and empathy for the truly marginalized, and the need for shame-free dialogue about a person's sexual needs and necessary adjustments.

Back then, when the AIDS epidemic swept through New York, I'd never thought that the Supreme Court of the United States would rule on this day that lesbians and gay men had a right to marry and be recognized as couples in every legal sense of the word. I don't think anyone of us would've thought this historic moment possible in our lifetime.

I feel overwhelmed with emotion. Many of my friends share their exuberance on my Facebook newsfeed. I reflect on the LGBT community's extraordinary progress since the first night of Stonewall Riots on June 28, 1969. Not even a half-century, and we've truly arrived.

Except that we haven't.

The LGBT community is commendable for their efforts to be more accessible and inclusive. Many of my Deaf straight friends are envious of the fact that our Pride festivals often have ASL interpreters onstage. Diversity is a marvelous concept. It means that we must pay close attention to those who are underrepresented in our community and work with them for better inclusion and enlightened understanding.

But there's a teeny-tiny problem. In an essay for *The Chronicle of Higher Education* ("Why Is Disability Missing From the Discourse on Diversity?"), Lennard J. Davis points out that:

> While our current interest in diversity is laudable, colleges rarely think of disability when they tout diversity. College brochures and Web sites depict people of various races and ethnicities, but how often do they include, say, blind people or those with Parkinson's disease? Or a deaf couple talking to each other in a library, or a group of wheelchair users gathered in the quad? When disability does appear, it is generally cloistered on the pages devoted to accommodations and services.
>
> It's not that disability is simply excluded from visual and narrative representations of diversity in college materials; it

is rarely even integrated into courses devoted to diversity. Anthologies in all fields now include theoretical perspectives devoted to race, gender, and sometimes social class, but disability is almost never included. Indeed, in my field, literary theory and cultural studies, *The Norton Anthology of Theory & Criticism* had only one essay on disability in its thousands of pages, and that was removed in its second edition. (Full disclosure: I wrote the essay.)

I recently gave a talk about disability and diversity at a major university, and a scholar of African-American history seemed nonplussed that I would consider disability as on a par with the oppression of people of color. Indeed, one famous disability-studies scholar who taught at a historically black college was denied tenure (subsequently reversed) for having made the analogy between race and disability.

I would argue that disability isn't just missing from a diversity consciousness, but that disability is antithetical to diversity as it now stands. . . I would add that diversity also represses difference that isn't included under the better-known categories of race, ethnicity, and gender. In other words, diversity can exist only as long as we discount physical, cognitive, and affective impairments. . . .

Courses on diversity are intended to celebrate and empower underrepresented identities. But disability seems harder for people without disabilities to celebrate and see as empowering. The idea presented by diversity is that any identity is one we all could imagine having, and that all identities are worthy of choosing. But the single identity one cannot (and, given the ethos of celebrating diversity, should not) choose is to be disabled. No one should make the choice that his or her partner be disabled, or that their child be born with a disability. So how could disability legitimately be part of the diversity paradigm, since it speaks so bluntly against the idea of choice and seems so obviously to be about helplessness and powerlessness? If diversity celebrates empowerment, disability seems to be the poster student for disempowerment.

Even though a good 20% of Americans are disabled in some way, we are rarely acknowledged. And when we are, our existence is often a source of inspiration porn, especially on social media. In a scintillating piece ("Despicable Memes") for *Slate*, Scott Jordan Harris writes:

> Social media exerts pressure on users to create or share posts that are immediately eye-catching and different, and to present them with the wittiest captions they can compose. Many of us who are disabled will always be eye-catching and different. And perhaps that is why we are increasingly mocked in memes. Other Internet memes do not mock people with disabilities but instead subject us to a peculiar kind of veneration. They are known as "inspiration porn," and many disabled people, including the activist Stella Young, who gave a TED talk on the subject, strongly object to them for the stereotypes they strengthen. An example of inspiration porn might be a photograph of a child playing wheelchair basketball, or of man with no legs doing pull-ups, with the caption "What's your excuse?"
>
> As a metaphor, a man with no legs doing pull-ups possibly has some slight value—it could suggest making the best of the talents you have, not mourning those you don't— but as an image of a human being, it's shallow and unhelpful. It suggests disability can be overcome by blunt effort. Many disabled people, me included, have conditions that mean we cannot undertake strenuous exercise. I could stand up from my wheelchair and walk a short distance, but I could never manage a pull-up.
>
> The "what's your excuse?" culture hurts us by suggesting we are making insufficient effort not to be disabled. If we were better motivated, it implies, we wouldn't be in such difficulties. . . . Most obnoxiously, inspiration porn suggests that disabled people only exist to inspire the able-bodied, just as memes that mock us suggest we only exist for their amusement.

Thus I proclaim: no more inspiration porn.

☙

The concept of "normal" is a very dangerous one. It implies a standard that one must meet in order to be accepted. In fact, if you think about it, the expectation of "normal," however defined by any religion or society, could be considered *the* root of all prejudice, including homophobia, ableism, racism, audism, ageism, and so on. Disability is a slap in the face of normality.

We are much more than wheelchairs, hearing aids, canes, oxygen tanks, and service animals. We are *you*, and *you* are us.

The mix of disability and sexuality may be too much for those raised on the Hollywood- and adult film industry-inspired standards of beauty and stamina. We disabled are not superheroes nor as helpless as you think, and we are tired of being Oscar bait for able-bodied performers. You won't find stories here to inspire one to seek salvation in the arms of Jesus, or about people who've conquered their disabilities to become "normal" again. We disabled are used to living with hard questions out of necessity. We are a nagging reminder that not everyone is welcomed into the open arms of the LGBT community. Of course, we do appreciate the efforts at accessibility being made at various Pride festivals and other events around the country, but if we remain seen as unworthy of your friendships—romantic and otherwise—not much will change.

And yet: I keep faith, much like how so many of us held steadfast in our long struggle for marriage equality, that things will—unfortunately *very* gradually—change for the better. It is critical to maintain an ongoing conversation within the LGBT community what it means to be physically, mentally, and emotionally different. It is like coming out all over again.

I remain grateful for the existence of two anthologies in particular: Victoria A. Brownworth and Susan Raffo's *Restricted Access: Lesbians on Disability* (Seal Press, 1999), and Bob Guter and John R. Killacky's *Queer Crips: Disabled Gay Men and Their Stories* (Routledge, 2003). (Disclosure: I have two pieces in the latter book.) Here, through the fantastic work of 48 writers in poetry, fiction, and nonfiction, *QDA: A Queer Disability Anthology* expands on the dialogue that these two prior collections began by including non-binaries and respecting gender fluidities. This book is a snapshot of the queer disability community right now. It's my hope that *QDA* will similarly inspire future collections of conversations about queerness, disability, *and* other intersectionalities.

Here we are, coming out not only as queer and disabled but also as *human beings* in these pages. We are all made of stories. Yet, as with any meaningful social change, mere "understanding" on your part isn't enough. Stop keeping us at arm's length. Interact with us. Make friends. Maybe you'll fall in love. (Hey, you never know!)

Loving one another without fear, stigma, and embarrassment shouldn't have to be this hard. Ignorance and prejudice are the worst barriers of all, and the fix, happily, doesn't require a doctor.

Raymond Luczak
Minneapolis, Minnesota
26 June 2015

Truth or Dare: Image Descriptions

First Panel. A girl with thick, curly hair wearing a t-shirt and shorts sits almost cross-legged on a bed against a hazy background. Above her are the narrator's words: "I had my first gay moment in fifth grade without realizing it."

Second Panel. A half-circle of five girls sit on a large bed in a room. The girl from the first panel is the second from the right. Above them reads: "One night all the deaf girls had a sleepover at the most popular deaf girl's house. Naturally, we played Truth or Dare."

Third Panel. The narrator continues: "One girl had developed very early, so compared to the rest of us, she was Angelina Jolie. Naturally, she was dared to flash us." On the far left, we see the back of the girl flashing her breasts at the other four girls. The first two girls on the left are in shock, covering their eyes. The narrator sits quietly as the girl on her left covers her eyes. Words like "EEEE," "FLASH!!!" and "AAAA!" are strewn around the girls.

Fourth Panel. The narrator says: "Everyone screamed and covered their eyes. It never even occurred to me that this was the socially acceptable response as opposed to staring. Which I did, shamelessly." The narrator's face is imbued with a deep blush. Someone off-panel exclaims: "Oh my God! Bex's looking!"

Fifth Panel. The narrator concludes: "Total pandemonium." As she sits still with a slight frown, the other four girls leap about with crudely-drawn expressions of horror and shock amidst oversized words such as "EEEEEEE" and "AAAAAA" cast like a rollercoaster in the background.

JAX JACKI BROWN

The Politics of Pashing

I have been doing a lot of public pashing of late with my girlfriend. She and I have pashed in the usual places: cafés, train stations, parks . . . just everywhere and anywhere, really. You know how it is. (For the record, a kiss is quicker, whereas a pash is prolonged, possibly more passionate and well usually involving more tongue. I like the word "pash" because it created nice alliteration.)

Maybe we are in a lust bubble, or maybe it's because we are in Melbourne, Australia where it's "hip to be queer," but we haven't noticed any visibly homophobic responses. We have seen a few shocked faces, staring as our lips part, but I think that's due to something else entirely.

See, there is something about me—other than my bright red spiky hair, and propensity to pash women with reckless abandon—which makes me stand out in a crowd (or should I say sit out in a crowd?): I'm a wheelchair user.

I'm used to feeling as though I'm on show—watched, observed, and positioned as the "other" in public spaces, which is a common experience for people with visible difference. I play with the fact that I'm eye-catching. I dress up for it. It's part of why I dye my hair so red; why I wear my rainbow neckerchief, leather jacket, and Doc Martens; why I overlay this body—this delightfully different body—with signals of queer sexuality. I like to trouble the assumption that people with disabilities are asexual.

People with disabilities are routinely viewed as not having a sexuality. I want my body to state clearly that I have a sexuality, and that I know what it is and how to use it! This pride-filled proclamation of my sexuality is also an act of resistance against the myth that those of us with non-normative bodies are sexually undesirable, weak or passive.

For this reason, every kiss is a statement. So when she bends down to take my face in her hands, and I run my fingers through her hair as she carefully avoids touching my spike (because she knows that would be messing with a key aspect of of my identity), maybe we are kissing in a way that looks so outside of what people are used to, that we don't get the hisses under the breath. Maybe we shake up the understanding of which bodies can be sexual so intensely that people become speechless.

This is an example of what I refer to as my "crip privilege"—the few perks that living with a disability affords you. You get to go to the front of the queue, you're let in first to the special seating at the movies, and so on. When we make out, people struggle to process how we kiss, let alone how we have sex. Queer sexuality and disability places me so far outside the realms of the everyday that it renders people silent. It is a display of queer, non-normative, crip lust that most people don't want to think about, leaving me able to pash my lover in public without a nasty comment.

This is part of why I'm proud of my differences—they allow me to live and love in unique and interesting ways. But like anyone living with a marginalized identity, maintaining pride takes practice, and sometimes it can feel like a never-ending battle. Sometimes I don't want to know that publicly kissing my girlfriend is eye-catching because most people haven't seen a dyke in a wheelchair having a pash. Until disability and sexual diversity become more visible in the media, my kissing in public will never be a simple act. My pashes will always be political, enacting a complex interplay between my queer and disability identities, and my pride in these two parts of myself.

Publicly kissing my ex-lover, who also had a visible disability—now there was an act of resistance! Our kisses were about as unconventional as you could get, and very wet (mouth control wasn't a strong point for us). We kissed to turn heads, and we kissed to fight against the myth that nice girls don't kiss like that, and nice girls certainly don't kiss each other like that.

We also kissed because we couldn't keep our hands or mouths off each other. I love feeling so into someone that I don't care where I am, or who might be watching. I know this speaks to my privilege of being able to be out and proud—I live in a metropolitan city, where if someone did say something homophobic, a passing ally may call them on it.

I'm also very aware that over 50% of women with disabilities are single, and for many, finding healthy, respectful relationships is a life-long struggle.

Finding people to pash has never really been a challenge for me. And while kissing in public holds the weight of my marginality, it also holds the promise of losing my mind in the moment, and transcending my markers of identity, even as they continue to be re-read and reinscribed by outsiders looking in.

An unexamined public kiss is a privilege, enjoyed by those who are not marked out as the "other" by a stranger's gaze. For me, a kiss is a political act of lustful resistance, whether I want it to be or not because it highlights those things people don't want to think about let alone talk about—that people with disabilities are sexual and that some of us are gay.

KENNY FRIES

Disability Made Me Do It
or Modeling for the Cause

In 1991, I am living in Provincetown when I get a call from Tom, a local artist. Tom has been hired to do the drawings for an updated version of a well-known guide to gay sex. "I want to make sure different types of men are represented in the drawings," he begins. "I wanted to talk to you about how to best portray a disabled man having sex."

"Don't use a wheelchair to signify the man is disabled," I tell him.

"Where can I find a disabled guy to model for me?" he asks.

"Beats me," I say.

"Would you do it?" There is a pause. "I'll take photos of you having sex and use them as the source for what I'll draw."

"Sex with whom?" I ask.

"That's easy," Tom assures me.

Why did I so easily agree to model for the cause?

In 1988, I was working for a San Francisco theater services organization when I was asked out to lunch by a man interested in getting to know his way around the theater community. "I was an understudy in *A Chorus Line*," the man tells me as we sit down for what I expect to be a business lunch. "What can you tell me about directing a play in San Francisco?"

Over salad I tell him what I know about getting a start: classes, the theaters, some people I suggest he call.

After the waiter removes the plates from the table, my lunchmate looks across the table at me and asks, matter-of-factly: "Do you like to be humiliated?"

I know right away what he is talking about, where this conversation is leading, even though no one has ever asked me that question before. "Why do you ask?"

"Because I know this one guy in Los Angeles who told me that's the only way he can enjoy sex. Pain and humiliation bring up all the times he got attention when he was a kid, so he gets off on it."

For me the operative words are *this one guy in Los Angeles*. I could answer him by pointing out how many nondisabled men, gay or otherwise, enjoy experiencing sex that way, or offer him other enlightened responses, but at this moment all I can muster in reply is, "Really?"

In 1990, a nondisabled gay male editor who is interested in my work takes me out to lunch at a ritzy New York restaurant.

"I was very interested in the sex in your book," the editor tells me.

"Oh?" I say. As I eat I keep nodding encouragement for him to continue.

"I have a cousin who is disabled. We spent a lot of time together growing up in Texas," he says. "My family wasn't very happy about how swishy I was. We lived in oil country and I guess I didn't live up to, well, what they expected a boy to be. My cousin was my only friend. People are very interested in how disabled people have sex, aren't they?"

Puzzled, my first thought is that not many people would be interested in the way I have sex, being that my sexual practices are probably similar to the experiences of most gay men. My unspoken response is: No, most people aren't interested, but you obviously are.

Taking into consideration that I might have to work with this well-intentioned man sitting across from me, and that he is paying for this rather expensive lunch, I simply correct his assumption: "Actually, most people do not think of those of who live with disabilities as being sexual at all."

To St. Augustine, "beauty was synonymous with geometric form and balance." Regarding human appearance, the *Oxford English Dictionary* defines *handsome* as: "having a fine form or figure, usually in conjunction with full size or stateliness." Psychologist Nancy Etcoff describes the historical discourse on beauty as "an aesthetic based on proportion."

When I was young, before we went to sleep, my brother, three and half years older than I and with whom I shared a trundle bed, teased me about how short I was. "I'm not short," I replied, "everyone else is tall."

Now, when I wake during the night, I am surprised when I realize my body, lying so closely to Ian's, is of measure. Because above my thighs my body is of customary length, lying in bed with him I feel the equality of my body's size. I feel comfortable, at ease, something I do not feel when standing up and talking to someone at a party where I often don't reach anyone's shoulders, or when sitting down for dinner in a restaurant where usually my feet dangle from the chair, unable to reach the floor. In crowded elevators I am often unseen, relegated to a back corner where the view is more often the middle of someone's back, or below.

In 1991, the night before Tom's photo shoot, I begin to get nervous. I have not taken off my clothes, been naked and shared my body with a stranger for many years.

I can't sleep. Lying in bed, I think about the story of Thai Queen Number One. Thai kings were polygamous; each queen had a number according to her station. A long time ago, Queen Number One was on her way to visit the king in the ancient capital of Ayutthaya. It was a very hot, humid day and Queen Number One decided to stop at the river.

As she cooled off in the river, the queen's servants watched over her royal possessions. Suddenly, the queen began to drown. Because no subject was allowed to touch a queen, number one or otherwise, her servants were relegated to simply stand and watch from the shore. Did any of the onlookers know Queen Number One could not swim? She drowned.

The next morning at Tom's studio, I am told the part of the book that I will model for will be "Biting."

This doesn't sound too heavy, I think to myself, as I introduce myself to George, my partner for the session.

Even though it probably wouldn't have made me any less nervous, I wish I had asked Tom if he had told George about my disability before we met. Next time remember to ask, I tell myself, as if this session will be my first step in what is sure to be a nude modeling career.

I don't know George well enough, have never seen him until a few minutes ago downstairs—has he ever seen me and my inimitable gait walking down Commercial Street?—to ask if he has ever done this before. What I do know is that he has olive skin, tight curly black hair, dark brown eyes.

"Why don't you two get to know each other?" Tom says as he checks a light he's set up over the bed.

And before I can give Tom's suggestion a moment's thought, George has trampolined onto the bed and is pulling me toward him.

Here in bed it feels as if the playing field has been literally leveled. Despite my insecurities, even though a half hour earlier I did not know George, I am soothed by his fingers grazing my shoulder, the length of my arm.

Later that week, Tom calls. He wants me to come over to look at the photos, as well as at the drawing he has already begun.

When I see the photos and drawing in his studio, I am both surprised and relieved by my reaction. I recognize the images of myself in both the photos and the drawing as very beautiful.

A week later, Tom calls. "The art director didn't like it. He said that in the drawing the disability didn't read. He wants me to cut off one of your legs."

"My parents didn't let many well-known doctors do that when I was born," I tell Tom.

"Or I put in a wheelchair by the side of the bed."

"But that's the easy way out. We talked about this before I agreed to model."

"I know I did."

"What are you going to do?"

There is a long pause.

"I can put somebody's head on your body, then take off one or both of your legs," he offers.

"You can't do that. If you can't use my body as it is you can't use my body at all."

In 1993, the book on gay male sex is published and no drawing of me is included. Instead, accompanying the section on "Masculinity," there is, included in a drawing of a group of otherwise nondisabled men, one fully clothed man sitting in his disability-signifying wheelchair.

As I stare at the drawing, I realize that a man with a disability has once again been defined *as* his disability instead of being portrayed as a person *with* a disability. To the large audience who will use this book, this might be the only image they will ever see of a disabled gay man. And the message of the drawing: "Despite his having to use a wheelchair, he is a man, too," rather than "Here is a man who also uses a wheelchair."

Leaving the bookstore, I am sad at this missed opportunity.

Waking the next morning, I get out of bed, reluctantly. Who was I kidding? I ask myself as I get up to take a shower. Was modeling for Tom any different from my earlier sexual encounters?

Feeling the strong pulse of the spraying water run over me, I close my eyes and it is as if the water's heat slowly dissolves the skin of my limbs, then my bones, until I am one of those armless, legless, Greek statues—all torso—something akin to a male *Venus de Milo* who, despite having no arms or hands, the stump of her upper right arm extending just above her breast, despite her scarred face and severed left foot, despite having the big toe cut off her right foot, and a missing left nipple, not being real, is considered one of the most beautiful figures in the world.

BARBARA RUTH

Eight Ways of Being Disabled in Love

1.

When we can
I press
my back up to her belly
she spoons me
when we can
then she turns on to her back
as we readjust the pillows
our hands refind each other
and say what they want.

2.

We hand dance
in sinuous tango, fingers rising flamingos
meet again
flamboyant merengue.

3.

The hospital bed positioned at last,
lips, tongue reacquaint
hearts race
neck muscles tense
pain and desire
battle it out.

4.

Saturday morning
phone rings
a friend asks, "What are you doing?"
"Lollygagging," I tell her,
"We've been at it for hours."
We're such fine lollygaggers
we push/pull ourselves up
go the bathroom, brush teeth
crawl back under the covers.
My love says, "We need to get out more."
"Where would we go?"
"Demonstrations."
We chant our demands to the walls,
provocateurs of the bed.
We nuzzle
grab the trapeze
gingerly turn to the center
smoochy Saturday
stretches
and smiles.

5.

So careful
not to put weight
on a leg, a foot
so liable to spasm
not careful enough.

6.

Sex on the dvd
they make it look effortless

they never look like us.
"They're actors," I scoff,
remembering
when I could move like that
when what I did not know
hadn't yet hurt me.
She has no
"before disability" memories.
Ah, but when we courted
when we did lines of honeymoon hour after hour—
dark chocolate memories
make us laugh
rage
cry.

7.

It's the meds
the arthritis
the migraines
the cysts
the cerebral palsy
osteoporosis
depression
fibromyalgia
it's the seizures
the surgeries
tendons cut
hardware inserted
organs removed
incisions infected
it's heartburn
high blood pressure
hair falling out
it's the doctors
the wheelchairs

the crutches
the c-pap
the oxygen tank
it's the pain
it's the pain
it's the pain.

8.

Her skin smells of pears
I bury my nose in her nape
burrow under her curls, her clothes
to the skin of her,
rest in her scent.

Who Killed Frida Kahlo?

Who killed Frida Kahlo? Who shall we blame?
The official cause of death *pulmonary embolism*;
what was the motive? Who stood to gain?

Who killed Frida Kahlo?
She said she'd practically been murdered by life.
Can "life" be made to stand trial?

Two great accidents felled her;
the second was Diego.
Did Diego kill Frida?
When he fucked her sister
did he literally break Frida's heart?

Did the doctors kill her?
—here were so many—
Take a number.
Who wants a piece of Frida Kahlo?
Take her toe, her foot,
take the tibia, fibula, the disks from her spine,
rip the babies out of her womb.
Cut Frida open
wrap her flesh in steel corsets
hang her on pulleys—call it therapy.
Did Frida die by hanging?
If that was the punishment
what was her crime?

All the doctors agreed, she should not have a baby,

they forbade it
so of course she kept trying.
Miscarriage after miscarriage
between lumbar fusions and amputations
—they were always cutting something out of her,
rearranging the parts she had left.

When Diego proposed for the second time
he did it through Frida's "Doctorcito Querido"
who recommended they reconcile
"for Frida's health."
Is this an approved doctor-patient relationship?
Did Frida ever, in her adult crippled life
have an approved relationship?

Was Frida a good patient?
She was famous, if not rich, then not poor, certainly.
Did any of the doctors
want her for himself? Try to demand
medical monogamy?
With all her complications, surely there was enough
to satisfy all.
Who was the primary care provider?
Who the chief surgeon?
Who the most special specialist?
Who knew the most acclaimed, most advanced forms of torture?
Who prescribed all those sleeping pills? Who ordered
the endless ampules of Demerol?

What of her lover, her nurse?
Did she and Frida caress while the nurse injected
Holy Demon Demerol into Frida's poor body?
What did they do in bed?

Frida hurt so bad
so long.
She painted and drank and drugged and willed herself through
    the pain

and discovered, on the other side of her suffering,
more pain.

For years, she slept with the suicide monster
it took her where sex could not take her
and always was faithful:
Santa Muerte
the Golem
el duende
a being beyond male or female
good or bad
a being who loved her.

Frida was a bitch
she addicted herself to alcohol, tobacco
always took more pain meds, more sleeping pills
than anyone prescribed.
Always went back to Diego.
Rotting fruit for her womb.
Death as her third eye.
Frida reveled in the grotesque.
She exploited her suffering.
She made art
of what she had.

In the picture of Frida erect in her wheelchair
in front of a portrait of el Doctor Querido,
she's offering him her easel
an anatomically perfect heart
drip dripping its blood onto her chaste white blouse.
She painted her lovely, crippled foot
with its trophic ulcer tenderly carved
drip-dripping blood into her bath
her foot, a trophy
the surgeon finally won.

TRAVIS CHI WING LAU

Curvature: Learning to Stand Up Straight; or, Growing Up Sideways

Hard edges: a labyrinth of metal cubes the shade of rotted peaches. Here we are, the lot of us, bare-chested, in line toward the center of this hideous knot of concrete contracting in the wet of summer heat. The smell of cheap body spray because the shower heads are suffocated with the rust and mold of generations before us. The air thick with the collision of different bodies: of sweat, of obscenities and bad syntax, of boys who are too proud to admit how they fumble, feel, and fall.

And so I bend forward to touch my toes—a little spectacle for the pubescent audience whose bodies do not match my own. Mr. H. rakes the golf pencil across the thin carbon-copy page on his clipboard. I am a last name, a first initial, a student number, an ethnicity that is a conflation. Then, I am a set of measurements, a formal description of a lateral view, an unflattering portrait from behind. *I am seen at last*, I say to myself, but I guess I wasn't specific enough when I threw that penny into the wishing well. Always be careful what you wish for.

I hang there, and Mr. H calls Mr. M over for a second opinion. They take turns with a little piece of plastic in the shape of a half-moon. *Scoliometer*, labeled in bold. As I hold my position, I struggle to breathe through their indecipherable mumbling, the gravel of a chuckle or two. One of them slowly runs his hand down my back, following the meandering line of my spine. Fingers sink into the two raised areas of my back: upper right, lower left. A pat on the ass, and I'm told to unfold myself. But, even as I pull myself upright, I still feel bent.

Now walk. So I do, with my usual shuffle: short, anxious shifts forward. Glides, feather footfalls because my father always had heavier steps. What I did not know at the time was that I would spend years unlearning this walk—what one of the guys would call my "kimono trot" because that's the closest term he could come up with for a *chino*.

Enough pussyfooting, he used to say to me, as he downed his creatine shake. My teenage conduct manual came in the form of a wrestler who used to "blackbag" to meet weight requirements. You know, the proven weight-loss technique of covering your car in Hefty trash bags and sitting inside for hours until you sweat out everything inside. And somehow I'm the crooked one.

Two more beats, and I hear more mumbling. *Note the hips,* I hear Mr. M say. *Misaligned. Uneven.* I strain to hear the next word, but my inattention strikes again: I feel my foot catch on a crack in the cement floor, my hip locks, and I shift my weight abruptly to avoid falling. Misstep. I fall away from the dotted line chalked out on the floor for me to follow. Like I'm being pulled over for a breathalyzer, but all they're going to confirm is that I just can't keep straight. *Jesus Christ. This ain't no catwalk.* Yeah, Mr. M, I get it.

A short deliberation and exchange of notes, and the peanut gallery starts to get a little rowdy. I've taken a few too many minutes of their already interrupted flag football match. Between the two coaches, a little manual is produced and consulted. Conclusive. Signed and dated. They sigh a breath of relief. We can now all thank the Georgia Department of Public Health for a good day's work.

Better stand up straighter, kid. Or you'll need a brace. That'd be a real shame, says Mr. H with his Scottish brogue.

I mean, you probably already need one for that limp wrist. Call it a new fashion accessory, mutters Mr. M under his breath behind me. The baseballers throw their laughter at me like dirty bills.

Beat. Am I the only one who doesn't hear the high hat?

Mr. M's bruised rugby finger points me toward the exit. I can feel the leers and jeers as the sweat on my back clings to my shirt as I pull it back on. I see that even my pasty white doesn't match theirs. But I still pull my shoulders back and broad, stretch tall, and take long strides to the door. *Atta girl.*

Because you know, it's better to stand up straight.

KRISTEN RINGMAN

All I Have Is the Body

Music festivals are like breeding grounds
for beauty—the feminine kind—
the wild—the
every-girl-I've-ever-wanted-to-sleep-with crowd.

It's not just their gender or membership in
festival culture.
It's their style, their choices of colors,
layers, fabrics,
their voices that fly off like birds
(sounds I'll never hear),
so all I have is the body and its adornments.

All I have is that patch of leather,
woven threads, white lace, yellow silk,
green cotton.
Those copper wires wrapping the tan skin
of their arms, those dreadlocks.
Their blue hair and brown hair and red hair.
All I have is the tattoos on their backs
and hips and shoulders:
a rainbow-shaded phoenix,
butterfly wings, angel wings, dragon wings,
floral mandalas,
sunflowers, hibiscus.

I spin with the shape of them all.
What they don't know is
how well I can hear their bodies
so silent to themselves.

Meeting Emily

I like your teeth from the moment I see them.
(I mean the spaces between them.)
How each one is just a little bit
apart from the next.
Full, painted lips above and below.
And I'm crushing on you already,
between the fire and the neighbor's face
closing the door to the sounds of us,
conversations I can't hear.

When you first arrived,
I stayed in the shadows. I didn't
reach out to the edges of your short
perfect skirt, or the ends of your dark hair
where they brush
against the middle of your back.
I didn't yet know that you smell
exactly like my first girlfriend
(first girl I fell in love with,
eleventh human).
And I can tell your skin is just as soft
without even touching you.
I know it as if I've met you
by a canal, or down the lane from a stone church.
Already touched you. This is *déjà vu*, I swear.

I lazily walk up to you,
talk about something too personal
or awkward. Your lips move in return

but I hear
mouse sounds, no meaning—until they
pass through my brain's filter.
Every other word, I think you say
"mermaid."
You correct me with your cell phone
(because we live in a time filled with
electronic devices and acronyms).
And then you say, "Mermaids are cool."

And I become: "the deaf girl who thinks she
hears cool things being said, who gets to talk
with a hot girl at a party around a warm fire,"
Not: "the deaf girl, alone at a dark
gathering of lips and murmurs."

You changed it for me, Emily,
and this is my way of serenading you.

Because I can't forget the shape of
your lips, or the spaces between your teeth,
or the blue of your eyes.

I write clichés.
Because our lovers never leave us, do
they?

Like the sensation of freedom
we find while riding a motorcycle
through the Vermont hills,
or the pain of a new
divorce,
old lovers return
in the casual shapes of
the people we meet, and
it's hard to separate the past from the
moment—right now—with you in front

of me, reaching out despite my
too-early queries of sexual orientation
and my coy eyes, leering over you
like an animal.

And maybe you aren't here at all.
Maybe I've made you up in my head.

But then
I check my phone,
and there she is,
a new contact
called Emily.

I Chant

you can sing—native dancing spread wide
and I can only half-hear you, but I see—
you are a red-tailed hawk spreading over me,
twisting through me, made of wings—uplifting—threading
through my desire your hands travel me,
as if I were a country for your taking (or a body), I breathe you—
bask in the fabric of you (velvet) spreading wide, spinning, I spin
on the narrow bed
past the point of trying
so hard to read your lips, I spin
until we are upside-down and
nothing matters but your eyes staring into me—
seeing me—opening to me—wide—the sunrise
of our meeting spreading—lighting the world—tumbling,
tripping through branches, leaves,
t-shirts of skulls and bones and white against black against skin—
there it is: that skin again—your arms, strong like mine—we can
    support each other's organs like the pillars in a house lifting lifting
    lifting us
into orange sun and air and gray cotton clouds bursting behind my
    eyes in your eyes between in between across how to explain—such
    feeling:
your breasts against mine—each molding against each other warm—
your language the soundtrack of my language—lips over hands—
your tongue across me:
making its way from my breast to my shoulder to my neck to my lips to
    my tongue—inside me—your body pushes
as if all of you could penetrate, enter all of me
e x p a n d

fill in all the places where I was wrong or lost or empty—
a new home between
your palms and narrow fingers threading
through mine threading through me as if I were a wave and you
a surfer—your board half inside—dipped into me

stay stay stay stay
I chant
with voice
and hands

A Girl Through a Hoop of Gold

I first saw only the gold edges of you:
the you in a tight red leather tunic and chaps,
your dancing black boots,
the fire burning between your hands,
at the ends of a stick and then
along the edges of a hoop.

Fire turns your whole
body into a Baroque painting—
all darkness
and warmth.
I read you like a piece of art.
I dream
of being as close as
that fire—
hitting against your left hip
twice—making you smile
from comfort
or pain,
I cannot tell.

I can only half-understand you,
fire dancer, girl of my dreams.
I can only linger over you like
an animal, stunned
by your ability to move your body
in a way I've always dreamed
of moving mine:
like a belly dancer

or a snake.
You remind me of the cobras
I once saw having sex
in the long grass of South India.

And I don't just want you, fire dancer,
I want to be you.
I long for the ability to dance with flames
between my hands, floating up
along my ribcage, hovering
beside the hood protecting my hair,
while I listen
to the gasps from the crowd—
hearing sounds of awe—
so close—
to the sounds of love.

You've got it all,
don't you, fire dancer?
But maybe you don't.
Maybe you're broken, like me,
in all the ways people have always thought—
you'd be fine.

Sometimes, I think I'm you,
fire dancer.
I've learned to step
too close to the flames.
Sometimes not around them
at all.
I've had to leap through them,
like you, fire dancer,
a girl through a hoop of gold, trying
not to slip her hand,
not to fall,
or burn.

SARA IBRAHIM

When Love Touches You

When you are young, sick and disabled, your world shifts drastically. Most of the time, people simply don't understand. Those who are older tend to empathize, but they also sometimes recoil in fear. Fear of illness and disability has been a dominant quality of our ableist culture. To live in the margins of society is a strange place to be. You are always occupying a space that is rejected, and you are always in a state of exile. There is no choice in the matter, no matter how hard you try to resist rejection. It just is.

When I was first diagnosed with multiple sclerosis, I felt completely alone. Everyone around me started treating me differently. A few friends decided that God had decided to punish me for some unknown sin I had committed. To be gay was to be a sinner. To be disabled and gay sounded accurate. God worked in mysterious ways, they said. I was horrified and began to hate myself.

But then Love comes along. A love that picks you up, it picks up where it left off when you first got the diagnosis. Love waltzes in, and claims she needs to dance with you. She doesn't care whether you can barely move your feet. She confronts and questions you, while you're lying on the bathroom floor and refusing to get up. She says she will cradle you and put you to bed.

Love holds your hand and you let her. She reminds you of bravery, of confidence, and that no matter how ugly and rejected you feel, there are still arms that protect you. She becomes your ally and together you fight the ugly disease every day.

I found myself experiencing love and vulnerability. My body was almost always acting out, as my sexuality began solidifying. I was no longer ashamed of who I was. Once, I was walking with a cane, and a woman prayed for me to get better. A complete stranger prayed for me, for God to help me repent, to save my youth from utter destruction. She urged me to wear the veil, or to go to Mecca, where I would surely be salvaged.

The disease takes over, gnawing at your insides. It hurts everywhere. When Love touches you, you flinch in pain. It is no longer soothing. There is no more eroticism as your skin burns, and not in a romanticized way. Your flesh burns as your nervous system decides that it cannot handle the human touch. It is difficult to just be.

When the body starts attacking you, there is much psychological damage to deal with. There is a constant struggle for competency and self-love. Doctors frowned at me and I marveled at how detached they were. I was only a patient, a file number, subhuman. Hospitals scared me. They were a place for older people, for sick people, and now I had become one of them. I had zero wrinkles on my face, yet I felt thirty years older than I really was. I was only twenty when I lost function in my hands. My fingers refused to budge. They would not listen to my brain's commands anymore.

Love cries as she watches you writhe in pain at night. In the morning, she reaches over and asks you if you managed to sleep. And that's when you lie to her and tell her you're okay. Because watching those you love suffer must hurt her, too. She's too young to be involved in this burden that is you. Circumstances gave you this illness, but how can she consciously choose to be a part of your life?

And when my partner started having nightmares of hell and torture, my world started falling apart. She was afraid that being with me, loving me, would make me worse. It would mean that my body would continuously suffer. Our friends hated and feared homosexuality.

Family were, of course, repulsed by the very idea that people "like that" even existed. There was only us, and the walls that protected us, our castle, began to suffocate her.

The gaps and distances grow. There is an unhealable rift between you two now, and Love is getting frustrated. Love decides to leave. She packs her bags and leaves you trying to find Autonomy. There is only you now. Don't forget your medication, your injections, your vitamins. You were born queer. Already on the outside. What's a little disability quirk going to do to you? You pick up the pieces, and you move on. You stop resisting rejection, and hope to make a home of the margins.

They tell you to stop sulking, to go out and notice the beautiful bright rays of the sun. Just when I began to heal, to find a place for myself amongst the margins, I realized that I was able to build my own kingdom. It was a fragile kingdom, one that could fall apart at any given moment. Yet it was *my* kingdom. I built it from scratch. When my first love left, I thought the world would never be the same again. The darkness set in, and I believed I was unworthy of being seen, let alone being loved. There was no one who actually saw me.

But then the Goddess noticed me. She found me stranded, bleeding out, soulless, and kneeled down to examine my wounds. Her long and beautiful black hair made her look like an Arabian princess from an old fairytale. She was more real than any Scheherazade. Shall I call her Aphrodite, the Goddess of love? Or perhaps compare her to the boldness of the legendary Salome? She was neither human nor Goddess. She said she was here to take me home.

Next to her, I felt flawed and undesirable. She was the epitome of perfection. Her body could tell stories; she was art at its best, at its grandness, its rawness. It was unavoidable and inevitable: I had met the woman who saved me from my demons.

    We talked about how much she loved the sun. She loved going

to the beach. She asked me if I would join her. I had to tell her that I couldn't, because people with MS cannot handle the heat. Our bodies deteriorate under high temperatures, my nerve function is altered, my ability to see, walk, hear her voice, all of it is threatened by enduring the heat. When I told her I was diagnosed with MS years ago, and that I was "fine," her reaction was dangerously raw. She opened her mouth to speak, but she lost her voice. My pain, my silent suffering, had transferred to her. She had fallen in love with me, and here I was admitting my lack, all ashamed and flustered. I was afraid she would walk away. Who wouldn't? Better now than later, I thought. Better to give her the chance to escape, to exit.

And yet she stayed. She yelled at me to listen. To understand. To know that it was me, all of me, that she wanted. My second Love was the Goddess that surpassed human flaws and failings. And yet I blocked her. I hid from her when she asked me if I had always pretended to be so strong. I covered my face when she asked me if I was in chronic pain every day. And then one night, when the pain became so intense, all I wanted to do was die. I went to my neurologist alone, and my Goddess called. Angry at me for not reaching out to her, for not telling her I was at the doctor's, she insisted on staying with me on the phone, until I finished my appointment. Presence is important, she said. And she was present. She talked to me until she knew I could no longer speak. My neurologist told me there was no hope, no cure, and nothing anybody could do could help ease the pain. The lump in my throat would not go away, and my voice cracked when my Goddess asked if I was okay. I could no longer stand being alone, and I could no longer pretend to be Superwoman. It was real life, painful, bitter, and in your face.

My Goddess showed up at my doorstep by the time I went home that night. I collapsed on her lap while her eyes brimmed with love and tears. She was proud of me. Of who I was. Of how my strength had shaped me. And it was these exact words she whispered and fed into my blood: "Your MS is you, my darling; I can't separate the two." I was not a Sinner anymore. I was not doomed, and it was not hopeless. I had found a home that embraced me, that love that did not limit me, a woman that saw into my soul and gave my cells the oxygen they were deprived of.

I saw her as the Moon, and I don't mean this in a clichéd way. I cannot stand the sun. The sun burns me, hinders my nervous system, it kills the brain pathways. And she was the moonlight that lit my path.

But because life is no fairytale, my Goddess was taken. She had a partner. Yet she had fallen in love with me. I had pressed my wounds into her; she had wrapped her arms around me and found herself aching for more. There was nothing else we could do. She did not choose me in the end; she chose to stay with her partner. Was I devastated? Yes, eternally. I had lost my second chance at love. My second love gave me life, after death; she gave me dignity, after humiliation and shame; and she gave me the desire to live. I could not betray her. There was a surgery option, an experimental one, and there had been some deaths. As much as I was desperate for any possibility of a cure, when I heard her fear of losing me to death, I could not do it. I could not break her heart. To exit life was to betray her.

I had touched Eden. I had touched a piece of paradise, a love that does not look down on you, a love that does not shame you, does not reject you, and does not claim to be forever, either. We did not promise a forever. We promised a different equation altogether. Life was random, loss was inevitable, and age was catching up. Our souls committed to one another, a bond had tied us to each other, a deep form of friendship, understanding, and acceptance.

Our separation was not out of a lack of love or even a betrayal, but instead, it was because of this concept of time. I had missed my chance to be with her, and she could not leave her partner. And we walked away from each other, promising to find one another when the time was right.

When You Saw Me

I was blindfolded
When you saw through me the first time.
I felt you kiss my wounded body,
touch my scars.
Who whispered it to you,
How did you know what I needed?

The need running so deep, back to
the edge of an afternoon years ago,
red—blood radiating blood,
flesh,
beautiful
life,
sprayed across the lawn,
my gasping, trying to keep from leaving
trying to wake up from the dream
to stay there as you stay here
as you have tried to conjure a new dream for me.

Pressing me to give up my shame,
my queer shame
from a child living in hospitals,
taken away from family, from friends,
befriended by nurses with pills,
rectal thermometers, dressing changes
stuck, pulled lose from wounds,
doctors with metal probes
penetrating raw, living flesh,
touching nerves, giving flashes of light, the light of pain

like the light behind Florentine oils.
Gangrene, from the past, they knew
the fragrance of death,
a queer scent I still smell, can conjure up.

Touch me, say anything to me.
look at me when I speak.
You hear what I've seen,
see me, listen to me
not just stare at the metal brace.
I can show you what I am,
here, now.

Don't Forget Your Badge

For a few moments no more than that,
you can forget your bad leg—
when you get drunk,
get high,
read poems out loud,
do queer things,
tell the world to fuck off.

Maybe not forget, maybe just not care,
but it never goes away.
It's your closest friend.

Most people are very nice, but
someone always manages to bring it up,
maybe to put you in your place,
maybe to remind you what you are,
maybe just to be helpful, kind,
but you don't want it, help.
Help is an intrusion, a show of power.

You see, they don't know what you've lived.
You just want to be normal,
take a pill, be normal,
not a victim, not a hero,
not like a movie star—objectified,
just normal,
just someone who can take his pants off without explaining.

That Day

What I remember of that day—
his dark eyebrows, eyes,
broad smile
not shown often,
but hot, humid like heat lightning—
a promise
to be claimed.

What I remember of us—
his singing in Farsi, telling me I don't understand,
I understand—
a dance,
a grave sin
in his religion, in my religion.
his darkness
our eyes closed
his lips apart
for mine for mine for mine.

What I remember he asked—
a small joke about who is cut, uncut—
says he doesn't believe me,
asks to see it.
I let him, feel him touch it.

Feel him, touch him, knowing,
our bodies enfolded,
gone—for an afternoon.
Later he shows me pictures of airplanes.

What It Means to Fall

Soaring high above the world
a man with wings of flesh,
the wind against his bareness,
all-watching, hearing, yet
too distant to be seen

by men, he thrusts
and glides down closer,
toward the glowing land,
hoping to find another
like himself

caught by the wind,
released, he plunges
to the hardness of the earth,
the golden grass waves
false, not what he believed

those he desired
see his fall,
run to find him
yet stop short,
recoil from the broken wings.

The movement on their lips,
he cannot understand
what their glances
reveal, the satisfaction
of never knowing.

JOEL GATES

Outcast: Deaf, Gay, Christian

All my life I could never fit in anywhere. Not only was I the only deaf person in my family, I was also left-handed. Because of where my crown was, I also had to comb my hair in the opposite direction from my dad and brother. I felt very conscious about being different. We were a conservative Christian family.

When I was nine years old, I visited my neighbor's church. I felt God's presence in that church. After the service ended, I recall asking my mom if I could receive Jesus Christ as my Savior. She smiled and said yes, and we prayed together. I recall becoming a very different boy after that. I was really excited and wanted to go to church every Sunday. My favorite thing was AWANA, a Christian organization for kids. We gathered for AWANA every Wednesday night at a big church in Beaverton, Oregon.

I recall one day when I was about 11, I went to a soccer game with my best friend David. We sat in the rafters. I looked behind me where there was a cute man in his late 30s. I got an erection. I didn't know what that meant back then; my parents and I never talked about sex.

Around the same time, I had a speech therapist who came to my house once a week to teach me how to speak. He was a bearded guy with a round belly. I thought he was extremely attractive. He had a very positive, magnetic personality, and he loved his job. That was one thing I looked forward to every week. We unfortunately had to end our weekly sessions when my family moved to Alaska.

When I was 12 years old, my dad decided to move to Fairbanks. I was devastated to leave AWANA, my friends, and Oregon. In Alaska, I had no friends. I also didn't enjoy its cold weather. My dad had felt called by God to move there and begin his career as a dentist.

We went to a conservative, fundamental Bible-thumping church in Fairbanks, which I attended for the next 16 years. Growing up, I learned about how wicked homosexuality was. Homeschooled, I lived in a bubble, and my only community was church and my family.

As I became more aware about my attraction to men and how wicked it was, I became more miserable. I hated how wicked I was. I began praying to God every night to help me "resist my evil temptations and ward off Satan," since I was convinced that the Devil was tempting me with those evil homosexual thoughts. I wanted to be free from those thoughts. I was too afraid to tell anyone.

In 1999 I graduated from high school and went to the University of Alaska, Fairbanks (UAF). Around that time, my friends in church all began to marry. They moved away, had kids, got too busy, and had no time to see me anymore. My circle of friends quickly dwindled until I had only one friend left at church. He was usually busy talking with others; I was the only deaf person at my church, and none of them would sign while talking. So I just trailed off. I began hating going to church and hating myself. I could never get rid of my gay thoughts. I wanted so bad to be a part of my church, to do something for God, to serve Him. I really loved being a part of God's plan and wanted to participate in my church, but I had this one huge thorn that I couldn't discard.

In December 2002 I began playing a computer game. It quickly became an addiction. It was a portal for me to escape reality. I remember thinking to myself, "Hey, this game is great! It actually does help me not dwell on these evil homosexual thoughts! I'm way too absorbed within this virtual world I'm playing in! So this game must be good for me!"

My grades at UAF began dropping. I used to get As and Bs all the time. That soon changed. I began getting Cs and eventually got my first D. And then another. And another. I was failing.

I finally graduated two years late with a degree in math. I barely got that degree, however. *Barely.* I failed that one class that I had to pass, but the director of the math department waived it, saying that only one class was no big deal.

I didn't know what to do with that degree, so I continued going to college. My parents were frustrated by my gaming addiction. My dad tried to get me to stop it. He lost his temper one day when I was caught playing, and he picked up my laptop and threw it down the stairs, totaling it completely.

Did that help me stop? No. Less than a year later I moved to Oregon and attended the University of Oregon. I was majored in architecture. I struggled in my first term but managed to pass all of my classes. Unfortunately, during the three-week break between terms, I had so much free time that I got sucked back into gaming. I was so absorbed that I dropped out of school about five weeks into the next term. I didn't respond to texts or emails from my parents. They were worried sick about me. The university contacted my parents about my attendance; they were wondering where I was. I was in my room the entire time playing. It was like a drug.

Three years later my dad finally flew in to pick me up, forcing me to move back to Alaska. I went to UAF for one year, majoring in civil engineering, as architecture wasn't offered at UAF. My dad tried to help me finish my engineering degree so I could get a job and a life. I decided I needed to finish school, end my addiction, and try to have a better life again. Gaming was making me worse, and nearing 30 with no job or my own home was making me miserable.

A year later my parents suggested that I go to the Rochester Institute of Technology (RIT). Perhaps I'd meet some deaf people and make some new friends. I decided that would be great. Being the only deaf person at UAF, I was really lonely. In the fall of 2009 I went there, and it was great! Truly great. I made some new friends. My life improved. I didn't completely break free of my gaming addiction, but I was improving. I forced myself to go out as often as I could and socialize. My grades at RIT were okay, not the best, but at least I was passing most of them. I still failed a couple.

Early during my second year at RIT, I found out that one of my friends was gay. I was very surprised because he looked like everyone else. I was 28 at the time. He was deaf also. My first thought was to stop being friends with him, but then I thought to myself, "Why? All these years I'd been hating myself, and I was very lonely. I need friends, and he is a good man. Stop being judgmental of other people, and especially of yourself." I decided I needed to end my habit of judging other people, which was how my church in Fairbanks had trained me to be, to think, to act. It was second nature.

I hung out with him and met his friends. I soon realized that several of them were gay as well. It was as if a light had come on. I never saw these people as gay before! It's weird how one little thing could completely change how you see people around you. I had grown up believing that all gay people were like what I saw on TV and in the news: extremely effeminate, flashy glamorous clothes, drag queens, that kind of stuff. I wanted nothing of that life. I thought I couldn't be gay because that kind of lifestyle didn't match mine at all. I realized anyone can be gay—even those who live in the country and do not socialize much. Even those who do not have good fashion taste, shave daily, wear cologne, get their hands dirty doing farm work—they can be gay.

During my Christmas break, I searched for a dating web site, and found a site for older men searching for younger men, and vice versa. I was very nervous when I created my profile describing myself and listed what I was looking for. I wanted a Christian partner. As a result, I expected to get no replies. I didn't expect there would be many Christian gay men on that site. If he were deaf as well, that'd be beyond amazing beyond belief, as that'd be next to impossible to find someone like that. But I didn't mention that part.

A man emailed me three weeks later. He was a Lutheran who went to church every Sunday. He was hearing, but he was very willing to learn sign language if we ended up in a relationship. Jerry and I emailed each other once a day.

We eventually switched from emails to chatting online. I purchased a webcam so we could communicate while seeing each other face to face. I taught him some signs. We hit it off pretty well. I explained my situation about being stuck at RIT while he was living in Portland. I'd finish in late May, and I was considering the possibility of finding an internship in Portland.

I asked Jerry what he thought of me coming to visit him during my spring break. He was very excited about that, so I purchased a round-trip ticket to Portland. We finally met in person after about a month and a half of chatting for hours online. Meeting him in person was very different. I learned a lot of new things about him. We had a wonderful time together, and it was the best week in my entire life. That week went by in a flash. It felt like we were together for only a day! We were both sad that I had to fly back.

We continued to chat daily. Months went by very slowly. When May finally came, I packed up my things and mailed most of them to

Jerry's house. I told my parents that I was moving to Portland to look for an internship, which was required for my engineering degree. I told them that I'd found a cheap place to rent. I never gave them a hint that I was in a relationship. I was way too afraid to tell them!

Jerry understood my situation, and he was okay with me being in the closet. He told me that it'd be best for me to build a new family of supportive friends first before I came out to my parents and sibilings.

We got engaged on May 24, 2011. My parents flew in Portland to see me. Jerry hid in his room while they toured my new home. It was very awkward for me. I told them that my landlord was not feeling well.

It was very stressful for me to juggle between my parents visiting frequently and Jerry. It put a strain on our relationship. I could sense that he was getting drained from being back in the closet himself. That was not a fun experience.

Four months after we got engaged, he was diagnosed with an aggressive form of cancer. A year later he died. I was so devastated. His sister, who inherited Jerry's house, kicked me out, leaving me with no place to live. This happened four weeks after Jerry passed away.

Exactly six weeks after Jerry died, I decided to end my life. I just couldn't take it any more. I was all alone, in the closet, with no home, and couldn't share with my parents what I was going through without first coming out of the closet. I typed a suicide note on Facebook explaining to everyone why I was doing this. Before I hit "Post," I brought a bottle of whiskey and a bottle of ibuprofen to my bed. I hit "Post" and immediately downed the entire bottle. I gagged a lot—that was a very powerful, overwhelming drink. When I began to fade out, I swallowed about 20 pills. My phone went insane with texts and emails. I threw it across the room without reading anything.

A few minutes later everything went black.

I woke up in ICU about 12 hours later. The first thing I saw was my aunt's face. She was holding my hand and sitting right beside me. My dad's youngest sister was a lesbian, and she was happy to see me awake.

My first thought was, I failed. My attempt failed. And now everyone knew! My parents knew! I ran that thought over and over and over. The time went very slowly. There was a clock in my room. I would look at it, and when I thought an hour had passed, I'd take a look and only one minute or two had passed. No, that wasn't an exaggeration. It was the longest day of my entire life. Then I learned that my mom was on her way over. I was very apprehensive about that. I couldn't face anyone, didn't want to see anyone. I just wanted to disappear into a dark hole.

After a couple days in the ICU, I stayed in the psych ward for two weeks and was put on antidepressants. My mom stayed in Portland the entire time, visiting me as often as she could. She was really sad. Even though she still didn't support my "choice," as she would put it, she said she still loved me. My dad felt like I had betrayed him. My sister said I would not be allowed around her six kids unless I repented and turned away from the "gay lifestyle." My twin brother told me that whatever I decided, he would still love me. He didn't want me to attempt to end my life again because he would miss me a lot.

When I was let out of the ward, I took a taxi to my therapist on the other side of the river. I recall being amazed at how different Portland looked. Everything seemed surreal, its colors more vivid. It was like a dream. I stepped out of my taxi, thanked the driver, and entered my therapist's office. He was relieved that I was alive. I saw him for six months. I slowly got better.

I am now engaged to a man. We will get married in 2016. I am off antidepressants. I attend a gay-friendly church with a gay pastor. I transferred to Portland State University to finish my degree there. I will graduate in 2016. I am grateful to be alive. My relationship with my family isn't great. We're drifting apart. I haven't talked to my sister for over two years. It hurts, but what else can I do? My fiancé helps me get through this. Because of him, I eat better, exercise more, and strive more to improve myself and to mature. I am much healthier physically and mentally than I've been in a very long time. Perhaps ever. Additionally, I don't waste away my life gaming like I used to.

I've grown up all my life feeling like an outcast because I'm gay and deaf. And then I'm also a Christian, which most gay people do not like. It's been very encouraging to have a gay pastor. Without him, I would not have made it this far. I am much happier now that I don't have this burden of self-denial and lying to people.

ASHLEY VOLION

An Incomplete Story

I once lived in a bubble where injustices were stories on a page
Meant to be read
Childhood innocence
I miss the simple pictures in the clouds
Rolling hand-and-hand with a childhood girlfriend
Saying "I do"
But there is so much more to say
It's never as simple as it seems
You'll see

But I feel like I must come clean before
I end up at the starting line once more
I never aspired to be the hero; the trendsetter
If only I could melt into this
I would be okay

But fuck this!
This is my story and I am the author
I am not sitting back
I am rolling on
I exist

F.U.C.K.

Don't touch me unless you want to fuck
My new mantra
And I don't mean it the gentle way
Make me feel something
"But I'm afraid to hurt you."
What hurts is that fucking line
See people have never been afraid to touch me
Pat me on the head
Use me as a toy to shake, literally
Not in the sexy way either
They almost feel obligated to do this
The nerd in me wants to do a social experiment
The strong woman in me says back the fuck up
See the touch I yearn for does not see the "brave disabled girl"
Not even woman because in those moments, I am not a woman
    to you
The touch I yearn for is fiery red
It makes me quiver from within
We mesh like a wave colliding together
"Hey buddy."
"She's my friend."
Like it's a fucking badge on your scout's uniform
Instead fuck me
Throw me on the bed
Embrace me
Fuck me like we're not going to see the sun tomorrow
Touch me
"Isn't she the girl that researches disability?"

"She's in a wheelchair."
"She's so brave."
"She's getting a Ph.D."
That is not who I am
"You have the biggest fan club."
Are they willing to make me yearn to scream?
Are they going to explore me inside and out?
Yes, please touch me
Fuck me
"You're so cute."
"You look so young."
"You're so happy."
"You light up a room."
You don't know me
I'm not breakable
Kiss me from top to bottom
Flip me inside and out
Now what do you think of me?
I have a new mantra
Just fuck me

ANDREW MORRISON-GURZA

"Can You Feel That?"

As he looks at me, his hands moving up my thigh and touching me in all the right places, I am excited. I am hoping that he can tell that I want this just as much as he does—probably more. He slides his hands in my pants, and just as he is about to connect with me in the most intimate way, he stops. He looks me straight in the eye. It is at this moment, I am secretly hoping he is going to say something either vaguely romantic or deliciously dirty. I am waiting with bated breath, and then he says it: "Ummmmm, I am just wondering . . . Can you feel that?"

I'll be honest. I typically get asked this question at the *worst* possible moment of the sexual experience. Picture this: your lover picks you up out of your wheelchair and puts you on the bed, helps you take off your clothes, while somehow simultaneously removing his own; there is kissing, touching, and giggling. His mouth makes its way across your curved and crippled body; each kiss feels better than the last. Just as he is about to head to the southernmost point and envelop you, he asks you this. Right at that moment, you try to remain calm, cool. On the outside, you answer him, telling him, "Yeah, I can feel everything. Nothing to worry about at all."

On the inside however, this question can bring about many feelings for the queer, disabled person, and that is what I would like to explore. If we are lucky enough to discuss sex and disability at all, typically we talk shop: the logistics, the impossibilities, etc. We never consider the emotional impact of sex and disability on the individual experiencing disability. So let me answer the question "Can you feel that?" as honestly as I can.

Yes, I can feel that. I feel every touch, every twinge, and every tickle. It feels incredible to me because for once I am being touched out of desire and not duty. There is a bite of electricity in the air, because this is one of the few moments where my body, with all its spastic twists and turns, is naked and free. It is one of the best feelings that I have had as a queer man with a disability, because I finally have the opportunity to connect with myself, and my lover as a man—not simply a client or a consumer. No schedules, routines, or treatments here. In this moment, I am fully in tune with my disability and myself, and that feels liberating. I feel as though I have to grab onto this and never let go, for fear that when it's over, I might not ever get it back again. I feel like this is mine.

I also feel really excited that someone is with me, sharing this experience. I feel exhilarated that you might actually see me—for all that I am, and accept me as a sexual being; that you might actually see the deliciousness that is my disability. It is such a rarity that I get to have the light that burns inside me turned on. Normally I have to keep this light at bay, and so to be able to bask in its warm glow is a feeling that I never want to forget.

At the same time, mixed in among all the excitement, I also feel scared. I worry that by asking me if I can really feel it, you are checking to see just how disabled I really am. While in my case there is no sensation loss as a result of my cerebral palsy, as I am lying there, my toes curled over themselves, I am trying to figure out how to answer. If I say that I can feel it, does this make me more sexually viable and normal? In that moment, as you ask me, this I am trying to remain sexy and suave (how does one convey this when a guy has his head between their legs?), all the while worried that you might leave any second having discovered that "doing that disabled guy" was too much for you.

I feel the all too familiar pang of doubt, that you may only be doing this to "help me out" because I am so disabled, I couldn't actually get laid out of anything other than pity. As you look at my body, tracking it up and down awaiting my answer, I feel your eyes watching me. Are you realizing that my disability defies all the homo-normative stereotypes that you have been indoctrinated with? Have you figured out that I don't go to the gym five times a week, and that I will never be able to tone down my disability?

While you may just think your question was a harmless attempt to ensure that I am a worthy bedfellow and that "everything works" (seriously, you don't know how many times I have had to say that to a guy), please know that it carries so much weight. The question connects me to the importance of this experience. It reminds me that this is so much more than just a hookup. It is my chance to access my body and yours. This is my chance to crack open my creamy, Queer Crippled center and give you a taste of something you never even knew you liked (yeah, I am that good). It is my chance to show the both of us that I have sexual capital.

Lastly, your question connects me to my own internalized ableism. I am forced to feel that maybe I am not good enough for you because I am living with a disability. In the space between question and answer, I am considering all the things that set me apart from lovers past. My wheelchair sits in the corner of the room, an unshakeable reminder of both the opportunities and obstacles presented here. So don't worry yourself one bit. I can feel everything you're doing to me . . . and then some.

LUCAS SCHEELK

A Prayer for a Non-Religious Autistic

May my special interests combat depressive episodes
May my stimming fingers repair what self-harm has taken away
May my clothing layers be my armor
May my toes be graceful, sturdy, and stealthy for travel
May my pocketed stim toys provide comfort in public
May my routines keep me safe
May my routines keep me safe
May my routines keep me safe
May my sensory weapons—be it music, be it noise-cancelling
headphones, be it sunglasses, be it grounding smells—defeat the
presence of crowds, defeat the sirens, defeat the sun, defeat dissociation
May my self-love flourish, no matter how small
May my reminders aide my memory
May my reminders aide my memory
May my reminders aide my memory
May my hyperfocus enhance my self-education
May my infodumps release overloading information—verbal or
otherwise
May my heart shield when necessary
May my logic question and deduce
May my surroundings continuously rain when I am most in need
For I am worthy
For I am worthy
For I am worthy
May my repetition help me heal
May my repetition help me heal
May my repetition help me heal

I Do Not Want Children

Age: Old enough to know, but too young to know why

I do not want children.

Age: Prepubescent

I do not want children.

I watch my girl peers be educated by adults
To a future of motherhood.
I notice the lack of education directed at me.

Society does not believe disabled people
Can, should, would dare to be parents.

That was an observation I saw early on.

Sex Ed never included disabled people,
Just pictures of body parts and giggles.

Age: 14

I do not want children.

The longest 5 minutes of my life at that point,
Waiting to know if my body betrayed me,
Unaware of my potential future, if that
Would include the father's tactics changing
From emotional abuse & manipulation,

"If you loved me, you would have sex with me,"
To physical violence.

Negative.

Age: Teenage years

I do not want children.

I hide my autistic mannerisms from everyone I meet.
When I tell people I have no desire to have children,
I cannot begin to count how many times
People have told me that I'll change my mind,
"Someday, you'll want kids!"

Age: 19

I do not want children.

Progress, sort of.
A different man, in a different city,
A kinder man, a consenting form of love,
But the same test.
Since I went through it before, none of
The panic was present, but in the back
Of my mind I knew I was not meant to stay
In Glyndon, MN—where the only remaining good
Memory I have there was the birth of my cat, Juno.

Negative.

Age: Teenage years [part II]

I do not want children.

I do not want to spread my genetics.
I am defective.

I am a infection to the human race.
My autism is seen as a disease so I can't,
Shouldn't, wouldn't dare to have children.
I am the only autistic person in my family
That I know of, so at least when I die,
Everything that I am will die with me.
Estranged relatives might sigh in relief.
Society will say, "One more down."

Age: 22

I do not want children.

I began identifying as a man.
On the few occasions that I've told
People that I don't want children,
My stance is not challenged.
At most, there is surprise that I
Have no desire to "spread the seed,"
But that's mostly from people who
Aren't in the know that I don't produce sperm.

Age: 23

I do not want children.

At least it's no longer because of
The fact that I'm autistic.

I do not want children, because the world
Would not love them, since the world does not love me.

I do not want children, because I have no
Desire to give birth. The thought alone brings fear.

I do not want children, and for once,
My reasoning does not include
My own lack of a father.

I do not want children, because during the
Rare opportunity that I'm stable enough to think
Beyond the short-term, my future has never
Included having children, biological or adopted.

Age: 26

I do not want children.

It's starting to become
An ultimatum in relationships.
My peers's paths to parenthood laid out before them.
Next time, I'll save my partner three years,
Spare myself the heartbreak, and make that
My opening statement.

"I do not want children."

I hope that one day I find a husband
Content on having a family of cats.

MONIQUE FLYNN

Prom Dresses and Popcorn

My grandmother was an incredible painter. I have seen proof of this because of the paintings that survived. When she was seven months pregnant with my mother, she either fell or my grandfather pushed her down a staircase. My unborn mother barely survived and my grandmother became paralyzed on her left side. My grandfather left her, and when my mother was born my grandmother decided she wasn't fit to be a parent. She gave my mother to her sister to raise and became an alcoholic.

When my mother was a teenager she demanded to meet her father. He lived in Canada and my mother was living in the United States near the border. She snuck past customs and tried to find him. It was the middle of winter. She was freezing so she gave up and showed up at a relative's home in Canada. When she finally met her father the first thing he said to her was, "I didn't push her." My mother has never healed from any of this. Instead she wrote her own fucked-up story. She once told me I was born because she couldn't afford birth control. My parents had a shotgun wedding. My mother told me my father didn't want me and that she had proof of it in writing. She told me this when I was a child. She created a distance between my father and me that took twenty years to repair.

I wasn't raised to be lady-like. I turned out to be a bit mouthy. Some people call it voicing your opinion; I call it having no filter. I don't cook. This must be a genetic problem because my mother told me she once broke dishes when my father came home from work and asked about dinner. She is proud of that story. My friend Annie has a bumper sticker on her car that says: MARRIAGE IS FOR LIFE, DIVORCE IS FOREVER. I come from a forever kind of family.

Annie and I became friends instantly once we got past awkward introductions. We were both members of a therapy group and we met at one of the gatherings. There is really no way to casually introduce yourself to a potentially interesting person at a therapy party. For me it was more like a "guess who" game: Guess who is going through a divorce, guess who is having a nervous breakdown, guess who, etc. I managed to spark up a conversation with Annie and her husband. It turned out that we had a lot in common. We developed a friendship that has lasted for years.

Annie and I had the same counselor. We would call each other to share stories about our individual sessions with him. It became a contest of who had the wackiest experience of the week. Our group therapy sessions were filled with so much drama that Annie and I decided to show up with popcorn. There were men and women in the group sleeping together; it was a real shit show. Annie and I had our own problems, some of which people didn't understand. I can say this much, if you are going to disclose to a group of strangers that you have Bipolar Disorder you might as well do it in a prom dress. Sometimes people react as though you are a key player in a major freak show. It takes a lot of courage to face that kind of bullshit.

I called my parents from a pay phone in the psychiatric inpatient unit of a shitty hospital in Holyoke, Massachusetts. I was scared. I went to the hospital because I ran out of my medication and my psychiatrist was MIA. I told the doctors at the hospital my situation; I assumed I would be able to get my medication. I did not assume that two guards would approach me with a wheelchair to escort me to the psychiatric inpatient unit. I was terrified to be left alone with them when they took me in a wheelchair via elevator to the unit. I didn't necessarily want to run, but I also didn't want my freedom stripped away from me.

The room I slept in was cold and dark. I was alone until at some point in the middle of the night an elderly woman arrived. I don't know what brought her there, but I could tell she was in bad shape. I happened to have my Walkman with me and they let me keep it. I listened to Ray Lamontagne until I fell asleep. In the morning a doctor sent me home with my medication. I was not suicidal; I was not a threat to myself or anyone else. I was simply put down on someone's chart as having Bipolar Disorder and they sent the guards. A year later I saw Ray Lamontagne in concert as a celebration of my freedom.

I've been known not to open my mail. My mailman scares me more than my dentist and psychiatrist. Remember the monster under your bed when you were a kid? Well, the mailman is the monster under my bed, and I avoid him at all costs. This is how your electricity and phone get shut off. This is how your wages get garnished. The anxiety-producing pile at your doorway will inevitably destroy parts of your life if you don't address it. In a panic I once brought a pile of mail to my father's house. My father, stepmother, and I sat down in the living room with my bags (yes, plural). They are very organized people so the sight of my teary eyes and the piles I dumped on their living room floor were beyond anything they were equipped to deal with. My father is an accountant; I imagine the monster under my bed gave him nightmares.

My father and I met with my therapist many times. I would show up to the sessions with different versions of a plan to get my life together. My father tried to keep up. This went well until my therapist's wife left him. Honestly I think my therapist had a nervous breakdown. His advice began to alter; one week I needed to do one thing, the next week the complete opposite. When my father questioned him (god forbid anyone question him), my therapist responded with so much rage that we never went back. I am still afraid of the monster under my bed.

The psychiatrist at the mental health clinic drugged me up so that I could come down from the manic episode. With the new medication I was not able to function; I couldn't get out of bed. At the time it seemed like my only option. I saw a therapist and a psychiatrist on a regular basis at the clinic. I was still in a long-term relationship. I shared everything with my therapist. She shared with me that she wanted to quit her job. That was not helpful. She thought I should try different positions in bed to work out some of my relationship problems. That was also not helpful. I tried a day program at the clinic. I stayed in the program until they wanted the group to take a van trip to a local university to meditate in a garden. I was not ready for that kind of exposure. I was not ready to take that kind of ride on a "special bus."

During my recovery I read self-help books as well as books written by people with firsthand experience with Bipolar Disorder. One Christmas I asked my father for every book written by Kay Redfield Jamison; he bought the books. Looking back, I feel bad for the guy. Most of my family didn't know what was going on or what to do. I tried to shield my brother and sister from all of it, but there is only so much you can fit in a closet and I was already in the closet about being gay.

With time I was able to get back on my feet. I had to make a decision about what path I was going to take and came to the conclusion that living near my mother was not good for my health. I decided to move to Northampton, Massachusetts. I took a leap of faith moving there. I did so because of its reputation for having a great queer community. I came out of the closet. I found a psychiatrist who introduced me to a medication that changed my life. It was able to stabilize my depression without causing mania. For the first time in my life I felt hopeful; I felt like I stood a chance.

You were sitting across the room, I'd been checking you out for a while. "That is not a girl," they laughed. I ignored them; I was with the wrong crowd that night. There was no time for conversations about their perception of gender. I kept my eyes on you, your intensity was moving, and I was content with just watching you. Am I bold to say I see you? You are a woman who carries herself with pride and strength, yet it is your shyness that has captured me. At the end of the night you stood by the door, hands in your pockets, eyes to the floor. You waited, but I did not come.

Another night you sat alone at the bar, ambivalent. We struck up a conversation, and I watched you play pool. You tried to impress me by telling me that you are getting a chopper. I continued to listen when you were quiet, to your struggle, your desire. Am I bold to say I see you?

The trouble began somewhere between coffee and a 2 a.m. phone call. We shopped together for your first tie. I bought you a dozen of your favorite Italian cookies when you had a bad day. I wrapped the box in ribbon and made you a card. Am I bold to say I see you? Tattered, but so sweet.

As I scrubbed the kitchen floor, I saw you, and I thought that when I was finished, I would strip for you. Even when my clothes surrounded my feet, I would still want to strip. I was aching to be free; squirming under a rock I had not figured out how to lift. I wondered, Do you see me?

And now much later, after we both left town on our different paths, I see you and I so clearly for the first time.

The last time I saw you:

You drove me to that club by the river. I wore my new halter-top and tight jeans. The drag queen on stage threw me the spotlight. She and I were the only two in heels.

At the bar you flirted with a blonde in a white polo shirt; her hair fell just short of her cheekbones. I stood to the side eyeing a table of women, looked back at you, one hand in your pocket, a beer in the other, your eyes on another woman. I wandered to the back and into the bathroom. I pulled my hair up off my shoulders and fumbled with my lipstick case in front of the mirror. What am I not saying? An hour later at the bar you nodded toward me and headed for the door; I followed. On the way home you told me I didn't dress right, that I needed to dress like you. I looked over at you and said, Like hell I do because we were not the same. And then I realized what you wanted.

The fight was so bad you pulled over. You pulled over at 2 a.m. on Euclid Boulevard to cuss. Two men approached the car from either side. You kept at it so I reached over you to lock your door. We never forgave each other:

The last time I saw you.

My ex-wife and I were in marriage counseling long before we were married. Our first therapy experience was a disaster. We made the mistake of seeing the same therapist. We saw her individually and then together. During my ex-wife's individual sessions, the therapist would tell her to leave me. During our couples sessions, the therapist offered us suggestions on how to maintain a healthy relationship. We paid for two-faced advice. This does not come highly recommended.

We got married at half-time at a women's roller derby game. To make it happen we had to approach a badass group of derby women in an abandoned building where they practiced. It was a surreal experience. My stepmother hired an incredible photographer to document the wedding; our story ended up in a famous wedding blog.

I used to frequently visit my wedding photos to remind myself of the picture-perfect life I lived. A picture is worth a thousand words, but by the end of the marriage I had nothing left to say. I had to stop visiting my wedding photos. I had to start living my life.

ALLISON FRADKIN

Hear Me Out

I may be hard-of-hearing
but I've got pride
coming out of my ears.
That doesn't mean
communi-gay-tion
is always easy though.
I read lips, you read lipstick.
Let's hear it for the boy?
Here we go again.
I'll sing a different tune, thank you.
In fact, I'll tune you out.
Now don't tympanic—
it's no great hearing loss.
On the advice of Nellie Forbush,
I went and washed that man
right out of my hair and
eardrummed him out
of my dreams.
Sorry to hear that?
That's neither here nor there.
And now I think I'll
turn off my listening ears,
remove the cool-aid from the cups,
and hear what I want to hear—
something laudable,
not audible.
Because here's the deal:
I'm "hear
-ing impaired,"

I'm queer,
get . . .
Well, you've heard all this already.
Now hear this:
from here on out,
let's be all ears, not all fears;
let's differentiate, not differenti-hate.
If you don't,
you'll never hear the end of it.
Oh, you heard me loud and queer?
Good.
Glad to hear it.

DONNA MINKOWITZ

How I Got Disabled

I told Gemma that I wanted to break up but that I wanted one more date with her before we did. So we had one. It was ceremonious—she brought red wine, it was our best fucking ever, Gemma wore a dazzling white man's dress shirt and black pants for me. She hoisted my legs and arms around her and carried me into the bedroom like she was carrying me over a threshold. (Or like someone ferrying a sleepy child into bed.)

Two days earlier, my arms had become weird. I'd had my regular physical therapy that morning for a minor wrist problem that I'd had on and off for years. The specialist for this problemette, who was called a physiatrist, had sent me to a trio of phenomenally beautiful physical therapists. Now, physical therapists—I don't know whether you know this, reader—are often uncommonly beautiful physical specimens who rather resemble—this is really true—goddesses. Like goddesses in the sexist classical tradition, some of them are beyond all human ethics.

That morning the PTs were planning something new for me. The three gorgeous ones gave me a test that involved squeezing a series of heavy metal grips, then lifting some strange weights that looked like little hockey pucks. "This hurts," I protested. But the young blonde therapist said: "We're measuring strength; pain doesn't matter in this test."

I said, "I don't think I should take this test." The brunette made a tiny smile and said, "Everybody has to." It was a policy of the Zwieback Rehabilitation Institute that everybody had to be tested at regular intervals for Zwieback's prestigious large-data study. The jet-black haired one just looked me in the eye and said, "Squeeze."

I squeezed. And there and then, in the twinkling of an eye, in Zwieback's odd, white, plastic-Lego-looking complex in East South midtown, began something different, reader, than I'd ever known—at least directly, responsibly, consciously. A world of immediate pain and terror, irremediable, sharp, frumpy—sharp points not just at my wrists but going all the way through me, a cutting and smashing and burning I did not think I would ever be rid of.

What did I have? (What do I have, I should say, for certainly I have it still.) My problem is called Repetitive Strain Injury, which is a "musculoskeletal condition" people get from infelicitous repetitive endeavors of all kinds. Assembly-line workers, musicians, and chicken-pluckers are known to get it. In the digital era, secretaries and writers get it. I wonder if bad fiddlers get it, reader, from playing the same damn tune over and over?

(People get RSI of the feet, too, but I don't know from what activities—pushing old-fashioned sewing machine treadles?)

RSI—that is the agreed-upon abbreviation for it—affects nerves, tendons, ligaments, and muscles. (And maybe, I dunno, blood, bones, mind? What else could it possibly effect?) Actually, it has a new, scarier name that I find it incumbent upon me to share with you: CRPS (can it possibly be pronounced "Crips"?) for Complex Regional Pain Syndrome.

The people who have it look normal, and our backs, and necks, and arms can even be quite well-shaped and comely. We are likely to be slender, the "Know Your RSI" books say, and model workers. Women are alleged to get it more than men, either because we have weaker muscles or because we work harder and longer for The Man, or both. Shy people get it more, some authors claim, because we neglect to set limits. Overall it seems to be a disease of the small, obedient, and cute, at least if you believe the literature.

Helpless and slender? Do exactly what you tell them? Perhaps it is fortunate that the RSI tribe is a hidden one, like Jews and queers, my other peoples: you cannot tell us by looking. The "indications" of RSI are remarkably various, which is one reason some doctors think we've made it up. Just as those sex-drenched French feminists call women "the sex that is not one," meaning, among other things, that we have many, many different sources of arousal, RSI is the illness that is not one. Its effects are entirely different in different people. It is mysterious. People can get it very mildly, or they can never brush their teeth again. They can lift their arms two inches, or three feet, or only diagonally, or stiffly one morning and ecstatically and supple-ly the next. The line separating the sick from the well floats unpredictably. What might cure it, and when and if it'll get better, is extraordinarily unpredictable, too.

I was a little pissed off at the PTs right when it happened, but I couldn't get too excited about it because I was obsessed with getting ready for my last date with Gemma.

By breaking up with her but asking for one more night of sex, I felt in control, reader, like a sex seller who finally establishes it that all the sex in her life happens on her cue.

I was still trying to ignore what had happened, even then. "I really wish you would kidnap me and lock me in your closet," I whispered to Gemma. I'd seen the enormous wardrobe on her and Ann's parlor floor, and it was black-lacquered and beautiful.

"Me, too," sighed Gemma, peeling down my panties.

It was hard, actually, to comprehend that anything at all had changed. Gemma called the very next day to say that she had left her reading glasses in my apartment. "Go figure," she said, softly laughing. "I needed some reason to come over."

This time she brought as a chaperone her tiniest girl, whom I had never met. As I played with elfin, one-and-a-half year-old Cassima, Gemma played with my nipple. I should not have allowed her to—we were both very wrong to let her play with me in front of her daughter—but I let it happen anyway.

When exactly did what had happened to me dawn on me? From my desk calendar of that month—March of 2000—I can tell I got an emergency massage the following week from an expensive masseur, Lewis Fitzhugh L M T. And I canceled all my future appointments with the Zwieback physical therapists. But there is nothing else in my records to register undue disquiet until three or four weeks later. Perhaps my strange ailment got much worse in the intervening weeks?

It was a strange ailment, reader. The next month, April, showed dozens of phone numbers scrawled on my calendar—dim acquaintances, friends so casual they may not have known that they were friends. People from my college I hadn't socialized with in college, or since. The pain was making me want to be friends with everyone. I remember wanting to breathe on my writing students and somehow conjure them all into friends, like the ancient Greek guy who sows his dragons' teeth into warriors. I made a date with a sexy, plump, straight student, who was always writing about sexual abuse and her exciting, Hitlerish boyfriend, to buy hundreds of dollars worth of makeup at Bergdorf's. I never wore makeup.

The pain made me want to do anything.

I made a date to watch videos with another student, a beautiful 22-year-old who was always writing about physical abuse and exciting sex with her Ripper-boyfriend. It was against my principles to be friends with students, but I did it anyway because I could see no other way out. I needed friends that badly and thought I would have an in with them because I was their writing teacher.

Because for the first time, my personal magic did not seem to be functioning very well, and I actually felt the pain, honeybuns. I almost couldn't comprehend what I was experiencing—it was that new to me.

Reader, I couldn't do anything to make it stop hurting. I furiously researched who the best RSI doctors were, but neither of them could see me till a month later. Writing on the computer hurt so badly that I stopped doing it, and tried eking out words by longhand in a composition book, but that hurt almost as badly, and I would sit at a coffee bar and futilely try to scratch out a page, hurting in the wrists almost more than I could stand.

Next to that, not being able to take out the garbage or to carry groceries without pain seemed tiny losses. One of the Two Best Doctors, on the phone from a Paris conference, said I should just give up those activities. "Treat your hands like the royalty of all time," she said. I tried kicking my garbage down the stairs and down the block and a half to the dumpster, and taking the *New York Times* out of its blue plastic envelope in the mornings with my feet.

I couldn't read books, which felt crazy. They were now too heavy to hold. Cooking was hard because I couldn't cut most raw foods, and many vegetables and fruits had become too heavy. Pots were too heavy, as though I'd gone down a rabbit hole to a place where I weighed one tenth my previous weight. I had to hoist each potato into the microwave. The few times I tried takeout it was agonizing just to try to get the leftovers off the table.

Concurrent to all this, I started seeing a repellent and unattractive woman named Nancy. I had begun checking her out before going out with Gemma—when I'd found her hot for some reason—but now, finding her butch in an unpleasant way and skeletal, with a mug like a death's head, I wanted to have sex with her anyway. My idea, if I can reconstruct a plan that memory has mercifully spared me, was that this would further advance the personal sexual revolution I had apparently begun with Gemma.

Nancy was a friend of friends, an investment banker who liked to donate to leftist guerrillas all around the world. Her mouth tasted terrible, as though she had a large bacterial infection. Also, she had once killed a man in Greece, she told me, because he had been striding toward her about to do "something" to her, she "didn't know what." She had beaten him to death with a tire iron.

Before Nancy, I'd gone on several dates with Allia, an infuriatingly attractive Russian bisexual college student. Thankfully, I'd rejected her as polyamorous. Though I think if she'd seduced me I'd have let her. "I don't ever want to be your wife," she had grinned wolfishly me at the West 4th Street Q train station, "but I might like to be your husband," she said, staring at my breasts, meaning that she would have enjoyed having me as one of a stable of hundreds of nubile women and a few cranky Russian men. I don't know how I was able to resist her—she was just like Gemma, only younger. In addition to Allia, I had had some hopes of my 22-year-old student, Hermione—why, I don't know, since she was groaningly in love with her boyfriend. But the hint of a sexual something between us gave our friendship what to me was a comforting frisson; we watched sexy lesbian films on HBO together at my house and talked about sex a lot. Still, our friendship, and my risible hopes, went up in flames when we went to the movies together just a month into my troubles. It was raining and Hermione had become upset when I'd asked her to hold the umbrella for us for what turned out to be our entire walk from the subway. This was my first rain with RSI, and I discovered I couldn't hold an umbrella overhead without great pain for any amount of time whatsoever. I couldn't hold the snacks we brought with us or our jackets, either. "You—you can't do anything," Hermione had stuttered in anger and frustration. "I—I have to hold the umbrella, and the snacks, and everything." She was at the point of weeping. "Can't . . . can't you try to hold it a little?" she urged, meaning the umbrella. "No," I'd said, and she made a grim moue. She didn't want to hang again.

She wasn't the only one. Nancy came along at a time when several friends had extricated themselves from my life because the prospect of my needing help had just become too intense. Was I a demanding, needy, hard to deal with friend? In almost all cases, reader, I believe I was. The estrangements came quite early on, in that first month or so, when my condition was most terrifying and it seemed likely that the pain would never leave me. Sonny, my close friend from Al-Anon, had called every day before RSI hit (and not just for "program" reasons, either). After, he announced he could no longer be in contact with me. He "just had too much going on," he said. He looked uncomfortable when he passed me in the street.

Sonny was handsome and compassionate, a straight man who'd seemed a lot like a woman. He was the opposite of tight-assed. Sonny was a feminist who worked as some kind of fancy sound-recording engineer for a record label. The previous month I had been one of a handful of friends celebrating Sonny's 50th birthday with him, in a smelly diner near Madison Square Garden that he loved. Sonny was a fan of the New York Liberty, the women's basketball team lesbians love, and of *Buffy the Vampire Slayer*, my favorite feminist TV show of all time. We used to talk for hours, often about how hard we both had to fight to resist the urge to obey.

When I was terrified in the beginning of RSI I would call him, but he ditched me after about a week or so.

Nancy, with her unpleasant mouth smell and her Mafia haircut, helped to make my life comfortable and functional at a time when people were fleeing me seemingly by the thousands, like an especially brutal civil war. Trina, my brilliant Brit friend of forever, and Harry, with whom I'd watched heroic-fantasy TV for six years—six years of cheering on *Xena: Warrior Princess* as she fought the evil both within and outside herself—had both made it plain that I'd become an utterly unappealing friend.

Nancy didn't mind pushing my glass to the edge of the table where I could reach it, didn't react in horror the way most people did, when she realized that I couldn't pick up a sandwich.

I also had a few new friends—boring men and women I had courted in the first place because I'd hoped that boring people might be kinder. Certainly the ones I picked were. So the uninspired would come by and bag my trash, or bring me back a sack of food when they shopped at the Co-op. Laura and Ellen were a particularly kind, boring couple who were even shyer than me, and seemed to want to see me constantly. They were eager to buy me local veggies at the Saturday farmers' market, and to have me over to their house to eat well-prepared fish and to look at Ellen's paintings. Her moderately abstract art had sensual reds and blues and emotional, bleak whites; I liked them. But oh sadly, reader, it was dull to talk to her.

When she wasn't as bland as Kraft slices, Ellen went quite grim; she worked investigating child abuse in foster care. She saved lives, I am certain, but she mostly talked about the badness of people, and how welfare actually encouraged moral turpitude. Laura, her partner, was a silent grad student in English who managed to be colorless and soporific even on the subjects of literature and feminism, her two main areas of interest. Neither of them ever talked personally. When I tried to sometimes, the two of them looked flattered but scared. Dinners with them were safe and calming and only occasionally awkward.

Maybe morally good people produced good art, I thought hopefully, looking at Ellen's warm red trees, though I had never believed this before. Certainly I was feeling like I'd ODed on the immoral after Gemma. But my new physical problems were making morally good people a sort of urgent fetish for me. I felt vaguely embarrassed about it, as though I had decided that I suddenly required illegal, unpasteurized French cheeses at $150 a pop and no other kind.

I forgot to mention that RSI can also make your body extremely sensitive, not just make it hurt. So I went to the hairdresser's, normally somewhat painful anyhow from my old, familiar, mild RSI, and my head in the washer's hands made me feel as though I were being flayed. Even having my hair cut, from the pressure of the stylist's hands on me, or the force with which she applied the scissors,

This is because the head was connected to the neck, which was connected to the arms and shoulders. RSI was a system, as many shamans, doctors and massage therapists have tried to explain to me.

The hair salon people were annoyed, as so many people were these days, when I asked for special gentleness. "What do you expect me to do?" the 20-year-old shampoo man asked, petulant. My sister Josie, whose hugs had always been on the crippling side, was now so frighteningly painful that I actually asked her to go lighter.

That was new. I had hardly ever asked her to moderate any physically uncomfortable thing she had ever done to me, it turned out. I found this out searching my memory. I seemed to be remembering many things I had forgotten or ignored for long years, perhaps deliberately. It was dawning on me hazily that the few times I had asked my sister to moderate something—a touch, a noise, a bit of roughhousing—she'd been furiously angry, hurt.

Once Josie had paid my day fee to a fancy health club and sat so close to me on the locker room bench she was right up against my leg. Her thighs and shoulders were glued to mine. I could feel her heat and density, smell her breath. Her sweat smelled like cheese that had been put in the deep fryer. There was nothing sexual about it but it felt nevertheless like a boss's palm cupping my knee. There was the same sense of ownership, of psychological harassment, almost stalking.

I moved my legs away. She followed.

I put some room between my shoulder and hers. She closed the gap.

"Would you mind giving me a little space?"

My sister exploded. "What the fuck is your problem?" She was so outraged by my request that I wondered if she might have mistaken it for an attack on her weight. Josie was always angry at me for being thinner and also for being younger, weaker, and sicker. Josie's body was powerful, not just fat, and as long as I'd known her she had always seemed to be using her extra size and force to annex my space to her own.

It was not unusual for her to walk or sit so close to me that I couldn't move. The previous month we'd gone to Brighton Beach, and on the boardwalk she'd kept her shoulders and hips as if magnetically clipped to mine. Whenever I tried to move away, she'd stalked me. Again. Finally, I just resigned myself to having her stick to me for our whole trip to Brighton Beach. Perhaps she just wanted to get close to me and didn't know any other way?

But Josie liked to make other physical decisions for me, too, and reader, for some reason I would tolerate her making them. When we were in an airplane, she would kick my bag so far underneath my seat that I would have to throw my back out to pull it out. I protested, but still flew with her. You might ask why, or why I agreed to sit right next to her, making it possible for her to kick my bag where she pleased. Why I often rode in her car even though she usually wouldn't take me where I wanted. Reader, she would just take me where she wanted. Perhaps I wanted to be close to her, too, and believed this was the price?

We were bound together in a curious fashion, my sister Josie and I, like two toys on a shelf that are always fighting. She was the larger, more aggressive toy, and I was the toy who gets thrown around but is the other's brother.

Josie was my counterpart, or as Robert Graves puts it, my "blood-brother, my other self, my weird." The one who "often appears in nightmare as the tall . . . dark-faced bedside spectre, or Prince of the Air, who tries to drag the dreamer out through the window . . . [they compete] for love of the capricious and all-powerful Threefold Goddess, their mother, bride and layer-out."

"Layer-out" as in layer-out for their funerals.

We were violent rivals, although sometimes also peculiarly passionate friends—loving each other with an almost erotic intensity, as doppelgängers do, and lifelong enemies.

"Buddies two, me and you!" she used to sing-song to me.

Before biting me hard in the arm.

When we were children Josie used to hit me, and I was almost as scared of her as I was of my father. When I was in high school, she once tore up my writing. My eyes are brown, and my hair used to be brown, too, reader; once when I was 19 and wearing a brown T-shirt, Josie remarked to me, "Do you know what you look like when you wear brown, Donna? You look like a piece of shit." I never wore brown that close to my eyes again.

I was never as physically intimidating to Josie as she was to me. That was the main difference between us. But I do remember, in my 20s, on one occasion sniggering at her facial hairs. I also hazily remember, with shame, reader, kissing Josie's neck in an obnoxious way when we were teenagers. Er, that is to say, a kind of sexual way. And she hated it, of course, which was my intention. And the last time I have ever hit anybody, when I was 21, I slapped Josie because she had laughed at my karate moves.

How did we love each other? I had, as I have said, a great capacity for ignoring things that hurt me. When Josie was loving to me, which she was for long periods, when she would show her warmer, nicer face to me like the bright side of the moon, I ignored that there were times when it was not so.

"That was the bad Josie," she said to me once when I was five and she had just hit me. "I'm the good Josie."

The fact that she could so easily split herself in two terrified me. But I apparently divided her in the same way ever afterward: as though she were two people, so that when Josie was violent or insulting I regarded her as a completely different person than the one who had kissed and hugged me just an hour ago.

I kept hoping that the good one would return, and she always did for a while. But when she did, I always assumed she would stay. I ignored past evidence that she would eventually enact her brutal side again.

RSI changed me. I just couldn't bear the pain when she hugged me, and had to ask her to go lighter. She replied that she simply wouldn't ever hug me again, then.

I said, Okay, she shouldn't then. Saying no to her was new to me, but I didn't know what else to do. I knew I wouldn't be able to bear Josie's hugs if they stayed unchanged.

Josie was nonplussed. She was furious as well when I asked her, as I did everyone else, to hand me things up close so that I could reach them without damaging my hands. (For Dr. Mayhew, my new RSI doctor, had warned me that if I did things with my hands that were physically painful, I would almost certainly damage them further, so that, perhaps, I would become unable to brush my teeth or put my own clothes on, or feed myself.)

My sister was, in fact, infuriated by my RSI requests. On one of my mother's increasingly frequent hospital stays, the old-fashioned phone by her bedside rang. My mother was sleeping. My sister and I looked at each other. "Why can't you pick it up?" Josie screamed. "Yeah, I know you're not supposed to, but you can!" "You know I can't pick it up," I told Josie quietly. I think it was the first time I've ever looked her in the eyes. I could use only headsets to listen to calls now. If I used a pay phone, or any other old-fashioned receiver, it would flare me up for at least a month.

I did not damage myself further. Dr. Mayhew, in fact, considered it a sort of achievement, claiming I avoided further-hand-damaging behaviors better and more consistently than any of her other patients.

თ

May 2000: Evidently, I have a body that feels pain, to my surprise. What do I do about it?

I have always sneered at the parts of the *Tao Te Ching* that talk about how important it is to protect your body. "Restraint keeps you out of danger," Lao Tzu and the other old sages say, "So you can go on for a long, long time." But what's the use of going on for a long, long time? What does that have to do with courage—or spirituality? What does The Way have to do with preserving a stupid mixture of carbon, hydrogen, oxygen, and nitrogen?

The weird old Chinese poem says, "He who values his body more than dominion over the empire can be entrusted with the empire. He who loves his body more than dominion over the empire can be given the custody of the empire." Really? *That's* who they think should have dominion over the Empire?

But as I start having to spend my time telling people to push my plate of eggs up to a certain place so I can reach it, or to please not shake my hand, I find myself obsessively reading the parts of the *Tao Te Ching* I used to hate.

I've been having despairing sex and despairing dates with Nancy—getting her to take me out to dinner for my birthday and crying at the dinner because she says she feels very seriously about me and I surely don't about her. But even nice, obliging Nancy has sex with me one day in a way I hate. The subtle powers of fetish have been the only thing keeping me from unqualified misery as I've tried to ignore that Nancy is not Gemma—so I get her to shave my legs erotically in bed, I let her make me come again and again, almost numbly. I don't much touch her, reader.

(I find her terribly ugly, and I accept her adulation.)

One evening she gets a little aggressive, always the flip side of abjection as I ought to know. When I've had enough sex and I'm ready to go to bed, I ask her to stop. She does, but then a little later fondles my breasts very alluringly. Now I want more. She says, "Oh now you want it, huh?" and starts saying demeaning things to me as she touches me, calling me a nasty slut, ordering me to beg. I get thoughtful for a moment: "Hmm, I don't actually like that. Don't say those things to me when you touch me."

She complies, but "forgets" herself and does it again a few minutes later.

Quite suddenly, I'm done. I leave on the spot, although it's midnight and I was in my nightgown and about to go to sleep.

Where did that come from?

And I never see her again.

My new therapist, Olive, says, "Perhaps in general, you need to be more careful about getting people to stop doing things that you don't want them to do to you."

I have always hated fear, but Lao Tzu says, "When we don't fear what we should fear, / we are in fearful danger."

When I was close with Josie, I always had little bursts of fear and I didn't know why, so I ignored them.

Now, I'm not ignoring them anymore.

I must go to sessions with my first post-RSI-attack physical therapist, Billie Jean Raister, considered the best physical therapist for Repetitive Strain Injury in New York City, and maybe the world. Nice Dr. Mayhew, who still has not returned from France, recommended that I start with Billie Jean immediately.

Years earlier, by happenstance, I'd met Billie Jean when her former partner in a joint physical therapy practice had treated me for my early, mild RSI.

When I came in for my first appointment, Billie Jean definitely remembered me. But she seemed very annoyed, even though it had happened ten years earlier, that I had seen her partner, Alice, for RSI back then and not her.

"Why would you have gone to Alice?" she said, working her hands hard into the fascia of my arms, crinkling her nose. "RSI was never her specialty. It was mine!"

I stared at her thumb pressing on my arm. The therapist continued. "She was never, ever known for RSI. You should have gone to me. Why on earth would you have wound up with her?"

I coughed. "Er . . . I think you were all booked up that first week."

Billie was still mad. "Alice thought she could grab you." But she got on another subject now, "The Japanese just brought me to teach all their physical therapists about RSI, they think that I'm the best one in the world."

Suddenly, she caused wrenching pain in my palm. "I'm the one they brought to Japan. I can do things no one else can." She took my hands abruptly and placed them on her own hips. I believed—still believe—that she just did it to stretch me, but I hated having my hands against her curves. As she twisted and stretched my arms against her, she made my hands fall again and again against the rounds of her breasts.

Even though I hadn't been the one to put my hands there, I felt a lava of shame. I tried not to have my palms and fingers touch her in any of those soft places, but it was impossible. It felt like being treated for RSI by having my mother make me feel her up.

Two sessions later, I spoke up. "Could you please stretch me in a different way? I know you don't intend anything bad by it, but it makes me uncomfortable to have to touch your body that way."

"No!" Billie Jean surprised me by her adamance.

The next session, I decided to be absolutely frank about my needs. "I'd like to ask you to find a different way to stretch me because this way makes me very, very uncomfortable. I'm very sensitive to touching certain parts of other people's bodies because I was sexually abused."

Billie made a snide face. "That's what I thought." She sneered. I looked at her blankly. "Well, I'm not gonna do it any other way because that's the only way I can do it!"

I canceled all my future appointments with her and found a new physical therapist who didn't insist on stretching me that way.

D. ALLEN

Possession

The pain is not personal. I am incidental to it. It is like faith,
the believer eclipsed by something immense ...
> —Tom Andrews, "Codeine Diary"

I.

Often I confuse pain with a poverty
of love. *I don't have hands today*
means I can't use them to touch you.

This is its own truth. But hands in pain
are unequivocally alive: stone altars
whose many candles blush and flicker.

You reach for my fingers;
a smokeless heat rises.

II.

Controlled grasping is the hand's
coveted achievement, a series of
movements by which we bring

our desires nearer. What is the word
for my index finger, then, when it
hovers below your collarbone,

moves across tattoo and skin
as if painting your body with light?
Attunement. A plucked steel string.

Pain, my teacher, reminding me
how little we can live on.

III.

Today in the museum I found
an ancient pair of ivory hands curved
but not clasped behind glass.

Egyptian Clappers, the placard calls them.
Hands held in the hands to make
the sound of applause. I think of

young Tom Andrews clapping
for fourteen hours, world record broken
despite his hemophilia.

The carved clappers speak across space
and time. *There are other ways.*

IV.

My surrogate hands
are not ivory; they are not
so ornamented as these.

They are not blown glass
or wood or burnished gold.
They are, my love, made

of water. My surrogate hands, which
you may touch whenever you
desire but never grasp,

are castles of salt and foam.
They will always hold you.

V.

Suspended with fine pins
over dark velvet and glassed in
by a diligent archivist—

burnished, lacquered,
and folded into a gesture
of supplication or surrender—

radioactive with pain—
my true hands could illuminate
every hallway in this museum,

beside them the curator's note:
Light, translated, is light.

GREGORY VILLA

Limp

Okay, sit down, shut up, and take a deep breath. Geez, you guys. You'd think that the scariest thing in the world is a less than perfectly functioning dick. Believe me, by the time you're my age, you'll have stared at enough overly-relaxed "love tubes" (including your own) that you could start up something like a slightly underinflated Macy's Thanksgiving Day Parade.

Okay, here's the deal. I'm a 67-year-old gay guy who's eaten his high school weight in cheese curls and ice cream and retained way too much of it. Plus I smoke like several chimneys, and that lovely little combination means that parts of me don't work as well as they used to. We talkin' knees, eyes, and penis.

No lie—back in my day I could use my hardon to hammer nails, poke your eye out with my ejaculate, and come so often you'd think I was a taxi. These days, not so much.

And all of the examples I've listed are, well, self-inflicted. If I'm pissed off that I can't even *see* my one-eyed wonder worn of joy anymore, the sidewalk is right outside the door waiting for me to start walking my girth off. Diet? Well, I know this lovely little guy who cooks the most *amazingly* delicious healthy food, so there's an opportunity (and we're not just talking cuisine, if you catch my drift). As for the smoking, I've just discovered this cool app that tracks how long it's been since I've smoked, how many of the bleeding coffin nails I *haven't* shoved into my face, and what's proved most effective, how much money I've saved by turning down the Camels.

On the other hand, there are contributors to my "erectile dysfunction," as the ads say, that I can't control. My days of improving the gene pool of the herd are long over, so my internal clock's telling me that my animated ivory doesn't need to go stampeding trough the savanna anymore. Also there's the matter of my prostate. Currently my urologist and I are tinkering away, figuring exactly what's going on in that glorious little bulb of joy, and deciding if this is something fixable by diet, medication, surgery, or what have you.

By this time you've probably noticed that what I'm talking about isn't really a disability.

Well, my disability relates to my mental illness and bouts of severe depression. You've heard the joke, no doubt, about how "depression doesn't run in my family, it gallops." It's settled down for a good long stay on *both* sides of my family. One of my parents was in and out of psych wards, ECT included, for years. For decades the secret on the other side of my family tree was that my grandfather spent years in an asylum in Georgia. When I learned this last bit, I cannot tell you how relieved I was, because in my case, depression and mental illness came with deep, unrelenting shame. Being a gay kid growing up in a somewhat fundamentalist religion had nothing on the shame I felt for being that broken.

Depression felt like an icicle plunged into my guts—an intense core of pain and unworthiness. I recall a friend taking me to a doctor, having finally convinced me to get out of my apartment, and saying, "This isn't Greg, he's always been so happy." My thoughts were, "Nope, this is all that I am." I felt like a malformed embryo floating in a sea of bile.

Of course, I was wrong. It's taken me years of therapy to get here. And "here" may be a temporary location. I have a chronic disease, and I have to work at staying well.

And that's where the final impediment to my hard throbbing pogo stick of lust comes in.

I have to take medication to keep my mind from going "Ka-*plang!*" all of which (and I'm not kidding here) make sex somewhat problematic.

And you know, I can deal with that. It's not as stark as either I shove these pills down my gullet or I'm out walking the sugar beet fields in the middle of a blizzard, but I'll take a bit of impotence to say sane.

But you know, it's not like I'm gonna become all monastic and turn into St. Francis of the Abstinent. It may take me a couple of days to work up to an orgasm, but Holy Fucking Hannah, they're intense.

So see, things could be worse.

LIV MAMMONE

Vagina Resigning

My vagina has put in
for a transfer from my legs.
"Irreconcilable differences," she says.
"They're crooked. Criminal. Either they go, or I go."

Rigidity keeps them splayed, a cold couple in separate beds.
At six years old, the tension
between them reached such a pitch
my vagina started to fuse shut, went mute.
My mother slathered her daily in estrogen gel
and she exploded.

Now she sings opera—
speaks Hungarian with only just the slightest
Long Island accent, designs her own wardrobe
of eighteenth century gowns
insists all Georgia O'Keeffe's flowers
are portraits of her.

She says she's overqualified to work with my legs.
Their bad attitude is affecting the higher-ups.
My right hand hooked on relaxants;
my back collapsing into its low self-esteem—
she can't work under these conditions.

At weddings, while I dance all night,
my vagina tells me I look like Shakira.
My legs turn me into something like
a baby pony on three shots of Jose Quervo.

When my vagina makes my toes curl,
my legs won't let them straighten again.
I have to sit up and pull them like artichoke leaves

When the lady conductor on Long Island Rail Road
asks for *proof of my special needs*,
my legs spasm their shame while my vagina
quips, "My special needs include:
cannoli cream, poems by the Earl of Rochester, and
an orgy with the entire Huston family."

In Times Square last week, a shirtless, drunk fratboy
with a sign around his neck advertising
FREE HUGS AND SEX TIPS
flinched away from my legs,
his douchebaggery silenced.
My vagina bitch-slapped him.
She demands to be objectified like any able pussy in America!

She wants to go clubbing; throws
spiked platforms from Trash and Vaudeville
at the wall next to my head while my legs lay stiff
and snoring by the bedroom door.
I try to explain that I can't
apply winged Nefertiti eyeliner or punk faerie
lilac highlights with one hand.
Can't clasp necklaces or keep loose in stockings
I am not the woman
she'd be proud to wear.

The blame for all this falls
on my legs. She calls it a
crippled cunt conspiracy.

But she thinks I am worth more than books,
blogging, and being called cutie pie
by a homeless guy or some gamer with a fetish.

My vagina thinks I'm sexy.
She says it's not her fault
if my legs can't support that.

Spell for the Hairy Girl

crop circle   column wreathed in blossom
Eve   she wolf   mossy stone   unconcern
     surgical scars kept warm kept hidden
bearded Lady burlesque yellow grass   high wind
gender juggler   Medusa peeking through kneeless jeans
cancer cream   tarantula
hot wax only used in prayer
safety among men   anemone home to your clownfish
     Paula Cole   Riot Grrl   animal shawl
dirty homegrown strawberry

mother's bent and slavish back   plague rat
     hospital gown happy trail   inmate
intimacy   lacework   thistle bouquet
     Ursa Major   fanged mouth in parenthetical fur
witch's tit   Whitman's beard
human woodland

truth:
nymphs wouldn't have skin
like a rounded sea stone

Prematurity

The baby was blue.
I was blue when I
was born. My skin
was a terrarium of
veins. They shoved
(saved) me into the
incubator. We buried
the baby under a
Japanese maple
sapling. I was born
in October on the
first cold day. Mom
gave me up when I
fell in love with a
woman. Dad locked
all the doors and un-
plugged the phone.
The left side of my
brain is a strangled
runt-kitten and God
is a genderless glyph.
The Rasta man sitting
outside Atlantic Terminal
is shouting, "And in the
beginning there was
the Word and the Word
was with God and the
Word was God!" over
and over and I am

praying it's the last
cold day. My blood
becomes glue. Mommy
prays the rosary while
driving in case we crash.
Says, "I worry I won't see you
In Heaven." Said, "I don't
want to be your mother
anymore; it's too hard,"
when I spoke of my lover,
so I smashed Jesus's face in
all his thousand places in the
house I didn't. I cut my wrists.
In my head I cut my wrists. Dad
wanted to name the baby
Max. The doors were never
locked. My brother once
choked my mother in her
car and we almost drove
into a pole. Dad
wanted to name
the baby Max.
Maximilian or
Maxine. I was
born in July. I came
too early. I spilled
the secret; we
planted the
Japanese Maple
for the baby.

SaraEve's Skull

is an endangered sea anemone
on a bleached stone against the polluted sea
of Jersey's sky. The reefs don't don't know they're going

extinct—or do they? She and I both read that article about old subway
cars tossed into the ocean to give coral a new place to call home.
Shells of those rattling shuttles under us where

no one ever gives her a seat are being put
to better use, letting everything swim in.
SaraEve's skull

is the last bird of its kind
perched above a polka dot dress.
But I don't have figurative language enough

for the fuchsia of her mouth, housing its brave as fuck
tongue. She wears her hair as a cockatoo's proud comb,
swept sideways, a shade too hard

to be called lilac; tossing it as she laughs
her last-hours-at-the-fairground laugh.
It's a grape soda volcano:

a royal-robed comma on her forehead,
so the sentence of her striving
never stops. And through that window on Avenue

A, the scars that ribbon her scalp
into a Fabergé egg with a fairy wren flapping inside
hold my eyes—that little purple bird swirls

a witch's brew of symptoms. SaraEve's
hurricane brained and I'm sitting in a cafe catching
light off her prism, wondering if that Dr. Seuss

colored Truffula tuft was the bow
inviting the doctors into her gift.
Did her neuro paths leak starfruit juice

onto latex gloves
when they tried to unspool them?
She's part peacock, part parrot, part lark.

SaraEve's scalp, scar
spangled banner, making all the angry

history in my skin hiss and sting, desiring
to split at their seams.

Advice to the Able-Bodied Poet
Entering a Disability Poetics Workshop
for Jennifer Bartlett and Shira Erlichman

- Let's just save time—yes, I *have* seen *Rain Man, The Miracle Worker, My Left Foot*, or, more recently, *The Theory of Everything*. I wanna fuck Daniel Day Lewis too, but can we not?
- If all the several Black Friends and the Special Needs Kids everybody's mom/cousin/friend/friend's mom/cousin's friend's mom has ever worked with got together, they could overthrow the government and we'd see some real change. Those people aren't reference points for me. There are no reference points for me.
- This isn't a *Whose Life Sucks More?* game. We aren't sitting around doing shots of Jack Daniels and tortoise or hare racing our way to some oppression finish line. You have seen moments I can never imagine.
- When asking about my disability, please remember you have Siri at your beck and call, and that what you really need to know will come up in the poems.
- Similarly, if you decide you need to ask my diagnosis, I can guarantee those ugly-sounding words are all I have in common with whoever you know. If you don't know anyone, asking me *What does that mean* isn't ingratiating. I'm not a painting by Warhol. Asterisk: if you're just meeting me and that's your opening? That, or *so what happened to you*—you're suspect. I have a favorite band, a gaggle of furry children. Let's start there.
- The words *disability, disorder*, and *disease* aren't synonymous.
- Don't ask if able-bodied people have really said and did jaw-dropping things in my poems. It's hard to invent ignorance.
- And while we're at it, let's talk about language. You're here for

that above all, right? Me too. But *I* get to decide how it's done, not you. If I say *cripple*, it's because I like how the consonants break like bones. I'm not handing you a membership card. If I say *Call me "special needs" and I'll roll over your foot*, it doesn't mean that softness won't comfort others. Political correctness is kind of like using correct pronouns. So many words have been made up and thrown onto my flesh. None were my name.

- Your ear will need to curve around the rhythm of speech. Your pace will hunger to leave me limping. You will want to catch me as I lurch forward; lead me by elbow or hand; not to repeat yourself; to talk as fast as you do out there. Slow down. Slow everything down.
- If you didn't get the above reference to pronouns, I'll write a separate piece for you.
- The phrase *but you don't look sick* can go fuck itself with a moving train covered in chainsaws.
- Don't use the word *inspiration* unless you're talking about Walt Whitman, Langston Hughes, John Keats or Jesus.
- Matter of fact, leave Jesus out of it altogether; he's busy enough.
- It isn't a wheelchair; it's a fully automated battlestation. It isn't a cane; it's a dousing rod. It isn't a limp; it's a swagger. It isn't a stim—it's how my fabulous self is pulling magic out of the air.
- I'm not your metaphor. Phantom limbs, deafness, or blindness as figurative language in your poems will result in unhinging my fucking jaw.
- Silence is a clichéd cliché that can't expire fast enough.
- If you find yourself saying something that begins *with no offense, but*, I want you to stop. Take a breath. And ask yourself these three questions: *Does this need to be said? Does this need to be said right now? Does this need to be said right now* by me? If the answer to any of those is no, return to Start. Do not collect $200.
- Laugh.
- Be honest.
- Your head had best be a microscope. Ask yourself why you're here. But question my motives, too. Slam your hand hard on my buttons.
- Some kind of dragon needed slaying to get to this room, whether

it be the nasty bus driver or thoughts of suicide.

- Speak for me, not over me.
- Yes, I can have sex. I hope everybody in here writes a jam so graphic it makes your goosebumps mambo just so you never ask a disabled person that ever again, unless you're offering. Some of us fuck differently from you, and we're all the better for it.
- I don't think shy people become poets, but in case you are, you best chill if you fear the body. If I'm gonna write about a colostomy bag in free verse or a pantoum about how hard it is to negotiate my period on crutches, I wanna do it in peace.
- You need Advil? Guaranteed, somebody got you covered.
- Getting here is hard. Even if the workshop is in my living room, getting there is hard. So somebody's probably gonna show up in pajamas, crocs, mismatched socks, unshowered, hair falling loose from ponytail—whatever. Either they're embarrassed or don't give a fuck. Either way, they don't need you mentioning it.
- If I have to leave the room while you're reading, sorry in advance.
- Let me point out that Tiny Tim has been fucking me over since 1843. If I'm happy, it's taken for a miracle; if I'm not, I remind them of all they have and all the work they have to do. I could be a big smile, a raised fist, an eye glittered with tears.
- My middle finger raised against assholes who should've known better is the source of my inspiration.
- This is the place I come to sharpen my teeth; to weep until I am the Danube. I don't care if you're frightened.
- Trigger warnings. That is all.
- Halle Berry, Harriet Tubman, Orlando Bloom, Bill Clinton, Agatha Christie, Charles Darwin. A lot of your faves are disabled. Just like a lot of your faves are actually bisexual. (More breaking news at 11.)
- And while we're on that, being disabled doesn't mean you've checked off your minority box on the form. Just saying.
- I'm flawed. Sainthood is boring.
- I don't want to talk about me. How's my stanza structure?
- Intersectionality is not just a buzzword. It's very real.
- I will ask if I need your help. Repeat this a billion times.
- Related note: you wouldn't grab someone on the subway. You'd

let your face smash into the pole before steadying yourself on the person next to you. So why in the name of God's teeth would you touch me or whatever apparatus I may have without asking?!

- Remember: you're one slip in the shower, a doctor's visit, a missed turn away from being me.
- If I fall, the way you gasp hurts worse than impact.
- I'm not blaming you. I'm saying *Pay attention.*
- Inevitably, someone will be forced to stop coming. Email them; that'd be cool.
- Even if you pity me, don't mess around when it comes to editing.
- Your body is so damn fucking beautiful. It's like nothing else.
- Please remember that compliance with any or all of the aforementioned will not result in praise of any kind, cookies, medals, or otherwise. Thank you.
- People are like poems. They don't get finished; they just stop.

KIT MEAD

Missing What You Never Had:
Autistic and Queer

There's a big LGBT and queer community in Atlanta, and I can't find it. I'm also autistic and I can't stand noise. I signed up to be part of the LBGTQ group on campus once, but fled because they were already friends and loud, and I was all fluttering hands, stuttering words, hide from the loud. It felt like my last chance to make a connection with my uncertain queerness, questioning gender, knowing I wasn't straight.

What does it mean to not be able to find a community you feel you should be part of? It means a lot of things. Because everything is influenced by my autism, and not everything is influenced by my queerness. It means that I feel I have failed at being queer in some aspect because many queer events are too loud. I would exist in a state of shutdown at those events. I can't go to Pride parades. I couldn't go to any of the events at my college. No one really asked for my opinions on making those events more accessible, because I exist as an invisible queer.

So here's what it means to be autistic and queer, and also not be able to find a queer community:

1. People don't believe you're actually agender (feeling like you don't have a gender) and sexually queer and not straight as hell because you're autistic.
2. You feel like you're missing an integral part of being queer by not having a queer community around you.
3. You feel like an invisible queer person.

The Invalidation of Autistic Queerness

I did meet someone interesting on the Internet and we're having a great conversation on being queer and autistic. Sometimes people don't think I'm actually queer, so I considered it a great relief to meet this person. We're having interesting conversations on how queerness gets considered symptomatic of autism and difference rather than being a difference in its own right. Melanie Yergeau, autistic activist, wrote this in "Neuroqueer Rhetorics: Gazes, Spaces and Relationships":

> "You have a male brain," the therapist explains. "That's what autism does to you." Or: "Autism makes you think you're queer."

None of my therapists told me this, perhaps because I didn't realize my queerness until late in high school. I started finding words to describe things then. No one had ever explained to me that I might be queer even though I had few "infatuations" with boys. And even as I stared at one girl's hair in the sunlight to the point of distraction in class. Simon Baren-Cohen's work created one of the ideas behind autistic people having "male brains" and invalidating their queerness. Baren-Cohen wrote that autistic people have "extreme male brains," leading off on a wild chase for many to claim that any deviance on the part of autistic people can only be the result of autism's symptoms and behaviors.

Since time eternal or at least the 1940s, people pathologized autism. This includes Leo Kanner, who named it early infantile autism. Later, Bruno Bettelheim took it further, calling autistic people empty shells. And autism and queerness have been inextricably tangled since Lovaas took the "effeminate boys studies" designed to make boys who displayed so-called feminine traits (if one buys into gender roles) stop displaying those traits and applied it to autistic people in what now gets called Applied Behavioral Analysis (ABA). The language used in the effeminate boys studies still sounds familiar for what ABA targets in autistic people: the elimination of certain autistic "behaviors." The language of the effeminate boys studies pathologizes feminine behaviors in boys the same way the language of ABA targets repetitive motions and lack of eye contact in autistic children.

So when I tell people I'm autistic and queer, what will their reaction be? Will I be welcome in their spaces? Especially when I ask them to turn the volume down or reduce the emphasis on so much talking.

Missing Queer Space

"Well, how can you miss something you've never been part of?" would be an easy question to ask of me. But of course I miss it. I missed it from the moment I signed up and then could not participate, watching from the sidelines like an injured athlete. And I miss knowing what could have been rather than what was. I feel like I am missing an integral part of me being queer by not being in queer spaces. I only had one person to celebrate with when I cut my hair short in a pixie cut, and we cracked jokes about my hair being excellently queer.

I can't find the queer community in Atlanta. I would not know where to start. There's a LGBT Pride parade I cannot go to, bars I cannot go to (because I would not interact well), and I don't know what else there is. No one ever educated me on the queer community in Atlanta.

I feel like a fake queer.

It makes me feel fake that I cannot take part and never could participate in some of the things the queer community on my campus did with blaring music, dances, and hauling off to Pride parades and putting up a LGBT history month panel, where disability wouldn't be included, in the student center.

I have a disabled community. At least half my friends on Facebook identify as autistic or otherwise disabled. Sometimes we talk about being queer. But I'm not part of a solid queer community.

Invisible Queers

This makes me an invisible queer. Scattered articles across the Internet bring notice to certain disabled queers or LGBTQ feminists of a certain type. But mostly, I see able-bodied ones. My disability is fairly visible. I squee and pressure stim and script and have erratic conversations about the problems in mainstream feminism with one of my friends.

I don't write about my queerness as much, because I can't find the queer community very much, and so I don't know who would listen. I write myself off as invisible sometimes, and other times I am made invisible. I don't write about my queerness as much, because I feel like it'll be written off by a community of able-bodied queer folks, or even written off by other disabled queer folks as symptomatic of autism.

My autism blurs into my queerness. It does not cause my queerness, but they tie together. When I cut my hair, it was not to look queer, though that was a bonus side-effect. It was because it was brushing the back of my neck and sticking there unpleasantly and creating a sensory hell. I wear loose clothing, t-shirts, and "guy jeans," and people said I look queer. Tight clothing is sensory hell.

Sensory hells create themselves in my environment. I have sensory processing disorder as a part of my autism, meaning that I perceive things with my senses more than non-autistic/non-SPDers. I have oversensitive hearing and tactile defensiveness, among other things. I do not touch and receive touch easily, and I do not walk into loud spaces easily.

And I miss things I am not part of. Social interactions feel crushing.

I want to walk into a queer community in my town and know I will be welcome for who I am.

ARTHUR DURKEE

Switch

Some old friends seem to think it's like hitting a switch,
and you reset to what you were before. Reset, reboot.
As though one treatment was enough to cure the plague.
As though none of what has gone before had gone before.
As though you could throw the switch and be what you had been,
before everything. Before everything happened. A simple switch.
But in the mirror you look older than you really are, lined down,
face aged, stiff, care-worn, beard and hair whiter than yesterday,
than in quick memory. You never get out unscathed.
In the meantime, having circled so close to that black hole drain,
close enough to see through the grate to nothing dark inside,
when you return to old venues full of old friends and dramas,
nothing clicks, nothing connects, nothing seems to matter.
You can't care about paying bills, buying groceries, weeding the garden.
Life becomes meditation. I am a monk in my own home, ill long enough
to lose track of what others say really matters. Time away
from the flurries of the ordinary dramas of other lives
makes them seem small, irrelevant. I suppose I must call back
friends who called awhile ago to ask how I was. It's just too hard,
though, to keep telling the same story. Friends who think the switch
has been thrown, one treatment and you're well again, are so tiring,
overwhelming, exhausting to seek out. Needy people are enough
to drain what's left right down that black drain, suck dry the juices
of available attention. Instead I'll spend an hour by a silent river,
in sun, with trees, listening to birds and brooks, having survived.

Scars

Long line along the right wrist, where
the sharp edge of a door caught, tearing.
Line of unknown origin making a ragged T above
the first line, like a knife wound. Pool of an L
on the middle digit. Older scar, from hitting a locker door
in high school. Naked at that moment, exuberant,
talking to other boys, flinging hands about to make a point,
point of the metal locker catching and scraping.
Point of a blood transfusion needle entry, pointless mounding
of wound and dimple of scab becoming scar. Already bleeding
away into wind and water. Itch of tracks on inner
elbows. Itch at night, before rest. Other scars to come.

Breast and belly, long lines and broken wounds.
Something of a knee problem. Crackle and pop of cartilage
grinding into bone, chips embedded in the connectors.
So it goes. Accumulation of memories gonging in marked skin.
Back of the hand a map of places where scars were acquired.
More scars to come. There will be blood, and sinew, and fatty tissue
to be torn through. There will be road lines across the lower belly.

A photo of a friend, naked in a field, walking stick in hand,
intense eyes eyeing the camera, aging, fit, hiking, a little fur
on the body, a little flushed with walking, a little dewed with sweat.
It's a beautiful portrait, face and eyes lively, lived-in, sensual, exuberant.
And the long scar across his torso, from clavicle to base of sternum.
A forgotten operation, mostly ignored in an outdoors life.
How many teenage boys have open-heart surgery and live another
30 years in perfect health, that near brush, long line of old incision

the only memory left of trauma? A repeat event would be more mortal.
We all survive things we can't embrace, can't imagine.

The scar on the naked hiker inspires: you can live on,
live through this, make it into an old scarred memory, stubborn survival
that gives an excuse to tell a story to make friends squirm.
Mostly we cannot imagine scars on the other side: how to get there
is a void, uncertain and persistent, a hole in ahead-memory, a blank
white sheet of rose-paper. Pull sinew out of its nut-hatch, its fibrous
anomaly. Recognition that the scar on the other side of survival
is a meadow we can't imagine surveying. Not yet.
The condition of a belly scar is a mark you've made it past.
The gates are guarded by converted demons who've changed their
     ways.

God of thunder, god of light. Some scars fade out, given time.
Stitches turn to the thinnest of lines, blooms in the crisis of flesh.
Never used to be needle-shy. A time in a hospital, they'll send you home
when you can walk again. Healer healed. Park that portable IV
by the pissoir. Might as well drain it directly. It's morphine makes you
into a worse poet, looped on limericks and asinine alliterations. Now,
     standing
before the mirror, naked, looking over every inch of skin, mapping
a catalogue of near-misses, almost-dieds, close encounters, slow
     seepages.
Slow breath, a little shuddery, as you realize just how close you came,
that time or another. Something dark behind the eyes, rarely seen,
rarely let out of its cage. Last battened weather-beaten door of privacy.
The worst scars are never visible to anyone on the other side.

Perfume of the Desert

Even though it's rained hard these days, I sniff a whirl
of alkali dust in air blown all the way from Nevada to Lake Michigan.
No wind strong enough to scrub it loose. Tang of dead cities,
eroded metals pooled in temporary lakes that lead to no ocean.
I've lost all ability to tell potential lovers what they do to me.
I'll settle for crumbs from the dancefloor sidelines. You lose
the will to risk when rejection is inevitable. Small consolations of
higher forms of love, spiritual, intellectual, distant, worshipful,
the perfume of the desert, either tang or memory of tang, a cup
long drunk, long hungover, long regrets in echoes of a breeze
combing its fingers through hair of trees. Such hard work to resist
this sudden pathetic wail that comes over you with its
demanding memory. I haven't got much left to offer anyway.
Solace comes from ignoring people and talking with redbirds.
The safest muse is distant, the muse you watch from afar,
the one that doesn't threaten immolation, moth wing to candle
bright as fusion, soaring in too close. I'm immunized
by being phoenix-burned. Let's rename these birds,
give those green tall stands which brush the wind
a new name, a heartwood name. I'll leave a mark
along a trail, a maze to master if you can. A milkweed
where there should be cactus, a stink of burning stone,
gypsum, salt, or terror. Stand on the ridgeline, take in blue air
hazed with wind and distance, its scent of dry lake dust.
Dance alone beneath such alien stars, sparks loose
as wind in trees, where none can hear them sing.

Hidden

He drove an hour up the East Bay for sex with me.
After emails, we chatted on the cell as he drew close.
Once at my door he beamed with grins, excited, eager.
I greeted him in shorts and tee, with hugs, with hope.
But when I shed my shirt, pants gone before, he spied
what clothes till then had hidden. He said, "Oh no,

I can't deal with that. You should have told me,
before I drove all this long while." Not completely rude,
he stayed an hour to rest and talk before he drove away.
The night was warm, the sea breeze gentle, cool.
My clothes were off, so I left them off. "Fuck this,"
I thought, "I'm not getting dressed again for you."

Aerial View of the Terrain

Hardness has become a way of life. A test of metals.
People think I'm all better but I'm not
even halfway home, and it gets worse before
it gets better. I'm in a small desert hotel room
feeling sorry for myself. The body struggles on with living,
determined, always optimistic. But I can't seem to locate
terrain remotely near to happiness. How to start the day?
A walk clears the thicket of words.
It's an offense to carve your name in sandstone
cliffs, such hubris equivalent only to
a glacier's fond erosion of everything.
I'm back to petroglyphs, beautiful mostly because
they've endured, mysterious in content, unfathomably aged
little icons carved into living rock's varnished patina.
What can I leave that could endure as long?
Not everything has a given name. Or needs one.
I dreamt I jumped into the sky and flew off
above the street, evading telephone wires and other obstacles.
In the city's canyons below, people began to look like black crabs
trying to pull me back down into their bucket of daily dramas.
But I am already flying away.

Seeing Bone

Losing armor is not dying. There are gaps between bones.
These fingers held together by nothing so much as will.
I've seen the cold dissolving of this flesh into electron clouds.
Seen flesh made galaxy, self spun into void.
Lost arms to aspen, thighs to red mesa sandstone.
Once or twice, at least, an emptying of self into self
into void. It leaves its marks. I'm not afraid to see
my own bones, I say. There they are. Is that blue halo
radioactive particle spin? Maybe it's just the X-ray light
from a long billion light-months powering its way
through gas cloud and flesh alike.

I am fishbone and horn and antler.
Make a fist in a night of burning horses. Still, they run.
A skeleton of ceremony, to want these marrow-bound books.
Open this heart, break through these glowing ribs,
fire within like sun, light within all bone.

tenderest of gifts

your arms around me in the shower
hands on my breast, slick fingertips on trembling skin
hands washing my hair, head back, eyes closed
hands gentle on my belly, pregnant pause
to caress a birth-giving world, feeling the baby move
hands playful dropping lower, to my root
warm penis pressed to thigh, promise of lightning—
long years no one has held me, touched me, to caress
O wilderness of years since anyone washed my hair

at 4 am I must untangle tangled limbs
to go deal with tiresome physical needs
and again as we awaken after dawn
I'm unused to your astounding patience
—how. . . ? —because it's part of you and I love you

when clothes came loose and fell
you did not fear, the first who has not fled—
caught by surprise, to feel accepted, tenderest of gifts
how can I say how touching you heals me
embrace me as I weep, naked beyond skin

CHRISTOPHER DEMPSEY

Deaf:Gay

I was deaf before I was gay, and deaf is on the body but gay is within the body.

Growing up deaf was a singular experience. I never met another person with hearing aids (HAs) until I was about ten. He was severely deaf and had been to a residential school. He used lipreading, basic spoken vocabulary, and some signs to communicate. The next person with HAs I met when I was 13 was much more deaf than I, and she spoke what she heard: a flat featureless voice at odds with what I heard.

I'm oral. Speech is my preferred and dominant way of communicating with others. I was taught to speak when I was starting out school—using large black and white labelled photos of everyday situations, I repeated words after Mum. This was the result of an "oral" policy in place by the early 1970s; both deaf (oral) and Deaf (signers) people were encouraged to use speech. I am fortunate to have enough hearing, at least with HAs, to know how to speak and be oral—the modulations and pitches needed to navigate a hearing world.

The only "sign" I learned was fingerspelling. A popular TV presenter used Sign as part of closing the show. This had an effect on school children everywhere, who dutifully learned fingerspelling and practiced. It was one of those memes that spread like wildfire throughout that cohort. But despite that, I never learned Sign. I was a product of a period of time that privileged speaking over signing.

Without HAs there is a world that only I know. Muted sounds are a blissful place, because noise is intrusive and demanding and oh so loud. That muted place is a place inside me. With HAs there's another world, a hearing world, but I hear only a part of it, never the full extent of it. Sounds are always mediated through an assemblage of electronics, plastic, silicone, tubing, and batteries.

Growing up, I developed requirements and rituals. A set of rules: No HAs in water (give them to Mum when swimming at the beach, she'll look after them for you, or wrap in a t-shirt). New earmolds every six months. Batteries always nearby.

Being deaf was a way of being until I started to realize I was gay. That I was attracted to men, not women. The earliest manifestation of this was at seven years old when I went gaga over a very handsome young man visiting from overseas and staying with us for the summer. But I didn't know, or realize, that there was a name for this behavior; I didn't understand what I was doing. All I knew was I loved being around him.

When I was 14, I knew I was gay, different from my schoolmates at our single-gender high school. Two years of questioning the self, figuring things out, coming out to parents and others. A slow construction of being gay. The rules, rituals, the social roles in different settings. Was this process easier for the fact that I was already an "other," an outsider by virtue of my deafness?

Being deaf is a physical feature. Being gay is an inherent, intrinsic feature. Both mark me out from the norm, from what is "normal." In that sense, the necessary survival mechanisms are the same. One is a reliance on the self. My self has a heavy load to bear. It bears the disadvantages of being deaf (not hearing things, unable to participate fully in conversations, can't get the joke said quickly, concentrating all day long, etc.), and the disadvantages of being gay (until recently, denied equal civil rights in marriage, the butt of jokes, the insecurities of dating and forming relationships, etc.).

I've developed a very strong sense of self in response. A view of the world that I'm normal, and everyone else is abnormal. This sense of self developed before I was gay, when I was just deaf. My deafness feels completely natural to me—how can it be otherwise? Conversely, everyone is abnormal because they don't have a diffability. (The word "diffability" comes from the phrase "different ability.") This sense colors my gay worldview. Everyone is gay unless proven otherwise. Critically though, I normalize both my deafness and my gayness to cover the world, but my deafness/diffability is situated in something that is natural for me, and abnormal for everyone else, whereas my gayness is situated in a world of "normality," unless proven otherwise. Deaf is personal; gay is communal.

For the deaf self, survival is developing communication strategies: always placing myself in a position so that my good ear captures the direction of talk, not wearing HAs unless I absolutely have to, putting up with poor hearing situations because it's just easier that way, and critically, being acutely aware of my surroundings—I pay attention to people's behavior for fears and dangers are communicated through speech, and influences behavior. For the gay self, survival lies in being with other gay men, friends, lovers, organizations, and deliberate placement in certain places and situations.

I deploy my deaf survival strategies within the gay world. I cannot abandon them, for the gay world is hearing. My life is composed of deaf survival strategies within gay survival strategies so I can succeed in the hearing world, the heterosexual world, and the gay hearing world.

Being deaf, I don't need to come out. It's obvious. If I'm not wearing HAs in some situations, I have trouble, but eventually, at some point, I always have to put them on. Coming out is an act of being counter to a dominant normality—something which is not acceptable. A norm regarding the degree of physical or mental disfigurement has developed in recent years to permit diffabled people to be within the ambit of "society." The diffabled serve a function in society—a kind of there-but-for-the-grace-of-god-go-I prayer for the able. A talisman against misfortune for the able-bodied. Thanking Gaia for not having been infected with diffabledness. The norm, although widened today, still regulates the diffabled to the margins, that shadowy area where all diffabled people are permitted to function. To be. All diffabled people are stored there, so you find yourself with the blind, those who have learning difficulties, those in wheelchairs, the autistic, or those who have internal body problems. Oddly, I never met Deaf people in this area. Speech is the commonality among people here, so the Deaf would have been elsewhere. Fags are also stored here, historically marginalized to the shadowy fringes of town, the shadowy parts of our social structures.

Growing up, I rebelled against being shoved here. I did not want to be with the diffabled. I did not want the treatment that was meted out to them. A place to be pitied, where our diffability was held up as a marvel, "Oh, how normal you are!" "You speak so well!"—a place where physical accommodations—a ramp, a hearing loop—are treated as "special" and mark you out, and places you apart, away from power, and privilege associated with being "normal." I was treated by society as if I belonged there. I did not want to be a part of the shadows, so I had minimal contact with other diffabled.

Without HAs I present as a hearing straight white male to strangers, which is useful—but only to the extent that I have minimal communication with others. With my HAs, I'm a straight white male with hearing aids, which function as a visible mechanistic body marker. For those who know me, without HAs I'm somewhat annoying for them, as they have to adapt to me; speaking a little louder, slower, and positioning themselves close to me. I exercise the wearing of HAs as a power play, typically in the morning when I get up. I don't put them on because noise is unbearable in the morning, then I'll put them on to the relief of hearing family members.

Gay identity is presented only when I disclose it to strangers. Until then I am a straight white male, with or without HAs, unless they have bothered to Google me first and know that I am gay. There is no visible marker for gay; it is only revealed by speaking, or by careful observation over a period of time. The means of revelation are different from being deaf, ironically, through communication, that is, speech, for which I need HAs.

I still rebel against being placed in society's marginality, but today, I have a greater sense of empathy for those who are more or less forced into the margins. I'm acutely aware of their struggles for social acceptance and improvements in our social infrastructure. They too are people deserving of consideration. I have started to learn NZSL (New Zealand Sign Language), and work within my professional field to modify communications, buildings, and cultures to enable the diffabled to take part in society.

Deaf is to be in a world of hearing. Gay is to be in a world of heterosexuality. Being deaf:gay is to be in a hearing gay world.

MICHAEL RUSSELL

Torch

I.

It's hard to find a good man in this city
of spinning lights, fast forward footsteps,
forgotten meals.   The men come
   when you're thin and hungry,
manic as a strobe light.   He likes
     the beast in the bedsheets,
the sleepless nights, the constant
       rowing and rowing toward God.

Call me daffodil, sweetheart. Call me phoenix.
   Tell me you love me ten times over.
  Kiss me until our mouths become ocean
         and only the moon can pull us apart.

II.

I close my eyes: the flowers have burned, the land has burned,
our bodies, hand-in-hand, lie charred on the scorched earth—
and then you are sleeping, alive and well, your breath a quiet
   whisper.

I am a distant planet drifting away from you.
I am cold as Pluto. Do not follow me into deep space, lover.
Do not chase me as I turn my back to you,
stumble out of bed heavy as a manatee and weep.

III.

My love has been torched.

He's a tulip   hanging in the liquor cabinet.

My lips, firecrackers, explode

on a new man's face.   I bounce and stir,
my words   trip and stutter.

I am the wooden whip of wind on your cheek,

hurricane song, tornado-whistle.

I can turn like a car and crash right into you.
                              I am the unused
condom, the fistful of spent cash.

Watch how I glimmer and bedazzle.

IV.

Here I am again, head tucked between white sheet and white
    pillow
the sun glaring through the window like an angry lover.

The nurse in her white scrubs asks me why I'm not in group, I
    do not answer—
my mouth stitched with a thousand sorrows.

I have lost my love to gentler hands, to a man who can work
with more than words. I have lost my love. I have lost my love

to a cloud full of winter, to blizzards and snowstorms and
    Canadian frost.
My white skin reddens then whitens as I pinch it.

The walls, color of eggshell, calm me. They are quiet as sleeping
    babies.
They rock and rock and rock and rock and rock me to sleep.

He Called Me Bear

In the back of my head I see an animal.
I look to my chest, my arms, my legs—fur—am I an animal?

In the eating disorder group I was the largest
of the herd of males, a different animal.

He called me bear. As he nibbled on his blade of grass
I dived into the garbage can, bear-faced, hungry animal.

Ritual: I sneak into the washroom, let my fingers kiss
the back of my throat; dirty boy, filthy animal.

The stretch marks speak for themselves, my skin
soft as a teddy bear. Starve the animal.

Most days I can't keep the food down, it passes through me
like wind through leaves. I am a sick animal.

Ritual: I run until my paws are bloody.
Hungry—must catch the animal.

When people say you look a little thin,
remember what the man said in group: Michael, you bear, you
　　　animal.

NOLA WEBER

The Worst, Most Faithful Friend

The pain started before I learned to read, its sharpness mirrored by the crisp clarity with which I can still recall it. To analogize it necessitates an uncomfortable metaphor: a sewing needle pushed gently into the body, held still enough to blur the thin line between muscle, skin and underwear. A bloodless pinprick, this strange pain erupted and subsided without external fanfare; its piercing streaks emanated outward from between my legs, then reined in and settled somewhere deep inside of me. As a child I handled these attacks with unflinching stoicism; though was too ashamed and confused to spin them into words. Like oncoming trains, I could discern their presence from a distance. I could brace myself rigidly to the nearest chair, stare blankly at the floor, and anxiously wait for them to fade away.

Viewed in retrospect, these eerie episodes—which ceased before I began middle school—gravely foreshadowed an ailment that would take a slow decade to surface, like quick and sharp allusions that flash conspicuously at a story's outset before its plot slips back, for a time, into relative normalcy. It is just as possible also that these early bouts were irrelevant flukes, and that the ties I grant them to my later diagnosis are a tenuous attempt at metaphor, a drive to encrypt bad luck within some larger meaning to override the body's frightening propensity for irony, for chance. Yet onward through my adolescence, my mysterious condition bound itself to me not always through the physical discomfort it wrought, but through the emotional pain inflicted by what was in its power to take away, forcefully and repeatedly, over and over again. Defined at once by its presence and all the consequent absences thereof, by its rigidity and its ephemerality, it has amplified the shortcoming of words just as desperately as it has implied the need for more of them.

There are two things wrong with me, if wrong is the right word, though they are intimately codependent. To make sense of the first, consider your eye. It rarely hurts of its own accord, though it is laden with nerves that can magnify, tenfold, the gentlest of ruptures: stray lashes, soft fingers, coarse yet infinitesimal specks of sand. To make sense of the second, imagine an object drawing nearer and nearer, so close and blurry within your line of vision that you feel its bristling certainty just before it touches. Your eyes, reflexively, will tense and close before it hits. Place the sensitivity of the eye between your legs, and this approximates the mechanisms of vestibulodynia and vaginismus, two concomitant gynecological conditions that make vaginal penetration so painful for me, my body shuts inward autonomously, and it is impossible. It is a reflex as natural as a heartbeat, as breathing, and despite numerous attempts at treatment, this part of me has never gone away. If not for my pain's unfortunate placement, perhaps I would not feel trapped into silence, afraid to name my anomalous state for fear of discomfort, denial, or ridicule. Yet it is precisely this culture of uneasiness that transforms my body into a quiet yet potent minefield, a means through which to explore the peculiar social and medical interplay of pain that is *loaded*, so to speak, far beyond its mere physicality.

For most of my waking moments I can pretend there is nothing wrong with me, though this fails to erase a more subliminal understanding of my difference. I may stroll down the sidewalk and notice, perchance, how innately I clench the muscles between my legs. I have done this long enough to not feel the strain. It is the relaxation of those muscles that feels more unnatural.

While my condition is ever present, I am not always in pain, as its hold on my body is phantasmal, as subconscious and continuous as blood through my veins. I could liken vestibulodynia to the sinister darkness of a basement cellar—a corner that watches and waits, that I tiptoe around, that I gaze upon curiously from a safe distance, that I try just as intently to not constantly stare at, that I inevitably must face from time to time. It is a mess of dualities: real yet invisible, pointed yet abstract, fleeting yet unwavering, there yet not. I rest in equilibrium between sick and well. What is my condition's hold on me, if not a distant yet malevolent threat?

It is hard to know quite what to call myself.

A *disease*, often, implies trajectory, not stasis. It can connote treatment, autonomous or medically induced improvement, weakening, death. A *condition*, on the other hand, holds two definitions, each evocative of the other: in medical parlance, an illness that can be controlled but not cured; in everyday speech, a standard of maintenance or stipulation. Whereas *disease* suggests a debilitating yet highly temporal state to which one succumbs or from which one transcends, *disability* seems to call for an intentional association between one's physicality and their larger sense of self. To self-identify as disabled—or its looser, more politicized counterpart *crip*—is thus to enter a relationship with the aberrant body, to *accept* as opposed to deny or correct it. Moreover, both terms evoke a permanence that supersedes more fleeting experiences of impairment; *disabled* in particular holds enough cultural stigma and clout to caution its flippant use. Applied to my own body, the term feels hyperbolic, dishonest, like a standard of experience not quite mine to claim, and one true only in the most literal sense—in the sense of not being *able*. It is strange how words accrue power when paired, how *disabled* speaks not only to a literal lack of ability, but to a sort of ostracization and consequent strip of power and prowess.

What complicates *crip* and *disabled* as specific embodiments, however, is that what is *normal* in physical terms is both subjective and undeniably nuanced. The term exists along a sort of gradient where only certain variations are considered unusual enough to necessitate their demarcation, which begs one ask precisely where normalcy ends and abnormality begins. In particular, contemporary queer and feminist theorists have been drawn to the disabled body for its potential to redefine physical and social standards of desirability, which complements both the recent emphases on intersectionality and postmodern interpretations of precisely what constitutes a queer body. Certainly disabled and queer sexuality share distinct qualities, and the social and physical complexities of each undoubtedly echo each other. Likewise, it is remarkably easy to conjure tangible examples that attest to the commonality of human difference. Aching knees, failing hearts, arthritic hands, wrinkling necks, and the slow, spectral disabling of the aging body come to mind as a mere handful of physical qualities. These emerge among us with enough frequency that it is easy to question whether *anyone* is perfectly well or able, their essence contained completely within requisite expectations. Perhaps an "able body" truly *is* a thing impossible, though perhaps we are not measured so much by our *innate* able-bodiedness—or heteronormativity, for that matter—as we are by the degree to which we can, with effort, acceptably replicate its likeness.

To propose that all bodies are in some sense queer and disabled is to prioritize a theoretical understanding of such identities over one with palpable social and physical consequences. Similarly, typifying disabled or dysfunctional bodies as queer devalues the term's clout among those who have long employed it to signify gender or sexual variance. Inherent in stretching *queer* into a sort of post-modern buzzword for all things ephemeral, unstable or indefinable is the danger of both diluting the term into ironic meaninglessness and usurping it from its original community—for if everything becomes queer, then how might self-identified queers self-define? Given this, my urge to at least consider non-penetrative sex's fundamental *queerness* is less an attempt at co-option than a desire to examine how it might subvert, or at least call into question, heteronormative paradigms. For just as queer sex can potentially widen the scope of which intimacies may be typified as sexual acts, so too does disabled sexuality allow eroticism's locus to shift away from genitalia to other parts of the body.

When I was much younger, my friends and I would hold sleepovers. We would lay on our stomachs, unhook our bras, and pull our t-shirts up to our necks. Gently and ritualistically, we would run our hands down each other's backs and arms, stopping with each swoop to the tailbone to glide back up to our hairlines' napes. I remember what I would always ask: that my friends draw rings around my ears with their fingertips, and that they teasingly pull my hair to achieve that perfect, elusive tension between ticklishness and pain, between too hard and not hard enough. I reveled in this touch, albeit uncomfortably cognizant of the way it hardened my breasts and forced me to hear my own breath, though it was a detached kind of pleasure, much less about the person who touched me than it was about the pure sensation. As I matured, this became the type of touch I would ask for when I wanted intimacy but no pressure to orgasm, when I was tired, or when my desire for sex between the legs began to wane, as it sometimes does when I am with someone too long.

These days we like to say sex can mean anything, that it is a social or even personal construct, a ripe and self-defined gray zone. Yet I am hardly immune to the satisfaction felt when I can say with certainty that I have *had* it, as opposed to the flimsy, unfinished feeling that accompanies forays onto my neck, back, or ears. Admittedly it can sometimes be hard to objectively declare whether sex with me has ever truly *happened*, though even this query depends on whether one perceives its defining factor as rooted in organs versus something more complex. Perhaps the most unfortunate lesson of my adolescence was the realization that so often, sex was less a celebration of pleasure than a series of clear-cut, inarguable benchmarks. Even still I sometimes wonder whether sex with me is sex at all, or if it is instead a mélange of lesser desires that dances slowly and tediously around the real thing. Perhaps I denigrate it into an endless tease of foreplay, one that never quite results in that gratifying, conclusive act deemed *genuine*, the act which seems to be all that counts. It is as if sex isn't *sex* until penetration occurs, which has only further amplified my unsettling intuition that it seems less about pleasure and more about procedure; less about intuition, more about conformity.

By the time I was eleven, I knew I was gay. Like I imagine many narratives of queer childhood must feel retrospectively, my sexuality's onset was surreal and gradual, like an elongated dream, or nightmare. Given that I had never desired male affection, I remember the terror and repulsion felt as I began to slowly ascertain my attraction to other girls. I remember the way it spurred in me such overt denial that I routinely listed to my friends, on my fingers, eleven boys who seemed theoretically attractive, whose tongues I thought I could at least passively tolerate in my mouth. Yet as each year passed, my feelings pushed harder and their pointedness became more threatening, transmuting from inarticulate longings to a disturbing onslaught of desires, the specificity of which I could not understand how I was possibly capable of imagining. On a few trusted friends, I practiced disclosing this pent-up yet overbearing reality, knowing full well that once the words left my mouth, I could never breathe them back in. Yet every time I sat on the brink of confession, my body would collapse in shaking convulsions, and for two years, I could not bring myself to speak.

I was fourteen when, in an inexplicable rush of bravado, I confessed to my mother while her apple juice pork chops braised in the oven. In retrospect the affair was morosely clichéd, and just as I had imagined it: a sudden, violent subversion of my childlike façade—its loss, but with no death, or at least not one that could be publicly mourned. Never before or since have I watched a person's preconceived comfort shatter almost visibly before me, as though my words had thickened the air between us into cracking panes of glass. My mother's near-instantaneous denial was almost psychotic, and her initial disassociation from me literal enough that for a time after my admission she requested I not walk too close to her in public. In a way, her behavior mirrored my own prior attempt to divorce a problem sexuality from a meticulously constructed heterosexual identity. Following my coming out, I could not help but wonder whether I was in fact the same person or if I had somehow managed, for three years prior, to have embodied two versions of myself.

Although my vulvar pain and sexual orientation unfurled into my adolescent consciousness somewhat independently of each other, their similarities have nevertheless compelled me. The onset of both occurred before I really knew, respectively, what sex and lesbians were, for just as I recall feeling nothing but a sharp and unsettling distance upon first touching my vagina and feeling its cold, unwelcoming pain, so too do I remember a strong reluctance to link the burgeoning knowledge of my own sexuality to any tangible identity. In both respects I occupied what I might retrospectively call a surreal sort of purgatory: an existential space between actions, feelings and words. As each "problem" grew more undeniable—and thus, increasingly unavoidable and obtuse—I fought hard against ascribing language to either theretofore-abstract state. In a strange way, it seemed, words made things real, and certainly more real than I wanted them to be.

I came out only shortly before my first sexual experience, which undoubtedly predicated how others understood the pain between my legs to which I occasionally alluded. For while my mother had initially discounted my sexuality on account of my gentility and delicate appearance, so too was my vulvar pain assessed as bearing some relation to my lesbianism, though often in contradictory ways. I was sometimes chided for my inability to satisfy a male partner, my sexual identity was just as readily denigrated to a coping mechanism, a façade to placate an impossibly realized heterosexuality perhaps rendered subconscious by my body's odd shortcoming. My physical limitation thus assured I could never excel at being straight, yet my unusual condition seemed *just* too suspicious not to question the coincidence that I was, in fact, quite queer. Such slights suggest more than a passing attempt to repudiate my own sense of identity, as they reiterate the social grounds on which sexualities are constructed and maintained. Further still, they conflate my gender expression with a sort of hopeless, romantic, innate heterosexuality—an accusation that continues to haunt feminine queer women, able-bodied or otherwise.

Perhaps this is why, in casual conversation, my vulvar pain and sexuality are not often co-disclosed, for it often seems one characteristic inevitably undermines the other: a lesbian who can't be penetrated lacks the sympathy granted to her heterosexual counterpart, and a woman who has never felt straight sex might not "really" be a lesbian. Like so many other ailments irrevocably gendered, classed and psycho-associated to debilitating effect, vulvar pain has historically been embroiled in a sort of prudent and paranoid femininity. Seeking treatment has thus entailed I navigate both a medical and social world that brands painful intercourse a heterosexual affliction, in tandem with a strong queer counterculture for which penetrative sex persists the reigning paradigm. In this way, my aforementioned embodiment between sick and well transmutes its significance from a linguistic observation to one more social and more tangible. It is as though I have managed, somehow, to be affected by a condition whose severity I cannot truly relate to: a lucky coincidence, or a perfect complication.

Vulvar pain places me in a constant limbo between the opportunity for disclosure, and the arguably privileged assumption of normalcy. This is both a blessing and a burden, as hidden conditions have the unfortunate tendency of being dismissed or denied until proven otherwise, or of having their believability predicated on their bearer's personality, reputation, and proneness to drama or honesty. Just as certain derisions from my past speak beyond their belittling intent and convey larger truths of how chronic gynecological concerns are considered, my forays into medicine are similarly telling. Whereas certain conditions can be seen, felt, and therefore less easily undermined, vulvar pain's physical invisibility ensures it is too often cursed by its own subjective nature. To validate untraceable pain necessitates a conscious belief-based affirmation, a move conflated with irrationality just as often as with faith.

A thorough analysis of vulvar pain's cultural reception, however, reveals more at play than simple denial, especially since the condition's primary symptom is so socially irreconcilable. While mind and body have been considered inter-reliant since antiquity, Sigmund Freud's nineteenth century theory that unaddressed fears, experiences and trauma can manifest into tangible symptoms remains a cornerstone interpretation of many vulvar conditions—though this is particularly true for vaginismus, the painful and prohibitive pelvic spasm for which no solely physical cause has been identified to date. Two decades of studies have linked the condition to personal or relationship conflicts, low self-esteem, an unfed desire for control, and myriad other psychosocial characteristics vaguely relevant at best, though more often problematically typifying. While such theories accrue context within the psychoanalytic resurgence that gained traction from the 1980s to the late '90s, recent conjectures continue to posit vaginismus as a fear-based concern, albeit one now conflated less with personal shortcomings than with a repressive or abusive upbringing.

A 2011 study linking vaginismus to moral strictures found that those with the condition "showed a generally enhanced disgust propensity and heightened disgust in response to sexual stimuli," and added that "the perceived 'immorality' of sexual behaviors . . . contribute[ed] to the defense reflexes . . . that characterize vaginismus." Similar to how vestibulodynia invokes a more nuanced understanding of the disease/disability binary, vaginismus's precarious status between a physical and mental affliction only complicates its treatment. The impulse to validate or dismiss its certain alleged causes can become increasingly touchy and increasingly situational, which compels me to question whether concretizing vaginismus's speculated origins offers any real benefit to its patients.

Underlining a tabloid-style fascination with the frustrated yet eternal "virgin" and subsequent dramas of childhood secrets and unconsummated marriages, interviews detailing the identities and experiences of women like me largely dominate vulvar pain's available body of literature. While it can be frustrating to feel like a spectacle— especially amidst the dearth of attention granted to advancing treatment for this type of pain—personal accounts can, at their richest, offer a candid glimpse into how we navigate our bodies through intimate and social spheres. I often sense within these interviews the familiar yet troubling tendency to place one's own life under a proverbial microscope, to feverishly trace backwards so that some psychosomatic or physical origin of pain may eventually be discovered. One woman, echoing a psychoanalytic conception of vaginismus, surmised she had developed it "at a very young age as a defense to a controlling mother . . . as a means] to provide a safe retreat, [and to prevent] disintegration of self." Another connected her pain to a childhood accident on a tree trunk, and still another considered her vaginismus fundamentally symbolic to her larger sense of self. "I do feel very strongly," she commented, "that . . . vaginismus is part of a much bigger problem [around] how I feel . . . and [how I] build a protective shell," and further conceded that her vaginismus "cannot be treated as a separate sexual dysfunction."

While such broad or unusually specific causalities provide ample room for skepticism, dismissing one's right to author a comfortable self-narrative speaks to a different sort of damage: the right to a sense of closure, and the right to assume mastery over the story of one's own experience. Admittedly, these women's aforementioned motions softly mirror my own means of coping, exemplified especially by my inclination to tenuously connect those shooting stings of my childhood to the pain that now has such a foothold on my adult sexuality. The psychological underpinnings which inescapably cloak my condition draw me in through their eerie echo of experiences and traits I would rather dismiss as arbitrary. Perhaps I, too, once fell crooked on a tree trunk; children hurt themselves so often that all but the deepest cuts tend to fade into oblivion. It is possible that my skin healed and my insides did not, and that had I played differently, sat differently, somehow moved through the world more carefully, I would not be as I am today. Stories can provide closure and circuitry, even if recited alone or adhered to quietly in private. Yet whether they offer a sense of ownership and empowerment or reify existing feminine clichés of anxiety and insecurity may depend on who constructs them, and how they are deployed.

I began treatment soon after my diagnosis at age seventeen. In 2006, this involved a combination of psychotherapy, topical numbing cream, pelvic floor exercises, and vaginal dilation. Every evening—from my senior year in high school to my first few months in a crowded Chicago college dormitory—I would lay on my back, squeeze my pelvic muscles as hard as I could and release them, again and again, thirty or forty times over. Had the spread of stinging nerves between my legs never existed, these exercises may have granted me greater control over vaginismus' involuntary muscle spasms. Perhaps, had that been the case, the three cold rods in my vaginal dilator set may also have been effective. Dousing the smallest one in lubricant snuck home from my school's health services center, I recall many long hours spent naked on my bedroom floor, transfixed in competition with my body's taunting stubbornness. The objective was to start with the thinnest size, grow impervious to its pain, move up one dilator, and continue forth until I mastered—or could at least withstand—the largest size in the box.

There is something apathetic about this form of treatment, as if a patient's capacity to hurt is forgotten once they are out from under their provider's hands, or as though a doctor would expect anything less than for their underling to look past their own discomfort and consider pain a necessary indicator of dedication, of progress. Likewise, it is easy even for those with an otherwise healthy dose of criticality to become deludedly enamored with a physician's instruction, if not since their own health is allegedly at stake. Yet I doubt it was at all considered that sticking a dilator between my legs required ardor and tenacity tantamount to running a knife along my very own skin. I cannot quite say why I self-inflicted this pain for nearly two years beyond that I was told to do so, and that I complied despite the glaring illogicality that my problem would somehow recede faster the harder I made myself hurt.

I remember those rare moments when I garnered enough strength to stick the smallest rod three inches inside of me; I would let it hang, suspended temporarily between the sting of its placement and that of its removal, as though my body never wanted to let it go. Briefly I would bask in this in-between, in the eye of the storm, where pain brushed only at the sidelines and through which I could taste some distorted version of normalcy. In that moment, I would tell myself: this is it. *This, I would think, is my taste of that everything.*

I was twelve when I first touched myself deliberately between my legs; not for pleasure, but for menarche. These are the pieces I remember sharpest: the tampon's straightforward sleekness and simplicity, coupled with its snide refusal to disappear inside of me. My body's calm, pinkish warmth transmuted, instantaneously, to a limp coldness. The painful shock of a shattered preconception, of missing the last step on a blackened stairwell, of thinking something should be there and jarredly finding it is not. The disquieting sensation of silently probing the body of a stranger who just so happens to be you.

I was fourteen when I first let the girl who wanted to have me, try. I remember how months prior, alone in my room, I had practiced running my hands over my body so I understood all the best places to touch. I remember the round, carpeted steps that led down to her basement, the dusty mattress, the mustard walls, our sleepover, the indescribable warmth of two bodies in symmetry, of skin completely touching. Then, the crash: one icy finger forced up inside me like a hot knife—the same specter of two years prior, only now in real time, with real consequence. I remember my adolescent self-reassurance that sex made pain and pleasure look and sound the same, at least from the outside. Internally, I wanted to divorce my own body.

In the bedroom I have tried hard to forget about myself, to transcend thought and become immaterial, yet I know it is my own subliminal awareness that so strongly drives this pursuit of corporal distance. It is useless. Every new time is like the last time, reified by every time before it: rising from the deepest tunnel of my insides, a foreign yet cunning pleasure, romantic in its distance. Accompanying it, my own stern prohibition: do not respond, do not touch. But sex is so irrational. In its moment I convince myself that I am cured, that there is nothing wrong with me, and I try what I know will fail. I am always sorry yet can't seem to learn, as though I believe my body theoretically, but never quite in practice.

I have written before that a chronic condition feels both human and alien. In certain moments, it is like maligned yet reliable family; in others, it becomes a soulless and unflinching parasite. In some ways it is both. Realistically it is neither. Vestibulodynia is a simple yet inexplicable overgrowth of highly sensitive nerve endings that span my lower vulva, sensitive and numerous enough to ascertain a sharply prohibitive burn, to slam shut from even the carefullest touch. Vaginismus is a steadfast and trusted reflex, evolved by my subconscious to shield me from the trauma of penetrative sex. I do not understand why my brain is my body's fiercest, most steadfast guard, as though the two are not born of the same cells and survive off the same blood. Nor do I understand why my body grew nerves it did not need to, and grew them—it seems— just so they could hurt me.

I find it more sensible sometimes, or at least more satisfying, to direct anguish at a foreign object: an infection, a virus, a thing that pushes its way in and threatens to overtake. At the very least I can perceive myself as divisible from it, superior, instead of brood over why my body would be so stupid as to mis-wire itself, why it would coalesce in the womb bearing its own propensity for pain. Others like me, it is noted, may yearn for Cartesian dualism, for "the ability to disconnect the troubled body from the real, essential self, [to hold] an assurance that our bodies, to twist the well-known phrase, are not ourselves." This war between two forces, conjoined in the same skin, is that with which I both strongly identify, and just as strongly question.

One surgery exists for vestibulodynia's most stubborn cases. Called a vestibulectomy, it would entail the extraction of much of my lower vulva. It is hard to pin down its actual success rate, and harder still to gauge whether *success* in such a context refers to a lack of pain or gain of pleasure. While the most promising estimates espouse positive results in seventy to ninety percent of cases, the vestibulectomy as a procedure echoes vestibulodynia's public obscurity, as much available information exists only through online hearsay. Lurking behind usernames and minuscule profile pictures, anonymous voices regale botched results, almost-successes, miracles, happy husbands, ice packs, blood, unusual scarring, excruciating bathroom trips. Thousands silently ask—perhaps rhetorically, perhaps pointedly—why so few medical professionals seem willing, initially, to dub their pain as physical, and why so little attention has been paid to developing a more transparent course of treatment.

To know that I could be "fixed"—however small the chance—only further cements my own suspension between sick and well, though under this framework, through my own lack of agency. Impossible penetration is a stasis, not a slow debilitation; I could live into my hundredth year, my good health none the wiser to my body's strange anomaly. Surgery in my case thus loses temporal urgency and becomes, instead, a novel wish, a lingering *what-if*, for to be operated upon may not reinstate a sense of normalcy though might instead allow me to feel some heretofore elusive version of it. Yet there is an artificiality to invasive medical procedures, and one that feels contentious to name aloud, given surgery is now so commonplace and rarely seen as anything but beneficial. As French philosopher Jean-Luc Nancy once noted of his transplanted heart, the life gained though surgery is one unnaturally granted, sustained by extemporaneous medical variables far beyond eating, drinking and breathing. In a considerably lower-stakes though vaguely similar manner, I consider surgery a fake alteration of my own circumstance—physically, though by extension experientially. I often wonder whether I am "like this" for a reason, and as evidenced by the preceding pages, it is a dangerous question . . . though one I cannot help but still ask. I do not know whether to accept myself, or to be dissatisfied; whether to embrace the potentially subversive eroticism of vulvar pain, or try my best to assimilate. I do not yet know, either, whether mine is an identity or an ailment. It can be hard to draw a line between the two.

While I have tucked the prospect of surgery in the furthest corner of my mind, it always holds out its hand, ever ready for me to risk it. Occasionally my impulsivity will snap me to do it, and I counsel myself back against this hope by imagining a knife that cuts into the delicate skin around my vulva, extracts a pinkish slab of my body, and sets it on a sleek white tool stand. I imagine this strange yet powerful piece of my self—my life—being thrown away, incinerated with a fetid pile of undesired human flesh. It makes me sick. So I mete the scales: I was born healthy, able to walk, strong, sharp. I have not broken any bones, have not had any wisdom teeth pulled, have not had my appendix out. I can count the times I have vomited on my own two hands. So I cannot "have sex," so I will never *know*. Those are just my cards, I say. For better or for worse, like everything else.

For better or worse, like everything else. Or so I try to tell myself.

KENNY FRIES

Body Language

What is a scar if not the memory of a once open wound?
You press your finger between my toes, slide

the soap up the side of my leg, until you reach
the scar with the two holes, where the pins were

inserted twenty years ago. Leaning back, I
remember how I pulled the pin from my leg, how

in a waist-high cast, I dragged myself
from my room to show my parents what I had done.

Your hand on my scar brings me back to the tub
and I want to ask you: What do you feel

when you touch me there? I want you to ask me:
What are you feeling now? But we do not speak.

You drop the soap in the water and I continue
washing, alone. Do you know that my father would

bathe my feet, as you do, as if it was the most
natural thing. But up to now, I have allowed

only two pairs of hands to touch me there,
to be the salve for what still feels like an open wound.

The skin has healed but the scars grow deeper—
When you touch them what do they tell you about my life?

Dressing the Wound

When you take off my clothes, the fire
heats my skin. I surround your nipples

with my toes. In front of me, your lips
find my scars, peel back my broken skin.

Why do I let your kiss expose my bones?
Trembling, I hear them crack.

When I open my eyes: my feet, twisted,
in your palms. Molded by your fingers,

my six toes. But . . . *gentle*. When you hold
my legs, it is my heart your hands enfold.

Beauty and Variations

1.

What is it like to be so beautiful? I dip
my hands inside you, come up with—*what?*

Beauty, at birth applied, does not transfer
to my hands. But every night, your hands

touch my scars, raise my twisted limbs to
graze against your lips. Lips that never

form the words—*you are beautiful*—transform
my deformed bones into—*what?*—if not beauty.

Can only one of us be beautiful? Is this your
plan? Are your sculpted thighs more powerful

driving into mine? Your hands find their way
inside me, scrape against my heart. Look

at your hands. Pieces of my skin trail from
your fingers. What do you make of this?

Your hands that know my scars, that lift me to your
lips, now drip my blood. Can blood be beautiful?

2.

I want to break your bones. Make them so
they look like mine. Force you to walk on

twisted legs. Then, will your lips still beg
for mine? Or will that disturb the balance

of our desire? Even as it inspires, your body
terrifies. And once again I find your hands

inside me. Why do you touch my scars? You
can't make them beautiful any more than I can

tear your skin apart. Beneath my scars,
between my twisted bones, hides my heart.

Why don't you let me leave my mark? With no
flaws on your skin—how can I find your heart?

3.

How much beauty can a person bear? Your smooth
skin is no relief from the danger of your eyes.

My hands would leave you scarred. Knead the muscles
of your thighs. I want to tear your skin, reach

inside you—your secrets tightly held. Breathe
deep. Release them. Let them fall into my palms.

My secrets are on my skin. Could this be why
each night I let you deep inside? Is that

where my beauty lies? Your eyes, without secrets,
would be two scars. I want to seal your eyes,

they know my every flaw. Your smooth skin, love's
wounds ignore. My skin won't mend, is callused, raw.

4.

Who can mend my bones? At night, your hands press
into my skin. My feet against your chest, you mold

my twisted bones. What attracts you to my legs? Not
sex. What brings your fingers to my scars is beyond

desire. Why do you persist? Why do you touch me
as if my skin were yours? Seal your lips. No kiss

can heal these wounds. No words unbend my bones.
Beauty is a two-faced god. As your fingers soothe

my scars, they scrape against my heart. Was this
birth's plan—to tie desire to my pain, to stain

love's touch with blood? If my skin won't heal, how
can I escape? My scars are in the shape of my love.

5.

How else can I quench this thirst? My lips
travel down your spine, drink the smoothness

of your skin. I am searching for the core:
What is beautiful? Who decides? Can the laws

of nature be defied? Your body tells me: come
close. But beauty distances even as it draws

me near. What does my body want from yours?
My twisted legs around your neck. You bend

me back. Even though you can't give the bones
at birth I wasn't given, I let you deep inside.

You give me—*what?* Peeling back my skin, you
expose my missing bones. And my heart, long

before you came, just as broken. I don't know who
to blame. So each night, naked on the bed, my body

doesn't want repair, but longs for innocence. If
innocent, despite the flaws I wear, I am beautiful.

KRISTEN RINGMAN

Twenty-Seven Nadines

Min älskling, there was no other way I could have fallen so hard.

I knew this the moment I first became lost in the lines of you: your shadow against the sunset, your brush strokes on the canvas, and then, the edges of your body where they meet the ground, where they meet my skin.

I run my fingers along my forearm. It feels the same as yours. But it's not.

Min älskling, I've got to be honest with you, once and for all. I'm not human, but I'm not so different either. Humans have always felt weirder than other humans sometimes, haven't they? I know they've all felt lonely.

My kind—skogsnymfer—are never lonely. But I was born unlike anyone else in my family. I couldn't hear the birds or the wind through the trees. The creaking of the branches. The river tumbling over rocks, falling into a great pool. My family's ring of infinity elms was near the waterfall. Everyone used the sound of the falls to find their way home. But I never could. I couldn't use any sounds because I was deaf.

A deaf skogsnymf was never heard of before. We asked Odin. We asked Freyja. Neither of them knew why it happened. Humans were deaf sometimes—skogsnymfer were not. I was born different. Automatically apart from my kind.

And I only fell farther and farther away.

Some of the reason was you.

I feel I owe it to you to tell you how many time I've actually loved you. Not the one you, but many copies of you. Twenty-seven so far.

☙

Humans don't know this, but every time they're forced to make a big decision, they feel torn in half, split between two passions, two choices, two roads. They never choose only one. They can't. Another dimension splits open and the one human becomes two.

When skogsnymfer come close to the other worlds, the parallel ones, we just move into them. We don't split and we don't die. Being deaf, I've gotten hit by so many cars and trains because I've crossed from one world to another at the wrong place. A place that is a forest in one world and a highway in the next. And I don't die. The impact forces me back into the world I was trying to leave, and sometimes it forces me into another world altogether.

I've chased you, Nadine.

I've run after your shadow in the darkness. Like that time when your friend died. I followed you into a dark place. A world where everyone was a slave to someone else. You lost me there. I followed the shape of you down a narrow canal, wedged between a church and a string of apartments made of stones. I was attacked before I could catch you. I still remember the hands snapping my bones, the smell of coffee from a nearby café, and the chemical taste of the canal water as I slipped out of that world and into the sea.

And just like that, you were gone again.

Sometimes it takes me weeks to find you.

Sometimes months.

I'm desperate now.

It's been three hundred and four days since I last saw you. I'm scared I won't find you again, so I lurk in all of your favorite coffee shops and bars in Munich, Paris, Vienna, Amsterdam. I pass as human so much more easily having loved you for this long. Having memorized the way you sip your wine, the way you laugh, the way you hold your head when you're thinking about something. The way you stare off into space while daydreaming of your next painting. The way you wander, as if your home is everything and nowhere. As if each new place is also old, familiar. I've learned to be bold in a way no one of my kind has ever been.

Skogsnymfer don't travel very far from their trees. They cross between the worlds, but they stay mostly in their home forests. I rebelled before I even knew you, because I never felt at home with my family. In any world, there are skogsnymfer that I know, have known for centuries. But they don't understand me.

I don't mean we cannot communicate.

We don't need speech. We just have to think and we are heard. I have all the voices of my family in my mind. Their whispers say, *Anja, stay. You should not go far from the waterfall, from our elms, especially you. Because you are broken. Because you can get hurt more easily than we can.*

For a long time, I listened. I stayed by the falls, using the river and the beeches to slip between the worlds. I wandered downstream, upstream. I climbed the beech trees and the elms. I climbed the ravine in summer, in winter, in fall.

One day, I wandered all the way to the bay. I saw the ocean for the first time.

After seeing so many copies of my own forest, the sea was like an alien thing. I didn't understand it. It was scary, so I looked away.

I looked into the window of a shop that sold your paintings. The first part of you I saw was the painting of a skogsnymf standing against a tree. You gave her strange ears and the wrong skin, but in the slashes of blue and green, in the dark, ragged edges of the trees, I thought I could see a piece of your soul.

You were different. Like me.

I didn't even know if you were male or female.

You were *N. B.* Two letters and a painting I wanted to keep, but I don't live in a house like you do. In my home, your art would only get ravaged by the rain and snow.

I kept going back to the gallery.

I searched for more of your work. I even went inside and wrote on a small piece of paper: *Does this artist ever come here?* I asked.

The young Swedish girl was polite. She shrugged. She didn't know. I kept returning.

It was one year before I got an answer.

She is coming next month, she wrote.

Skogsnymfer don't measure time very well. I couldn't switch worlds while I waited. Sometimes, in the shifting, time skips or falters. I couldn't take the chance of missing you.

When I first saw you, it wasn't at the gallery. It wasn't even in that seaside town.

It was by the falls. Tourists always find their way there. Mostly they complain that the waterfall isn't impressive enough and the hike down to it is too steep.

You came alone. You had a backpack with a travel easel and brushes and paint. I realized it was you when I snuck up behind you as you painted the falls. I watched the way you held the brush. The way you made the lines.

You were just doing a landscape, but I could tell you were thinking about nymphs. I felt it in the way you paused each time you painted a beech tree.

I had an idea then.

Skogsnymfer are only seen when they wish to be seen. I decided to conduct an experiment. I moved into your line of vision, stood against the tree you were working on, and then allowed you to see me.

No one else was there that day. No one heard you gasp, dropping the brush and knocking over your paints. I remember how beautiful the reds and yellows looked when they spilled over the brown leaves and green moss of the forest floor.

You spoke to me then, though I couldn't hear you.

I smiled and motioned to my ears.

That's when you surprised me with sign language. You knew it because of your brother. It wasn't Swedish Sign Language, but I didn't know that either. I hadn't tried to look for deaf humans. The farthest

I wandered from my forest was to the town by the sea. I saw groups of deaf people sometimes in passing. I liked watching their hands, but there was no reason for me to try and learn to communicate with them. I wasn't human. Skogsnymfer don't have human friends, and when they do, they're scolded by their family. They're reminded that they live so much longer than you. What is the point? Why would we want to forge a bond that will only be broken when you die and we remain?

Sometimes I wish I never showed myself to you that day.

Sometimes I wish I never fell so madly in love with you at all.

You were patient when I couldn't understand your hands. You took out a drawing pencil and your sketchbook, and you wrote to me.

As mystical as I must have looked in my tattered green and brown dress, my bare feet, you never thought I was actually a skogsnymf. I think you thought I must have been homeless. A wanderer, like you.

And you were right. From the start, you were right.

That day, you painted three portraits of me against the trees. Me as a skogsnymf. Without even knowing you were painting me as who I really am.

That was why I never knew how to tell you this. How to reveal my true self to you.

Would you have believed me then?

Would you believe me now?

Sometimes I forget where I am. I sit in cafés like a writer, scratching away at this letter. So I don't forget. Even though I can't forget.

I've learned to eat human food and drink human drinks, even though I don't need them. It's hard to do it without you, though, so I am often sitting in a corner table with a view of the door, like I am now, with a half empty cup of coffee for hours. Sometimes people approach me, usually men, but when I mime that I am deaf, they often go away. The occasional curious person who actually sits down across from me can be hard to escape. I write to them that I'm working on a very important letter, so I need to be alone, but sometimes they cannot stop writing back to me, asking me questions I don't wish to answer.

Sometimes I stand up and leave. I go to the next place, the next favorite, and start again.

This is Amsterdam. I remember from the smell of the weed a few tables away from me. It's soothing. It reminds me of the forest. It reminds me of the first time you handed me your pipe. That was the fifth Nadine. Yes. (And the eighth and the twelfth . . .)

The fifth Nadine was one of your wildest. You brought me to all the darkest, reddest bars. The ones where people could practically have sex in the corners without anyone noticing. Alcohol affects me strongly. I cannot drink much of it at all, and never while out wandering, even with you. I get so dizzy, I can't even move without falling.

But that evening by the canal, when you handed me your pipe, I breathed in the fragrant smoke, and the world seemed friendlier. Humans didn't look as threatening. The water, the stones, the city trees, and the lamplights all sparkled with the same iridescence as a gathering of skogsnymfer in a ring of infinity elms.

I wanted to tell you then more than any other time in our lives together. I wanted to tell you who I am. I thought maybe, maybe then, your mind would be open enough for you to believe in me. To know me as I know you. To understand the multiplicity of life, of your own lives, of all the magical things that exist on the Earth alongside you.

But I was scared.

I had only been romantic with two of you by then. Nadine three and Nadine five.

So I did what most people do when they smoke together.

I kissed you. I held your hand. I followed you by the water. I followed you across the city. And everything was magic, because we were there together, seeing it sparkle, seeing the beauty in every doorway, every piece of gray stone, broken and not. Every line was exactly how it was supposed to be.

I half-wish for a smoke now.

But I'm alone. And I don't think it would show me the magic of everything without you.

So instead, I stand up, I gather my notebook where I write these words to you, and I move on to the next place.

ʚ

It's hard to escape the smell of weed in this city, but I find another of your favorites tucked away down an alley. Hardly anyone is there, and the server looks bored. I order chai and sit in a blue corner.

The eleventh Nadine brought me here for the first time. You were coping with losing your dog. We sat here at this very table. You stared at the blue walls. Your hair was blue, then, too, and you wore all black. A hooded sweatshirt that fit you perfectly. You always had one of those, in all of your lives. It's strange to think that hoodies are one of those things humans cannot stop replicating. Hoodies and coffee and jeans. Sometimes humans disappoint me with their imagination, but you never did.

You always made your own dresses out of random fabrics. Sometimes they were velvet, sometimes cotton or wool. In every world, you're different than anyone else. In every world, you color your hair or cut it in unique way, or shave it off.

In every world, you paint differently, but there are always paintings of skogsnymfs in your work. Sometimes only one painting or two. Sometimes hundreds.

They're never accurate. They're never exactly how we look, or act, or sit, or stand.

But you cannot stop painting them. Painting me, I suppose. The way I cannot stop chasing you, regardless of the fact that each time I find you again, I must win you back. I must sign the right words, and sometimes your brother has died, sometimes you forget how to sign, and I must teach you the language you taught me. And I do it. I remind you.

We don't always become lovers. But I never needed that. Many times just being with you was enough. Sitting beside you with our feet dangling over a canal. Standing with you on a bridge, watching boats pass below us.

The twentieth Nadine was a Nicholas. A man. I almost didn't recognize you. But then I saw your paintings. I saw my face in one of them. And I recognized the lines of your body, even though they had changed, through the lines of that painting. And I loved you. I didn't care about the ways you transformed yourself, because you always transform, and I love each of you. All of you.

We were lovers then. For years.

Until your parents called you from Germany, and you had to go home, but you couldn't bring me there. You cried with me. Your body trembled in my arms on your bed. You asked me to wait for you to return. You promised.

But sometimes life gets in the way of promises.

Your father was dying.

I waited for a long time. Until the day you called to say he was gone, and you were broken, and then I knew you had split again, though I admit, I felt you splitting from leaving me, too. I slipped out of that sad world then. I slipped into another, where you had long hair and full breasts, and you fell into my arms with the feeling that we had always known each other. You didn't understand that your feeling was true. We had been together for more than fifteen years by that time.

The last ten of you I have known were all my lovers. We reached a point where, soon after meeting, we would fall together, regardless of who you were dating or even who you had married.

I write this, Nadine, because I need you. I don't want to wander alone anymore and I can't go home. I haven't seen my ring of infinity elms in ten years. I only returned with the seventeenth Nadine because you begged me. You wanted to go to the place where I was born, and I told you a romantic story of my parents having me by those falls. In the spot where I first saw you.

I tried hard to avoid my family while we were there, but I couldn't do it entirely.

My mother spoke to me from the trees.

Anja, she said, *where have you been? Why have you left us? Who is this human? What are you doing? How are you okay? Come back! Right now! Stop your wanderings, and come home.*

I cried and cried until she stopped talking to me. Until she faded away, though I could feel her sorrow in my bones. It hurt. It hurt like nothing else ever had.

I made up a story then, too, I told you the memories were too much because my parents had died. Because seeing those trees and that waterfall only reminded me of them.

And my story was true.

In my head, my family have died. They hadn't been my home for a long time, and even though my mother's pain doesn't hurt me now, I still hear her sometimes, begging me to return. Sometimes I tell her I'm sorry. Sometimes I don't say anything back at all.

This pain of being without you now is much greater than the pain I felt by the falls. The pain feels like a shadow. And I know it's because I do have a home now, and that home is you, a human, an artist.

We don't get to choose our home. I realize this now, while writing on a black table beside the blue walls. I brush away tears. (Yes, I cry now. I've learned to cry like a human, too.)

Somehow, my tears open the door at the front of the café.

I know it's you immediately.

You've got a black hoodie on again and you're struggling with a portfolio. Your hair is tied back and you've just finished a cigarette. You look tired. You look as weary as I feel.

But I'm not weary anymore.

I'm not lost.

I'm not chasing you because you've found me again.

I stand up, and I know that even though it's the twenty-eighth Nadine before me.

I am home.

You will know me.

I am home.

The Use of Blindness in the Text

Some metaphors for the body to dress
it in borrowed clothes: a puzzlebox, a battlefield,
a gift from an indifferent god. Consider your eyes,
which might as well be in orbit
around some far off star for all they're knowable
to mine, naked. Facial expressions wing
over my head like crows in the night. Mangled
analogies for the way I am: shorthand
for ignorance or poor planning. A lack
of attention paid. The reality is baroque
with specific vocabulary. My sudden double
vision was caused by a swollen cornea,
not an illustrative fracturing of the self. Reverse
the cause and effect. If you invoke a simile
for schizophrenia, I will scream. Not in my name.
I keep a list of things that look like other things
to the untrained observer: ignoring
a wave in the street. Failure
to recognize faces out of context. Not wearing glasses
when holding a book too close. Not good looks
for a young woman. I can't catch
to save my life. I can't keep my head
below my chest for more than a minute.
My acetazolamide habit is more
akin to breathing than manufactured dependency,
but I still rely on the kindness
of everyone. What does that say? Pick me
up at the hospital? Twice a year
and in emergencies (a head

injury, a yoga pose held too long)
my doctor's dilating drops roll in
fog and I fall like a trinket lost
in a bag of cotton balls, playing one
woman Polyphemus versus Odysseus
alone, addressing an empty theater. My literal
translation is plainspoken but unread.

Shadowland

Amid this tempest I move uncertainly,
always looked upon
by headlights that flicker
across my torso, wide-eyed clocks
with slender hands
that stare me down. Neon bleeds
hazy red into the street, dulling shadows,
distorting faces. This night is timeless; I lose
track in the dark
of what it takes, holds
back.
     Your eyes fall
into shadow in the pub's
smoldering glow, and you're sitting
to my left again, the bad side, wavering
in and out of sight. I have few signs
to follow—the slow drain
of your beer, the distance
between our hands—before I must guess
what has fallen
              into periphery:
    Your eyes,
the drive home, your hands, the road,
our voices. I cannot approach
with flashlight and loupe
to map you: lid, lash, white, iris,
pupil: the dark unknowable center.
Follow my voice beyond the car,
into the street

with its burnt out
lamps. Cast off
your contacts, listen
to them tick
against the pavement
like rain—how easily
they fall from you.

                    We are two
                    alone
inside the dark. Here
my hands will read you.

TAK HALLUS

Love Me, Love My Ostomy

What I learned when I became disabled was that gay men are even more shallow and fickle than I had ever imagined they were.

Don't get me wrong. I'm really glad I'm alive to complain about this.

I almost died. I had ulcerative colitis for 20 years and didn't know it. It only got diagnosed when it almost killed me. Emergency blood transfusions. Emergency diagnostic colonoscopy. My doctor said I should have died from anemia, if nothing else. Ten units of red blood cells over a couple of years, anti-inflammatory IV treatments, a crashed immune system, constant secondary illnesses, exhaustion, sudden collapse of will to live, depression, PTSD. It's a laundry list of bare survival. I had two near-death experiences.

Yet I made it. I lived. There was major surgery. Recovery. Big scars on my belly where my entire colon was removed. And the blessing of having to have an ostomy, with an appliance. I shit into a bag now. It's a high-flow ileostomy, so everything you've ever heard about ostomies is wrong, because all most folks know about is colostomy, where part of the colon remains. No such luck here. I have to empty the bag several times a day and night, I have no control over it, and I can't hide it. The appliance makes my belly stick out, and there's always a round bulge under my shirt on the right side, making a very uneven profile. It's not something you can afford to be squeamish about. You deal with it because you must.

That's why gay men are even more fickle and shallow than I thought they were. None of them, so far, has been able to deal with my ostomy, including all of the ones who claim that they can look past a disability if they really want to date a guy. Uh-*huh*. In my experience not one has been able to walk their talk. More than one has told me that it wouldn't bother them, like the ex-nurse whom I chatted with online for a while, but who never showed up. We never even met for tea; there was always some excuse or reason to postpone a scheduled date. Which to me seems far more dishonest and hurtful than straightforward, obvious horror.

Disclosure: when do I tell you I have this particular disability? Do I disclose it upfront when looking for men to date? In which case, I never even get any replies or responses. Or do I not tell them what the disability is, till we meet in person? In which case they without exception flee screaming into the night, hair on fire, never to be seen or heard from again. How's that for rejection?

Because it's not a *pretty* disability. It's not something anyone knows anything about. It's not a *popular* disability, one that generates pity and sympathy instead of horror. It's not a *fashionable* disability.

And it's mostly *invisible*—until the clothes come off. I can hide it under a loose shirt, and usually do. I've had men approach me in friendly ways, only to back away as soon as they know the Horror That Lies Beneath. It's not an *obvious* disability, like using a wheelchair, or a guide dog—so, in fact, some feel that I have been deceitful, and lied about myself and my nature. I've been insulted to my face that I was bad and wrong in that I should have told them upfront about the unpretty ostomy, so they wouldn't waste their time on me. How's that for rejection?

Either way I lose: if I disclose the ostomy upfront, they never even get to the point of rejecting me to my face; if I don't, they get insulted and claim that I lied to them. There's no win-win positive-thinking aphoristic easy answers to this piquant existential dilemma. As long as I have this ostomy, there's no way I'll ever have sex again. Some friends still tell me to Be Positive. Well, I'm glad I'm alive, I'm glad I survived the illness and surgery and recovery—I'm also frustrated as hell with men who don't have the stomach to stomach my stomach.

I'm strong. I'm tougher than anybody knows. I've had to be, to have survived. And survive I did.

The surgical anesthesia, meds, and PTSD have also left me with recurring brain fog: some days I can't make even mundane decisions, or remember simple things; which for the son of a woman who died from Alzheimer's is frankly terrifying. The lingering fog is also invisible. I have a genius-level IQ—but on brain fog days I can barely remember how to do anything. Some friends frankly don't even believe this happens. It's invisible to them.

Here's what ulcerative colitis does to you when you don't know you have it: it saps your energy and your will; it creates depression caused by medical lack rather than emotional trauma. It makes you believe you're a slacker, lazy, unambitious, lacking progress toward life's usual goals and lacking willpower to achieve them: because you can't do what everyone else does, you don't succeed in your career, you're tired all the time, and you don't know why. I am still undoing decades of horrible self-esteem: I am still wrapping my head around the truth that I wasn't a career failure, I was just sick. I was *sick*. My adult life was invisibly stolen from me, and the cure for my chronic illness left me with an invisible disability. This is just one of the numerous Catch-22s that make up my life.

When I now look with appreciative eyes at younger, healthier men, I am not envious of their youth, relative to mine, but of their vitality, their vigor, their life-force, their exuberant sexuality, their physical health—all of which was taken from me, gradually, invisibly, unknowingly.

Yet the men I would want to date all seem too squeamish to deal with this unfashionable, unpretty, unacceptable disability. They can't deal with the reality of me. My own life-force and sexual vitality have dramatically returned since the surgery: I now have the libido of someone much younger than I, yet there's no one to share it with. They all run off screaming into the night. That's not wholly metaphor: more than one man has arrived at my door to have sex, then immediately fled when they learned the reality of my disability. As I said, some of these have even blamed me for deceiving them.

How dare you? How dare you call yourselves open and accepting when you can't deal with my disability? The open horror is better than the lies and excuses about avoiding actually getting together, because at least horror is honest. You know where you stand.

Nonetheless I have been getting better since the surgery, even though I have big scars and this disturbing disability. I have been gradually getting stronger, and healthier—it is a joy to have a functioning immune system again. I have more ability for sex than I have had in a decade.

I'm frustrated, disappointed, and angry at the shallowness of my fellow gay men. Sexual frustration and rejection have metastasized into a prickly hedge of mistrust and doubt. Not of myself, but of you. You self-centered, squeamish liars. You lie when you claim the ostomy won't bother you. Your actions speak louder than your words, and your action is to run away as soon as you can.

To the next man who says to me that the ostomy wouldn't matter to him, I will say: Prove it. Just shut up and prove it.

Mercy, and my ability to be clinical, demands that I be honest: I know that most gay men, having survived so much hatred and fear in their own lives, are walking wounded with their own issues. Many of the most wounded can't deal with (unpretty) disability on top of it. Even if everything else about me is perfect for them.

The disabled community is often just as bad: because my disability is not obvious, and I can "pass for able-bodied" under many circumstances. Or until my energy runs out and I'm useless for any activity, which can still happen: you don't undo the damage overnight from 20 years of chronic illness. It's not the kind of disability that draws attention, sympathy, or pity—which is what I mean by "fashionable." Even within the disabled community, I have discovered a hierarchy of reverse-gamesmanship: who is worse off than others, therefore who deserves more attention. There are people I've met in the disabled community who sneer at my ostomy and scars as not being a *real* disability. I'm not disabled *enough*. After all, I'm still walking (except when I run out of energy), I'm not obviously disabled, and I'm able to do most of the things most able-bodied people can do (except that I can't, because I was sick for 20 years, and that time is gone, and I'll never fully recover). We are not all noble solitary warriors.

Here's my manifesto—it's very simple: Love me, love my ostomy. Don't pretend it doesn't bother you if it does. Don't lie—I'll know when you're lying. Do tell me what you think and feel about it—so we can talk it through, and maybe alleviate your fears. It's not the end of the world. After all, I've had to learn how to live with this thing. You could, too. If you choose to.

And yet, I dunno, maybe they're right? Maybe I'm not actually disabled? What is the critical threshold? Does almost dying count toward being disabled, or just toward being a survivor? What is the most important metric?

For that matter, am I queer enough? I can "pass" as a straight man much of the time, not because I try to, just because my gayness isn't obvious (until you catch me ogling guys, which I do all the time, but *subtly*). Even my "sensitive artist" friends didn't figure out I was gay before I told them.

In my pockets, along with my wallet, phone, coins, and a luckstone or two, is a roll of medical tape: just in case the ostomy appliance starts to come loose and leak around the edges. Because I've become physically active again, appliances usually last a week or less, and when they fail, they fail with spectacular leakage and odor. Yes, that's right: the shitbag stinks. When the appliance fails, and if I'm away from home, I can use the tape to hold a paper napkin over the leak, in theory, until I can get back where my ostomy supply kit awaits. The process of changing the appliance requires about half an hour of time and necessitates a shower. Skin protector liquids and powders also have to be used, as yeast infections are common.

Physical activity can loosen an appliance. You can catch its edges on a table, or when lifting a box of books, or if you bend and turn in just the wrong direction. Can you imagine if the appliance failed during vigorous sweaty sex? Could the mood be maintained till I was done changing the appliance? I doubt it.

So let's get real: it's not difficult to understand why the men who might otherwise date me will not because of the ostomy. I can be very clinical: I've had to be in order to get through the medical journey, surgery, recovery, and disability. Will a man I want to date stay with me long enough to learn to be equally clinical? So far, at least two gay male nurses have told me that it wouldn't bother them—still, we never got together, and they were always "too busy." Right. I do understand the problem. But understanding it doesn't make it less frustrating.

I'm disappointed. I'm disappointed in all the gay men who claim to be able to date a man with a disability, but when the clothes come off, they won't, or can't, or don't. Few things piss me off more than this.

So it goes.

I'm still waiting. And I'm not holding my breath for Mr. Right to show up at my door anytime soon. Go ahead, prove me wrong. I double-dare you.

CYRÉE JARELLE JOHNSON

Flashback, Porchlight, and Rivers

she played me her blues
deep into the coffee brown
dirt of the Oakland evening
her voice sculpting the fanged roots of a tree
named diaspora

she called out the names
oh yes she did

flicked her thumb
back and forth
and back and forth
across the warm wood body
leaning open on her lap

the strings ting-a-linging
out the sounds of her two syllable name
deceptively seeming like just one
twinkling sound
ting-a-ling

just to tease
a femme like me
the jealous type   maybe
who's poetry
may only be
a way to make them   crazy

and

grrrrl, you don't even know
don't even
know
know
know
cause nobody but my Jesus know
how deep blue my blues go

but you pluck and strum your blues
and I fuck to numb my blues
my deep blue blues
like the bruises on my shins
where the prednisone
has made my skin thin

and my
heart
and stomach
ache
with blues

when my rashes burst
I ooze
the blues

grrrl, you don't even
know
no
no
cuz nobody but my Jesus know
how deep
my deep
blues go

and I see
your tiny legs
and heavy shoes

and I want
uncontrollably
I want
cannot find the peace for all the wanting
which your voice burned into me
like a tea kettle
from stove to leg

like the way
the
night pills
morning pills
just in case pills
too too much pills
and too too much
blues

that your
just below the navel voice
erupted

clove oil
all over
my clandestine passion

but somebody else gets my lovin all the time
who is probably
well enough
to stay on
their unsnapping knees
all
night
long

I guess
I'll
just be thankful
for the music

but don't nobody
but my Jesus know
don't nobody
know
no
no
how blues my deep blues go

and the way she
was
rocking
holding
loving it
made me wish
I was some warm stringed gourd
remembering rhythm
as roots

instead of a house of soundless brick
and mortar

smelling like dust and death smell
iron clasps
my face a clenched fist

my blues
like a chasm
that Jesus could
but does not
fill
deep and wide
deep and wide
and dry

just plain
and unpainted
like the feeling

in my belly
when you played it

I guess I'll just be thankful for the music

JASON T. INGRAM

They Called It Mercy

My flight from Alaska to Northern Kentucky left late at night, so when I got to the airport I fell into a daze. It was like I was there but not there. I was so overwhelmed with fear, confusion and second thoughts about what I was doing, I retreated somewhere inside myself like a turtle. I tried to remind myself that I thought I was doing the right thing. A part of me was mentally exhausted from fighting my feelings constantly, so when I sat down at my departure gate, my mind was out of control. Every man who caught my eye made me think of taking him to a private place. Then I was afraid of what I would do. That caused more anxiety on top of my lust. I was 31 years old.

I could not sleep at all on my long flight to Seattle but managed a few winks on its last leg to Cincinnati International Airport. That next day, still in a daze, I studied over and over again the complicated pick-up instructions and found the place where I would take a van for the ranch. It was a cold winter Ohio afternoon, and even though I was coming from Alaska, I hadn't expected such harsh weather. I finally spotted a large maroon van with an adorable older driver, who was my type. I immediately got afraid of my thoughts. Yet in the van, I felt at ease a bit since "Brother Jerry" had a calm presence, but at the same time, I could not look at him. I just looked down or out the window on this new part of the country. He then told me that he was assigned to be my counselor!

The trip to the live-in program site took nearly an hour. We arrived there just at the end of dinner time. They managed to fill a plate of food for me, which was nice, because I was starving. There was a student who was still finishing his dinner, and I was introduced to him. He was mean-looking with a light mustache and lots of tattoos. He just stared at me. That was when I learned I wasn't supposed to shake anyone's hands. In fact, I was not to touch anybody!

After dinner I was given a brief tour of the campus, which was an old cattle ranch. The sun was just setting, and the weather was bitter. I was taken into the counseling office for briefing. I was a total emotional mess. I was given a list of a dozen assignments, many of them due the first week including signing legal paperwork. I was to study the live-in manual, remember a long list of written rules, and sign the LEGAL RELEASE FORM. This form protected them from malpractice lawsuits and other legal entanglements. This scared me. This form seemed to give them the ability to do almost anything to me, and it took me quite a while before I read it and signed it.

One of the questions people have about the Pure Life's residential program is if they do force the students to stay there. The answer is technically no. There are no barbed wires or doors that lock from the outside. Men can leave without being chased by cops with big guns and slobbering barking hounds. The reality, for most of the students and interns and even some of the staff, is that if someone leaves, there is a very large chance of him being brought to financial and emotional ruin.

Later that first evening I was shown my dorm. While I was getting oriented, a pastor gathered up as many of those who were staying in the dorm for a brief meeting in the small commons area. The meeting turned out to be him just yelling at all of us about how immature we all were. I was terrified. The pastor had these piercing eyes, a thick New York accent, and a very militant forceful voice. He did not need to yell at us packed into such a small room.

While the men were asleep, I was a bit late in getting ready for bed. "Andre," one of the leaders, took me to the commons area. He told me that he had read my file and that he knew about my "issue." He explained that I had additional rules, like how I should sit, and I had to keep my gay background a secret. He spoke in a voice very close to a whisper. He was taller than me, and he was very dark and slim. What was strange about him, like so many in the ex-gay movement, was how effeminate he was. You would think, that if he rose to such power over the years in this organization, he would have changed his mannerisms to act "straight." My bed, number nine, was a droopy old bunk right over a student who had arrived shortly before I entered the program. He was a real "crusty." When he took his shoes off to lay in bed, his feet smelled so rank that I had to turn around so my head was facing the other way from where his feet were.

Later that first week I found myself unable to sleep. A man, detoxing off crack cocaine, was very vocal, and our stuffy and smelly room, containing 16 men, was at maximum capacity. The sound of men snoring and creaking their old army-style metal bunk beds would've driven anyone crazy. On this particular night, though, I snuck out to the next building where the counseling offices were, and I climbed to the top of the stairs where there was a locked door. I curled up into a ball near the landing of the darkened stairway and lay there terrified. I was trying everything I could to hold on and not lose my mind. I felt so cold, despised, and worthless that I wanted someone to take me to a mental hospital.

I learned very quickly to rely on my faith to endure this new environment. I found a place to pray, and one of the other students heard me. He joined me in prayer, and we were both hit with spiritual joy. It was very cold that night but we didn't care. We were overcome with laughter that we ended up sitting in the driveway near our dorm.

"Brother Mark" worked for the ministry. I found him outside near the parking lot and asked if I could talk. We found a place to sit, and he listened to me as I told him some of the things I had done earlier that same winter before leaving Alaska. I felt so ashamed of having played with a married man who was also a Christian counselor. Brother Mark seemed to listen; he did not judge, correct, or try to punish me in any way. Having that kind of kindness from a staff member made things bearable at times while trying to survive in such a negative environment.

Most of the time when I was in a counselor's office, the sessions were brutal, confrontational and sometimes abusive. During my first few weeks I had a number of nervous breakdowns, and one night I could not find my counselor. Instead I was offered to talk to another counselor working late in his office. After I began to share, he just looked at me and said nothing, so I nervously kept talking until he finally stopped me and tore into me. It was as if he hadn't heard a word of what I said, and because I had gone to him in the first place, which was considered wrong, he started insulting me. He told me that no Christian should be acting the way I was and that I was in "the wrong religion."

I was told that Pure Life Ministries (PLM) chose rural Kentucky because the area had a lot of laws against the sex industry. Cincinnati, Ohio, an hour's drive away, was the home of Larry Flynt, and by the time

I was in that area, politicians had made things very difficult for those seeking out sex-related businesses. PLM also got a great deal buying this beautiful old cattle ranch just outside Williamstown, Kentucky. PLM draws a lot of gay men even though they focus on general sex addiction. Students cannot share whether or not they have had gay issues. We do hear in some of their graduating "testimonies" of some gay attractions and experiences, but then again most men are told not to share that part about themselves. Of course, some men give hints and even disclosures of their pasts while in the program. Then there are those who are—well, you know, "obvious."

I could not believe how cold Kentucky was in March. There was snow the first week I was there, and I did not have a warm coat. The "warm" coat I had in Anchorage was a very expensive arctic parka that was good in extreme subzero temperatures, but I thought I did not need anything like that in "the South." Whenever a student, an intern, or a staff member did not need something, they would leave things behind for the new students. They called it "mercy," something we did not deserve but got for free. Many times men exiting the program left behind all kinds of nice things. I needed a jacket and a shaver, and I felt so blessed to get them.

When I was told that the electric razor and jacket were "mercy," I soon learned that all kinds of things were called "mercy." When someone did your chore for you, it was mercy. When someone donated a jar of peanut butter, it was mercy. In fact, there would be the word "mercy" on the jar to show the men that it was up for grabs. I love peanut butter, and I experienced God's sweet generous mercy in the form of a few jars of organic, unsalted natural-style peanut butter. A student from Detroit did not see it that way and stirred sugar and salt into one of the jars. To avoid this sacrilege, I crossed out the word "mercy" and put my name on the jars I found. I discovered that I had to put my name on just about everything I owned, ate, and bathed with to avoid my stuff becoming someone else's mercy.

There were not only the written rules; there were also verbal and unspoken rules. They involved how we acted, what we talked about, and what clothes we wore.

The complicated dress code also included whatever a random staff member didn't like. Sometimes a counselor would assume that a certain garment or accessory would represent the "old man," or my former life, and I was forced to remove it. They often made mistakes about these assumptions, including falsely accusing me in front of everyone in front of the chapel. Even if they were mistaken, I didn't dare speak out.

One time I wore a bandana on my head at work, and three guys in the program were making fun of me. Then I wore it on campus. "Brother Herbert" told me to take it off because he said it was "old man." The funny thing was that wearing a bandana was one of my attempts at trying to be more tough and not so gay-looking. In fact, it was a new look. But I took it off.

There were rules about facial hair. We were all to enter the program clean-shaven and stay that way for the first few months. If we wanted to grow any kind of facial hair, our counselor had to approve it first, and even then we had to ask what kind of facial hair we could grow. If you were too effeminate, they'd try many times to get you to grow a beard to "butch you up." But the rules about eggs were the silliest of all, and they were not written down anywhere. Each student was allowed two eggs every weekday. You could not save up yesterday's eggs and eat them the next day. If there were eggs left over on the weekend, the students had to agree how they would share the eggs.

One of their worst practices was called the "Light Session." It was an attempt to try and shed light on a student who was too stubborn, so they would try to break him by using insults and humiliation. We all sat in a circle in the dim chapel. In the center was a chair with a sign that said MERCY. Each student was expected to say three negative things about any man sitting in the middle. I admit that I threw stones of judgment like everyone else did.

The pressure to conform was quite intense. I felt like such an outcast because of my humor, the things I talked about, where I was from and other differences I had. Just before leaving Alaska, I had spent most of my time teaching children so I developed a very dry, simple sense of humor which came off as silly. Most people in PLM thought I was just plain stupid, and they let me know of this often. I fell back on my private "stupid tests" that I developed when I felt put down back in middle school. If I said something that someone does not understand, and if they thought I was an idiot because of that, I would add something really stupid to see if they truly thought I was that dumb. I found this especially true of insecure and uneducated men. If I said something that was beyond them, they automatically criticized me. Instead of trying to defend myself, I would say something intentionally ridiculous to see what kind of reaction they would give me. If they really thought that I was that thick and continued to insult me, I knew that I did not want to be with that person. But if they knew I was joking, I felt more comfortable with them.

I felt deep down inside that I had an untreated mood disorder, but I gave up on trying to get help and bought into the old-fashioned idea of just working it off and fighting it. Therefore I had conflicting ideas about work: on one hand, I thought I was indestructible and because of my faith, I could be anybody I thought I should be; but on the other hand, I was terrified of labor work. As I had plenty of years of trying to do labor work, failing that had made me an emotional mess. In fact, when I was getting a ride to the warehouse to my first job after only a few days into the program, I cried on my way there. It was so embarrassing.

My first job was at a distribution center for a swimming pool supply company. I learned how to "pick and pack" using a motorized pallet jack and tried my best to meet the high-pressure time quotas, moving hundreds of boxes of chemicals. In my first week there I hurt myself so I had to go to a clinic. Then the following two weeks I got hurt twice so they fired me. I was moved to another warehouse job, this time in garden supplies. Because of the stress, my lack of sleep, and the way my mind processes information, I couldn't seem to follow instructions very well. I was moved around to different departments, and I made a lot of mistakes. The more pressure put on me to work faster, the more accidents I had.

In addition to working off-campus, I had a long list of things that needed to be done a regular basis. They included praying with an assigned prayer partner, writing sermon notes, listening to teaching tapes, studying workbooks, and reading the Bible. Those involved in the program either sought out or created messages similar to sermons such as "Longing for Sodom" and Pastor Steve's "For Those Who Continue in Sin." One of our teachings was about "The Duty of Man," and it was all about fearing God, keeping his commandments and that God will bring everything into a judgment based on the end of the Book of Ecclesiastes. One of the most memorable sermons was given by Pastor

Josh where he gave the analogy of a rock cutter hammering away at a huge boulder. He gave us the image of how a skilled rock cutter could hit this rock a hundred times and not see it break. He further explained that it was because of many tiny fractures inside the stone that were not visible, but was destroying the huge object from within until it collapsed. He told us not to be discouraged at working at this 99 times because the hundredth time could actually work.

I longed for this breakthrough so I could be free from my attraction toward men. I thought it would come in a form of spiritual experience, or maybe I would just notice that several weeks had passed by with no sexual feelings toward men.

Once, after confessing that I masturbated in the shower before a chapel service, I was brought to Pastor Josh's office. He confronted me and asked me if I was going to take the program seriously. I nervously agreed, and I felt like a pea getting smashed by an elephant. Getting special "corrective" things to try to stop me from touching myself were also humiliating. They might as well have put a chastity belt on me!

The assignments demanded honest answers about my life. A supplemental assignment was called "What's Wrong with Masturbation" by Steve Gallagher. He stated that masturbation goes against God's purpose of sex; it's a form of self-gratification, goes with "lustful fantasy," "opens the door for the enemy to lead the person deeper into sin," and it controls a person. While discussing masturbation with Brother Jerry in counseling, he began to preach that I should picture Jesus on the cross and me with my "organ," masturbating to his face. I tried to keep from squirming in my seat, but even though I was loyal to the ministry, I did question what he said. As I thought about it later, I wondered who was the pervert? Was it me playing with myself, or some guy who talked about beating off in front of Christ himself?

During my first few weeks in the program, I was constantly getting hurt, but I soon agreed that "tough love" was the kind of love that I needed. When I made out a gratitude list, I honestly thought that the program was the most important thing on Earth. Before my family, those who were praying for me, and a few other things, at the top of my list was "PLM." I believed that the program saved my life, saved me from going to hell, and was saving me from my dreaded homosexuality.

I believed I had a warped mind. I believed I was deranged, perverted, twisted, wicked, and sick. I believed that PLM was "Spirit-led." I believed that my mental health issues and even physical health problems were just ways I was trying to get attention. I believed that searching for my father's love was what I was trying to find in homosexuality. I had a distorted view of my past ministry work, especially of the stressful mission trips I took. As I had acted sexually many times after each intense series of meetings, I saw myself as a fake. PLM pressured me to see my past in this perspective. I did not take into account my lack of self-care, my sexual repression, and a lack of healthy outlets as well as ignoring my mental health issues. Many people use sex as a means of dealing with life's ups and downs, exhaustion and elation; however, anything sexual in that time of my life was so forbidden that when I would "burn out," I would lose the extreme control I usually had over myself.

When I entered the program, I did not trust myself to handle my own life. I would not leave the program. I was not only determined to work the program as best as I could, I was also afraid to leave. I was afraid of failure, I was afraid to face other church people from my past, and most of all, I was afraid of being stuck in an unfamiliar place with no money and nowhere to go.

If a counselor was especially abusive to me, I tried to bring it up to another staff member. There was never an apology, and it seemed as if the leadership had no intention of dealing with the problem. In fact, the problem was always "self." Every time I had a complaint there was some sort of corrective action taken against me. For instance, Brother Andre was particularly mean toward me. I was given yet another assignment to do, which was to come up with an entire page of things that I was grateful about him. One of the things I wrote was: "I appreciate Brother Andre because he is an anointed and caring counselor; that sees emotional and spiritual needs, and is not afraid to help correct when needed and find an answer." If I dared to complain about anything, the problem would always somehow be me.

Although many sermons and teachings spoke against being judgmental toward others, the very ones who were telling us not to judge were in fact judging us. They said that we are to live a merciful life toward everyone and yet they could practice their own form of "mercy." They said that there is a bad side to mercy, that leaders could discipline their followers, so therefore punishment is another form of mercy. One student would joke that when he did wrong to others, he is "bad mercy."

Somewhere in the middle of my stay at the ranch, I became hardened. I went about my day constantly on guard wondering who or what was going to try and bring me down. It could be my job or other students, but mostly it was the leaders. My fear of them grew to the point that I no longer challenged their authority. I tried to act more like the others in order to fit in, and I kept quiet. I started to have a chip on my shoulder, and I became very sharp to my peers at times. Little by little I started to lose myself in the madness. One time, while I was to drive a new student somewhere and we were about to leave the property, Brother Andre stopped me and began criticizing me. The new student seemed quite shocked at how mean this leader was to me over practically nothing. When he let us go, I told the new student that they were here to break us down and that was an example of it. Within a few days the new student made a phone call to his hometown and told them what was going on. They convinced him that he was in a cult and that he needed to leave, so he did.

When a man voluntarily left the program or was kicked out, we were to follow a strange and unusual protocol. This set of rules were never written down. As students in the program, we were to excommunicate them, even if they were an intern, employee, or staff member. We were not to listen or talk to them, and walk away. There was a message given in the chapel mostly about why the person left, often given with very humiliating and slanderous remarks. They would use words like this man was "unteachable," "deceived," or "full of pride." The humiliated man would be escorted or driven off the property; many times he was just dumped at a bus station.

This happened to Brother Mark, who was so kind to me my first few weeks I was there. They said that he broke his five-year commitment so he must suffer the same kind of banishment even though his crime was that he wanted to get married. Even if a student had to leave the program while on the job, all of their personal belongings left behind became property of the ministry. It was another example of mercy.

One night that summer I took a little walk by myself and happened to find an enormous tree filled with thousands of fireflies. Having lived most of my life in the Pacific Northwest, I missed seeing lightning bugs.

It was also rare to see so many in one place. I was so elated that I said a prayer, and I felt like I heard the voice of the Spirit again.

After these months of constant introspection, soul searching, and purging of anything sinful from within myself, I actually felt like I was in a place where there was no more sin in me. I was nervous to share this with my counselor. I really felt like a different man. I felt excited that I had attained a new level of purity. I was on better terms with the staff, tolerating my job better, and stopped masturbating for days and even weeks at a time. The old Jason was gone. I was wholeheartedly a Pure Life student on his way to being an ex-gay leader determined to help others in pain.

Whenever I had a day off from work, I spent that day in prayer, worship, and Bible study. I prayed fervently for other students, old friends back in Alaska, and most importantly, direction in my life. Because I had such profound feelings and deep spiritual experiences during prayer, I truly believed that I was receiving pure spiritual direction. While talking to my counselor about my plans after graduating from the program, he insisted that I not go back to Alaska as only sin would be waiting for me there. I pointed out that my car and things were in storage there. But I was willing to make that sacrifice for fear of going into a homosexual lifestyle.

If we cooperated successfully with the program, we would graduate in six months. I had planned it that I would start the program in March and complete it successfully without having to be given the dreaded "extension," then just in time to start my piano teaching the beginning of September when school started. Yet PLM had other plans for me. It was getting well into August and nobody would give me my graduation date. I wouldn't dare ask because I believed that if I did, I would get an automatic extension. I had heard of stories like that. One man, within just a few days of his graduation date, treated a few of the guys on their way back from work to a game of miniature golf. As a result, he had to stay in the program at least another month. It was a shameful thing to be extended, and some men got extended up to a year.

One day, in a counseling session, I was given an extension for another month. I couldn't believe it. All because I confessed that I had a crush on another man earlier that month. I wondered why I was so honest. I felt like I didn't deserve that kind of punishment, especially over the fact that I had not acted on my gay feelings. He just told me that I wasn't where I needed to be. He thought it was about where my heart was at. I also was very clear that summer that if I didn't get back to Anchorage in time to start my piano teaching, I would have to give my career up at least for that school year. Then my counselor kept telling me not to go back to Alaska. He gave me an assignment that I was to write a prayer and a two-page speech; and that they needed his approval. I gave him my first draft, and he read parts of it out loud for me. I found it strange that Brother Jerry, an older man who knew how attracted I was to him, changed this one word: he read that I had been with "other men," instead of "older men," which I had actually written. Nevertheless, he made me rewrite the entire speech, removing any piece of evidence that made anyone think that I had even been with men. It had to be vague enough to imply that I was a sex addict who had problems with lust only toward women.

Then it was time: October 2, 2005. We had just finished a half-day of fasting and prayer the day before. Often on weekends, some students who had been there longer made a big breakfast for the newer recruits. I felt obligated to wake up early and served them. I felt like I was being a good example. After breakfast, all of the men crammed into the small cafeteria, which had been converted from the downstairs area of the old farmhouse. We had to wait until all of us men were together; then we got a little lecture about how to behave in church, a prayer, and discussions about who would ride with who as well as exchanging cash for gas money.

Grace Fellowship Church, a 45-minute drive away, was one of the few churches in the region that would have much at all to do with PLM. It was the type of church where its pastor Brad Bigney would simply excommunicate a member of his church by telling the entire congregation during a Sunday morning service not to associate with a particular person, and share the man's first and last name in addition to some disagreeable things he'd done.

I sat there in the service wearing my Sunday best. We were taken to these services on a monthly basis or so, and we had a special place in the front of the church where we were all on display. This particular morning I felt a great sense of accomplishment as I prepared to graduate from the program later that day. I was among the three who graduated that night after their Sunday evening chapel meeting.

After the ceremony, I asked a friend in the program to snap a photograph from my disposable camera of me just outside the chapel. We walked across the parking lot into the main house where we had our regular graduation parties. Students all have to put in a few dollars each to pay for the cake, ice cream, and soda pop. During the celebration I was somehow very downtrodden. I was relieved to finally be out of that place, yet I had so many confused feelings going on inside me. Judy, my counselor's wife, was there so I tried to start up a conversation with her. I was hoping to get a word of encouragement or maybe even a "thank you" for the fact that I painted and framed an original oil painting of two eagles soaring above a storm for her and her husband. Instead she seemed to pretend I wasn't there. It was very strange. I was finally allowed to hug people and even shake their hands, yet somehow I still was treated as if I had a plague.

After the party, I heard more encouraging words from other students as I made my way to my bunk for some sleep before my flight out of Kentucky. A one-way ticket to North Carolina, a place further away than I had lived before. A place where I had no history of my struggle between straight and gay. A place where I could start a new life. Perhaps I would find a wife and settle down, starting a family of my own. Yet I had the same feeling I had when I left Alaska: nothing I did seemed to work. If I just got on an airplane and flew far away, I would find something that actually did work. I was gay in every state that I lived in. Finally I got to start over again as a heterosexual.

Cß

As a survivor of the ex-gay movement, I often find I am afraid that if I give myself up to God, someone else will demand I give my life to them at the same time. There is also a fear of trust from having been in an environment like that: it's not only difficult to trust in God when he has been so misrepresented; it is equally difficult to trust any organization and anyone in authority.

I am now living with an older man whom I love very much. His presence is the greatest mercy I could ever want.

MAVERICK SMITH

Invisible Within the Ten Percent

Pride is a sponsored summer spectacle
where politics are crowded out by corporate logos
recognition of difference has been reduced to rainbows
symbols of inclusivity omnipresent on flags & banners

    Tolerance
    Acceptance
    Inclusion
    Celebration

Pride is a rainbow blanket smothering difference
it makes words palatable to diverse communities
but even as folks's lips shape these verbs for others's ears
ableism & audism are omnipresent during Pride

    Cisnormativity
    Heteronormativity
    Cissexist
    Heterosexist

able-bodied folk debate the impacts of these complicated concepts
safe in their seemingly welcoming spaces during Pride festivities
lived realities of dis/abled folk are omitted from these discussions
their intersecting oppressions are actively erased & invisiblized

    Societal
    Institutional
    Systemic
    Individual

the narrow exclusionary sponsored corporatized version of Pride
endorses deliberate discrimination providing only floats never access
yet dis/abled folk create places for their intersecting identities
within & beyond borders of state-sanctioned Pride events

QUINTAN ANA WIKSO

Charité

1.

She and I smoke from a pale pink box. She evens up a blue pack of matches. Within my Dubonnet floats a centipede. Her manicure taps the glass—it wakes. We eat alongside the Charité Hospital, and the discomfort of such proximity demands distracting pleasures: the soft pillow on the chair, the candle between us, crisp black charms of a pepper shaker, the restaurant strung with café lights, katydids in the river reeds that soften the concrete, flat-bottomed boats pass by: laughter, beer, children.

2.

All across the continent of summer, asparagus and potatoes pulled from the soil. Cows induced for the release of cream. To the south along the mountain's toes, salt dragged scraping from its holes. Surprised by transport. And now my salad arrives, prostrate on its plate, exhausted.

3.

Beside the Spree, a pair of pale eyes in the delicate face of a beauty. She hands me a cigarette, and I smoke three.

4.

The legs that are currently attached to my body are not the ones with which I am familiar, and certainly have not been mine since birth. These new ones surprised me in this evening's bath—an old, cracked porcelain affair. The water drained out past my ankles: mild, yellow, thin. These are some stony and nerveless things, poured into a mold, or else cast. Prosthetic, but unsubtle. Unlike the others: bony and serviceable and flushed and swelled and pumping with blood.

5.

She wears a yellow dress. Between the Charité and the Spree, my glass of Dubonnet. Within it floats a centipede, underbelly turned up to the sky. Clouds in Berlin unlike any others: huge, swollen, white. Where are the stringy pale ones, the vulnerable whisk of egg ones, the broken-feather ones of gray haze.

6.

In recent days, my old legs must have uncoupled from my hips, with a click of grease and a muscled wheeze. Separated at some station along my route. My arms and torso bound for investigation of atrocities—yet the embrittled remnant, allied in refusal, detaches on the platform in Leipzig. The tablecloth falls over my lap to hide the seam.

7.

She is five foot ten. She agrees to a second glass of Dubonnet. She is kind, and uncomfortable. Had hoped for some happier kind of evening.

8.

She has a faint blonde fur on the tops of her fingers, and it suspends a blur of dust in the candlelight. It is sweet. She is useless with euphemism. Like the others, she asks if my grandmother survived the experiments.

Like the others, she has forgotten that her death would have made my birth improbable. Yes, I say with practice. And then, no.

9.

There is nothing to be accomplished by summoning a waiter and exchanging the glass of Dubonnet, by requesting a cleaner drink: in other glasses, other insects. Within this one a thousand legs spread open, doomed.

10.

Below the table, my underwear disguises a sharp bend of hips that now seem to snap instead of fold. There are feelings I used to have down there that I want to recognize again. Her eyelids bear blue paint. A luminous glaze, near incandescent in the haze of my smoke. Despite the readiness of her cosmetics, there is no dancing tonight at the Ballhaus in Mitte, with its varnish-crazed floors dehydrated by feet from last century. My former legs would have taken me away from this place. But these have rooted themselves, and refuse to move. She checks the tint of her lips in the hand mirror, opens them to flash light on bright teeth—a rasp of pink tongue across their white.

11.

She says hers was an easy birth. She arrived right after everything had begun to get better again: there were vegetables sprouting in the Tiergarten, different uniforms to be sewn with new patches and badges. And buildings were going up, with lipstick-red geraniums and hydraulic elevators. Babies were raw and welcome. Her mother was frightened and pleased. Dr. Aquilin Ullrich delivered her in what was widely recognized as a very easy birth.

12.

At some distance, I feel my legs twitch in Leipzig, in an imagined sanatorium for the mutinous legs of Jews who have returned for questioning. For the appendages that have refused to walk any farther through the mysterious anguish of ancestry. There is a strained gruel of sunshine and my rebel legs are blanketed in soft blue linens, tucked up on a chaise lounge. Pain and numbness, an unsavory combination alleviated by violins, chipped ice, and violets.

13.

She is patient with my questions, although her hair falls in her eyes when she lowers her face. When she looks up, it's with a gift for statements of extrapolated fact. She believes Dr. Ullrich died without regrets. Before he reinvented himself, her mother's eventual obstetrician hid from arrest and trial in the mines of the Saar. The killings of four thousand five hundred schizophrenics were easy deaths. The rocks in the shafts were difficult to pick apart, and he cared about his fingertips. After all that, attending births is no big deal. He was lighthearted with escape.

14.

Here I am, unraveling. Her navel, tied off with a killer's string.

15.

Stretched out beside my legs in the Leipzig sanitarium—the thick-muscled, hairy legs of a man I met on a bus: his uncle the driver of a Hadamar gas van, his grandfather had been the boy who delivered the euthanized ashes of epileptics to their surviving parents. The seats on our bus were dark green plastic. I sat on my hands to still them. His grandfather had been a responsible boy, with soft hands known to be reliable, clasping the tiny urn on his bicycle as he shot across the cobblestones with a wobble. Accurate readings of street numbers meant a polite knock at the family's door. The man's nose blunted, a half-day growth of stubble at the base of his neck, a fresh tie and no freckles. At the stop, we didn't transfer as neither of us wished to go farther.

16.

Beside the Spree, dinner arrives with fresh glasses and cloth napkins. She believes Dr. Ullrich died taking pride in his accomplishments. Across the street at the Charité Hospital are offices that once welcomed the gynecologists' experiment: how best to prevent the imperfect from multiplying. Four hundred thousand proved the point: it is absolutely possible to eradicate hereditary diseases. Because depressed patients did not exhibit a will to live, Dr. Ullrich did not consider it murder. Everything salted to taste, then peppered. Seasonal asparagus with butter stains on the seam of my lap. He had no regrets. The children consigned to Chelm or to Brandenburg were then gassed. The first two hundred thousand were practice perfected. Tonight, she would have preferred to go dancing.

DAVID CUMMER

The Changeling

Were the lights out?
Rosaries wouldn't be pagan enough, was that it?
Or did the Elf Queen replace you so quickly
that your mother thought the oak branch was you?
Did they think you were broken when the few leaves withered
    like Fairy gelt?
Afterwards they swaddled you with cold blue wire.
That star pulled you away.
A forest rose up and died before the Elf Queen returned you.
Your mother sat there, a starving dog at her feet.
No Mab's ointment for her.
You stood there,
deeply-rooted,
thick-trunked,
the wind and the birds and leaves flying about.
You saw that she was only looking at the dry, splintery twig in
    her lap.

She had been dreaming of old,
the changeling she had,
but not the child who was.

CARL WAYNE DENNEY

Our Son Is a Beautiful Girl

Dominic is born on an August evening. A beautiful child, he comes out willingly, lovingly, and full of curiosity. The time spent in the hospital, located in Noblesville, Indiana, is uneventful.

When taken home, he is instantly captivated by everything around him—three older brothers, a vibrant and beautiful actress mother, and a hard-working father who runs the third shift at the local Deaf school. Both of his parents are Deaf, and his oldest brother is Deaf.

Home is where its forest green walls are lined with Christmas lights strung along its edges and books stacked on shelves everywhere, and surrounded with large pieces of artwork. The four-bedroom place has his brothers at one end, the younger brother in his own room, and the parents's room, where his crib is laid with blinking stars set above the bed.

Growing up, Dominic is quiet, always smiling, and chases after the cats. He rides his little Razor four-wheeler. He attends his brothers's athletic events and runs around the football fields and basketball courts. The father coaches the local club team to basketball prominence; the mother acts in the first few ASL Films.

After his family relocates to a new cozy house, Dominic has his own space and a living room full of toys and artworks and more balls—at last count, there are more than 40 footballs and basketballs around the house. His scooter is replaced by a bicycle, and a kiddie rim is set up in the backyard. Videos are made of him running and dunking the basketball. He dribbles the ball along the sidelines of his older brothers's games.

Then comes school—the Indiana School for the Deaf in Indianapolis, Indiana. In preschool, Dominic begins the long process of socializing, learning, and growing. But out comes unexpected anger, confusion, acting-out, bewilderment, frustration, and tears.

"Dominic sure doesn't like school," the father says. "What's wrong with him?"

"It's a phase," the mother says late at night, just before shutting the lights off for the night. "He'll outgrow it."

Yet comes the sullenness, the brooding, the refusals, the desire for something never seen before in the household: Barbie dolls, little baby dolls, treks into the girls' clothes department. When he is taken to the boys's clothes area, his outbursts turn hard, vile, scary.

"He'll outgrow it," the father says. "He's gonna be a tight end for the ISD football team."

"I don't know," says the mother, unconvincingly. "I take care of him most of the day now that he rarely goes to preschool. He doesn't communicate, other than 'milk' and 'binky.'"

The academic year turns into a blur of nonstop activity—sports of all levels for the three older boys, the Indy Hawks basketball schedule, ISD sports, and the mother's art classes. Then there is the increasing frequency of Dominic's destructive acts in the preschool classrooms. Whenever he is dragged to the school and set in the arms of teachers, the parents sprint down the hallway away from him wailing after them. But he rips and shreds bulletin boards into pieces. Texts chime in, the videophone blinks, and the messages say, *Come please pick up Dominic, take him home and to please work with him in controlling his temper, work on his attachment issues,* and so on.

"Something's wrong with Dominic," the father says, cradling him in his arms one late spring day. He no longer works at the Deaf school. He spends all his energies reading, walking, and coaching his beloved Hawks.

"We need to be patient," the mother says, watching Dominic carefully.

The parents have made amends already. Without discussion, reproach, or broaching, they individually and together purchase feminine toys: Barbie dolls, dollhouses, plastic babies, and kitchen-themed toys. The father has even gone out on a limb by bringing home a bicycle—pink-colored with pretty accessories—and gives it to Dominic. His eyes lights up as he smiles and signs, "Mine, mine!" He hops on and pedals up and down the street as the father sits on the curb, grinning.

The mother has secretly purchased clothes for little girls at Goodwill, KidsZone, and Once Upon a Child. The clothes are in a couple of sacks laid across a bedroom closet shelf. Every morning she looks at them and wonders if she should . . .

On a late cool summer evening Dominic, just before turning four years old, finds a few of his mother's wigs and puts one on. He runs down the stairs of the tri-level, clad in pajamas and with his favorite furry backpack made to resemble a bear on his back. He zips down the driveway and back into the garage, smiling, laughing, and bursting with joy. The mother smiles and signs to the father, "Happy?"

He turns away, eyes filling with tears, and heads into the rear of the garage.

Dominic turns four. In the days that follow, decisions are made: mostly one-sided decisions, met with apprehension and fear from the father; courage and determination by the mother.

"Dominic will from now on wear halter tops," the mother says. "He will wear girl shoes. I will make sure he wears half and half daily. This will help him go to school."

"I don't like it," the father says, shaking his head.

"I don't care," she says. "I want Dominic happy."

"He is happy!" he says. "He goes with us everywhere—he does what other boys do."

"Does he say anything? Does he really enjoy himself?"

"He doesn't say much, except that he's tired and wants to go home. Then he sits in my lap and falls asleep while I read."

"So, you're saying he doesn't participate, only watches, like he does here?" She says, pointing to Dominic, whom they could see through the front window, where he is astride his bike as his brothers try crazy skateboard flips off a homemade ramp built on the street.

"Well, we always try to get him on a board, but after a few times, he wanders off to sit and watch and say it's too hot and wants to go home," he says glumly.

"This is what we should experiment with—see what happens."

"No way!"

"Remember what happened at the tournament last spring?" she says angrily.

"Yeah, he got mad and turned the gym lights off!" he says, smiling at the memory.

"It's not funny!" she says.

Dominic had wanted to go home only a hour after arriving to watch his father's team capture the annual Central Region basketball championship. Dominic had a bright idea as to how to get his message across—he turned the gym lights off while the consolation game was nearing its end, and while his father was standing with his team along the sidelines ready to take the court.

"Well, it wasn't at the time," he says.

"What do you think he did when he got home?" she says, beginning to cry.

"Aw, don't cry. I know he didn't mean anything by it. He was just tired and cranky."

"No, when he got home—he put on the wig, and dived into his dolls and told me—directly, 'Mommy, I'm a girl. Why doesn't Daddy see it?'"

He holds her as she cries. He loves her more than words could say. He also knows how cruel life can be, especially for kids who stand out.

"Okay. I know your mind is made up, so I'll support you," he finally says, knowing how a community could behave toward those different. This was as different as can be, no matter how small it seemed.

"Dominic can dress like a girl here at home anytime he wants," she says.

"Okay, but only at home," he says, lost and afraid for Dominic.

The brothers are okay with it. The eldest says he would beat up anyone who insults Dominic. The second, a wiser one, says, Dominic is tough—he doesn't care what anyone thinks so he would be okay. The third one asks, Why?

"I don't know, Massimo," the father says. "Dominic is different."

"He's not a fag," Massimo says, acute for a seven-year-old.

He grabs him by the neck and says, "We don't use that word here, period."

Massimo squirms free. "He's my brother."

Dominic begins wearing halter tops, pink Vans, and hair cut a specifically girly way. The family sees improvement—not much more communication, but Dominic smiles more often. His outbursts are fewer, and he starts to talk with other kids his age. He plays with them in their games at school. He rides the bus more willingly to preschool.

The parents take him there more often than not, but to the outside observer, things seem to be going well for Dominic.

Yet things are not what they seem. The parents try to shield Dominic and Merle, the eldest, also a student at the Deaf school.

"Mom, someone said Dom is a fag." Merle says. "I set them straight."

"Did you punch him out?" the father asks, teasingly.

"No, I'm not gonna get suspended. I just told them straight up that Dominic isn't, and that he's just different." Merle says, "But kids are talking, and I just tell them to let it go as it's probably a phase."

"That's good," the mother says. "People will get used to Dominic and his unique funky ways."

Nearby Dominic is playing with Massimo. Dakota is out bicycling with his friends around the neighborhood. Noelle, the new baby, is asleep. She has taken Dominic's place in the crib. Dominic sleeps between his parents. More often than not, the father has started to wake up around midnight, walk downstairs to the second living room, and bury himself in the recliner. He sleeps better in spite of his nightmares over what will happen to Dominic, which he doesn't share with anyone.

Dominic becomes taken with Noelle. He begins to help his mother take care of her to the point everyone called Dominic "Mommy's Aide." He beams and demands to hold Noelle in his arms every evening. Noelle coos and holds his hands whenever he hovers around. They are inseparable.

The year goes slowly, lovingly. The baby amazes everyone; the family circles tighter around everyone else. The father struggles still; the mother watches reality television daily. The Indy Hawks fail in their quest for a three-peat USA Deaf Basketball (USADB) championship. Dominic continues to dominate everyone's thoughts. The family knows change in the air is coming, even as he appears content with what he has become: feminine and more and more into earrings, nail polish, and a couple high-heels he found at a garage sale nearby, which the mother bought without question.

Dominic goes to almost all of the mother's gatherings with her friends. He goes to makeup parties and has a blast. The mother's friends are understanding and supportive.

The father still takes him to the backyard hoop and tries to have him shoot a couple. Dominic kicks the ball away instead. The father tries to toss the old pigskin at Dominic, but he flings it over the fence.

The community swirls around them. People are talking.

A longtime friend, accompanied by her husband, meets the father before an Orioles varsity game and says he's going to hell for letting Dominic dress the way he dresses. The father looks at the woman's husband, a friend of his, who looks away. He tells her that if anyone talks to him that way about his son, he will—he brings his fist to within an inch of her face—punch him.

The mother goes out with the ladies; they ask her about Dominic. She explains the taping of genitals and the time they found him hidden away in a corner of the kitchen, steak scissors in hand, his own manhood in the other ready to be snipped away.

Horrified, the ladies say Dominic is beautiful, and to let him blossom.

The father is at the Orioles football game. He loves seeing his alma mater play football. He once wore the uniform with pride, and now he sees Merle play. He turns and spots someone he considered a friend in the bleachers sign to another man, "Dominic is a fag." After a quick internal debate, the father points, in full view of everybody in the bleachers, and clambers up the stands toward the man, "—the fuck you saying about my son?" Other men quickly circle him and calm him down. The other friend slinks away, forever banished.

The mother, Dominic, and Noelle spend a lot of time shopping together. They come back with bags of frilly pretty outfits. The father smiles, hugs them, and says nothing.

One Halloween, for the hell of it, the boys dress as girls along with Dominic for Halloween, and they have a blast. Despite his initial discomfort, the father finds it funny and enjoyable as the night goes along. The mother takes group pictures of the boys with Noelle in the middle and jokes she has five daughters.

Dominic has a godfather named Tony; the father and Tony grew up together. Tony is going through a difficult time in his life, but he stops by once a week to check up on the family and to tickle Dominic, who laughs.

The father, still struggling, asks Tony what to do about his son.

Tony says, "Leave him alone." He bikes back to Indianapolis.

The father has a close friend named Dorn. Dorn is 6'9", 230 lbs., and black. He lives nearby and often bikes over to have dinner with the family every Wednesday before the Hawks basketball league games at the Fieldhouse. Dominic adores Dorn, and he and Noelle climb all over him, who lifts them easily and with pride.

While driving Dorn to the Deaf school's Caskey Gym for the Hawks's practice, the father asks Dorn about his son.

Dorn has a ready answer: "Cherish Dom."

At night the father holds Dom and Noelle in his arms as *Sunday Night Football* unfolds on ESPN. He wonders what the hell he's going to do. It feels as if his life, full of jockstraps and balls and competition, is in free fall.

With Dominic in kindergarten and the eldest a freshman football player for the Orioles as well as the other boys in their sports programs and leagues, the father shuttles around from practice to games to a local basketball team he's just joined—older men who still think they got game. The father seeks escape and this helps.

At a league game, a man, who works as an aide at the Deaf school, teases Dominic with "You a boy or girl?" repeatedly throughout the game. The father gets tired of it, grabs him by the lapels, and propels him backwards into a wall. The other men intervene and calm the father down. Dominic and Massimo watch this and break into tears.

The mother watches reality television while taking care of Noelle as the father falls into his own fog. She like to keep a close eye on different shows, following current events, as the world spins ever so slightly on its axis—to the point she turns to an episode of Oprah.

When the father comes home, she says, "This is the show I want you to watch." She flips the DVR to the episode. He sits and nods, biding his time till he could get out of the house. As the show unfolds, the lady in question talks about her son who dresses as a girl. The father, a black man, nods supportively. They have written a pretty book in pink.

"That is Dominic," the mother says.

"Bullshit!" the father says, anguished.

He bolts from the house, drives to the Town Center where a bookstore is, and sees the book *My Princess Boy*. His hands shake as he opens the book to read. He sits in the bookstore as he turns the page. He ends up buying two and brings them home.

Dominic reads the book when he arrives home from the Deaf school. He smiles and says, "This is me!" He holds the book as he sleeps.

The mother delves into research about transgender children. In 2010, this is new territory for a lot of people. She digs long and hard on the computer. What she finds is alarming—rejection, bullying, and high suicide rates.

The father doesn't talk about it anymore. He just goes about his business—the Hawks are in danger of collapse. Scandal has rocked the team; players have moved elsewhere and joined other teams. The sons's grades are suffering. The eldest cannot play varsity basketball due to grades, the second one says sports are for idiots, and the third one wonders why Dominic isn't his little brother.

Noelle begins to babble, and Dominic is never far from her side.

The mother sets a great Thanksgiving table, and the mood is somber at home with everyone drifting, thoughts and words left unsaid.

The cold darkness of December sweeps the suburb where they live. The father goes to the Deaf school's Caskey Gym and surveys his team—a team tottering on ruin. The mother is home with the boys, who are huddled in the game room, a room changed into a palace to escape into the world of virtual gaming.

The mother decides easily and decisively. She goes to Dominic's room, empties the closet's contents into four large trash bags, and places them in the garage. Dominic gapes as Noelle sleeps. She beckons him into the bathroom.

The father drives home, once again wondering why he isn't someplace warm. He pulls up into the driveway, flings his basketball bag onto the garage floor, and notices the four garbage bags. He opens them and sees the clothes, wondering what the hell is going on. He takes out several items—the Colts jerseys, the Indiana University basketball uniform, the Colts sweatshirt—and opens the door into the kitchen. He dumps the clothing onto the kitchen table and notices Noelle napping.

He gives a small shout to the mother, who comes down from the upper floor. The father asks what's up with the clothes.

She smiles and flicks the hallway light as he stomps back into the kitchen to retrieve more clothing from the bags in the garage.

She flicks the kitchen light on and off to stop him and beckons him back. At the same time, Dominic comes down the stairs in a simple white dress, hair fixed up beautifully, and glowing. "Hi, Daddy!"

The father breaks down, tears coming out like a fountain, as he grabs and holds Dominic. He kisses Dominic as he hugs back fiercely with his small hands and thin frame. He holds and struggles to let go, afraid to lose Dominic, afraid to lose his son.

Dominic leans back and says, "I'm happy!"

For the first and final time, the father lets go.

Time passes so slowly that winter, Dominic doesn't go to school the first few days after the change. The father wouldn't let him go to school. Dominic has begun communicating; like water gushing from a break in a dam, he is talking, signing, and laughing. He feels free; he prances, dances, and leaps. Noelle and Dominic are inseparable.

The mother relaxes, busy with Christmas shopping, the annual Christmas family picture, and the Christmas dinner. She, Dominic, and Noelle purchase girl stuff—clothes, makeup, and posters.

The father visibly relaxes. He holds Dominic at night with his arm around him as they watch television. The parents do not really talk about the change but they are more relaxed.

The Christmas goes very well.

"What will the community think?" the father asks one night.

"Fuck the community—this is our child," the mother answers.

Then comes the new year of 2011.

The Deaf school is not prepared—hell, nobody is. This thing is so new—nobody even knew what it was. Not teachers, not counselors, not anyone.

The father knows change would be difficult, but with his mind made up, he would give Dominic full support from now on and forevermore. He watches Dominic dress proudly in the morning and walk with a bright smile to the school bus. He flashes a ILY to the father that early morning and hops onto the bus.

The mother has the foresight to email the Deaf school about the change and their decision to support Dominic fully. They explained that they, as parents, understood it was a new and scary thing. If they all worked together for Dominic, they could help Dominic be accepted. Heck, they all could acclimate each other for Dominic.

There are cursory responses. Nobody at the Deaf school says anything else. The community is in an uproar, but nothing is said to their faces, given who the father and the mother are. The eldest has only a few questions from his peers but it mostly goes well, with acceptance.

God bless the young.

The school calls a meeting to discuss Dominic, which does not go well. It turns into a shouting match between the father and the new elementary principal; both macho men, both strong-willed. One phrase taken one way nearly leads to fisticuffs and both being separated by the women in the meeting room.

The father takes Dominic home despite the mother's wishes for him to stay for the day.

Not even a week later, the Child Protective Services sends an agent to check out Dominic's well-being. The mother greets the agent, and the father is gentle, with documents pertaining to transgender, gender dispora, and, for the hell of it, *My Princess Boy*.

The visit is uneventful. The agent is friendly, asking Dominic and the other children questions. The parents, while interviewed, reply truthfully about their struggles and their final acceptance—in other words, stop struggling and let live.

The agent then explains that "transgender" is still a new word, and it is being studied, but it is not a danger for anyone and that she is glad that Dominic had a strong and loving home. That is what was most important—a strong and loving family who supported Dominic.

Yet at the same time, a certain restlessness takes place in the mother. She is tiring of the barely hidden scorn from others. Dominic has not been invited to a birthday party in over two years. He asked the varsity cheerleading coach if he could be part of the cheerleaders' skit featuring elementary girls dressed as cheerleaders, only to be rejected. Being a Bay Area native, the mother feels it is time to "go west."

The father is reluctant. He was a Hoosier with everything he wanted around him, and he had just fought his inner demons and beat them—hell, he conquered them. He has his Hawks, who are now righting the ship—with several retreads playing the season of their lives around Dorn; his thinking has never been clearer, and spring is coming—baseball, USADB, and skateboards and rollerblades.

"We're going to move to California, with or without you—Dominic needs a place that will understand and accept him," the mother says. She means it.

So they give up all of what they had built—the home, the teams, and the old lives—and move out west.

There, as the mother has proven correctly, is acceptance and a strong liberal live-and-let-live mentality in the Bay Area. Yes, it is expensive as sin, but at least, the school is great with counselors ready for them.

"First of all, stop calling Dominic 'him' and 'he,'" the counselor says. "This is vital in her development."

The mother nods; she has taken this to heart. The father doesn't argue; he is fully vested.

The school helps guide Dominic in terms of what bathroom to use—the girls. Terms where she can change into a bathing suit—the unisex one. Where can she sleep if we place her in the dorms, the mother asks, given that the Bay Area is pricey and the lowest affordable apartment they have found is a hour away.

Why, they answer—naturally—the girls cottage!

The parents sigh in relief. Their boys are enjoying California, its weather, and the skateparks. Dominic is happy at his—her—new school, and she has already gone to two birthday parties.

The mother is thrilled to be in her old stomping grounds; the father isn't, but he tries. He goes to Minnesota for the USADB tournament and leads his undermanned Hawks to a near-upset of the Deaf Sports Academy, a powerhouse West Coast team in double overtime. The Hawks then overcome Austin with their three Deaf Olympians in overtime after being down 22 points. They finish fifth, and he is honored as the USADB Coach of the Year. But he disappears from the tournament immediately after the last game, so the announcement is made without his presence.

He is holed up alone with his memories in his hotel room. This would be his last tournament and his last game with the Indy Hawks.

His love for his new daughter, who has added an "e" to the end of her name, has trumped all.

଼ଃ

After two years between the Bay Area and Kentucky, the Denney family relocates back to Indiana in January 2013. Their homecoming is quiet. The Indiana School for the Deaf welcomes Dominice with open and warm arms, allowing her use of the girls facilities and having her sleep in the girls dormitory whenever she stays overnight. She is treated fully as a female. She still struggles with her peer group, but she has more acceptance than ever and, at the age of nine as of this writing, is aware of her unique situation in life. She has never asked to be treated differently.

The mother, Tuesday Apple, remains a LGBT advocate and is staunchly supportive of Dominice and the children. She attends Gay Pride events with Dominice, and she hopes to establish a workshop where Dominice is understood more clearly within the Deaf community.

The father, Carl Wayne Denney, has returned to club coaching. He led his New Mexico Zia to the 2013 USADB championship and followed up with the Indy Hawks winning the 2014 USADB championship. He considers Dominice his heroine and is practically wrapped around her little finger.

Dommie and Noelle are the best of friends.

TRAVIS CHI WING LAU

Perspectival

Legal pad: // crammed beneath // a stressed // table leg // and the heavy // strokes of // what remains // forever crossed // and dotted. // The mug topples // and the colors, // partially separated, // blend briefly // in the interim, // the hanging space // where milk // and arabica are // forced back // into precarious // proximity // without the // possibility // of my pleasure.

Uneven floor: // I sit with // a slight lean, // a (disad-)vantage // point of the // park square // askew with the // day's burden of // grey and too // many footfalls that // do not breathe. // The photo // I snap // needs straightening, // but the tilt // does not break // the game like // a pinball machine; // instead, there are // lines that // recede // and come to // the startling fore.

With All Due Respect

With all due respect,
sensei, you were sorely

mistaken about the
very capacities of this

crooked frame you
refused to deem beautiful

before the mirrors
erected to play slanted

games of revelation—
there, fractures in

the wood are not
filled with gold,

but instead swell
to splintering,

until I collapse in
the manner most

conducive to your
prescriptions twisted

out of iron and
the scent of rice wine.

TORANSE LOWELL

Learning the Words

When I was 17, I started shaking, or maybe I always had. My hands were skittish animals, my body felt like a plucked string, vibrating from the inside, like I could feel my own intestines tremor where I laid a hand.

We were forever trying to pin me down, my mother and I, figure me out. Dizzy and faint, just look at my blood pressure, exhausted and listless, let's demand the doctor check my iron levels, coughing, we would discover was allergies. I had everything wrong that would count as nothing, I was fragile and fine, always fine.

We were Pentecostals, charismatics, praying to God for miracles. "Speak health," my mother would tell me to my scratchy throats and sniffles, "Speak health in Jesus's name," and that would be the end of it, and anyway, it was only allergies. That would be what she would tell anyone who asked, why was I sick, why was I missing work or school or church and from menstruation to headaches to exhaustion she would say, "It's only allergies."

So we prayed and I took her vitamins and I was never sick but always sick. And when the doctor suggested depression, suggested counseling, suggested it was mental, my mother laughed it off in disbelief. "You are the most content person I know," she told me, and I lived under that label because she said it, and she also said she wasn't wrong. So I slept without covers until the cold ached in my bones, and I begged God for flus and sniffles and I crawled into bed at eight, at six, at four to tell myself a better story. Because I wasn't sick.

We were Pentecostals, so I was supposed to be a Handmaiden of the Lord. A Handmaiden meant that I was pure, it meant that I was accepting my God-given femininity, it meant that I understood my future role as wife and mother, and I spent my days letting God prepare me for such. Except that I didn't. I fought, I raged, I stormed in silent rebellion against every submission sermon that tumbled from the pastor's lips. But it wasn't real, exactly. I knew my role. I knew what obedience looked like. I knew one day I was supposed to marry, not a Christian, but a *Man of God*, and if someone doesn't understand the distinction, they clearly aren't a Christian like we were Christians.

God loved a submissive heart, and God loved to test your obedience to Him, so I knew, I knew he would ask marriage of me. I knew one day I would look upon the face of the man I was to marry, and I would be terrified; terrified of him, terrified of everything I was supposed to be, I knew that I would have to be subsumed into him, lose myself to him. There wasn't a choice in this manner, because I loved God more than I loathed the restraints He put me under. If I hated marriage, if I hated the idea of childbirth, there would be God to say, "Do you love Me enough to obey Me, even in this?" And I did.

I'm focusing on school, I'd say. I'm focusing on work, I'd say. I don't have the time right now, I'd say. I'm just tired, I'd say. I'm just not hungry, I'd say. And my hands kept shaking.

There were demons in our house. We prayed them out, rebuked them, anointed our house with oil, but they kept coming back, and they loved my bedroom and my parents' bedroom, especially. They loved little girl flesh in the darkness, they loved my father's coarse skin, and I'm sure they would have harmonized with his shouting if he could carry a tune. There was a name for every spirit: The Spirit of Fear, the Spirit of Alcoholism, I was one of the few children privy to the secret information that demons were transferred from rapist to victim, demons created the lie of repressed memories, demons were behind accusations against the dear Men of God.

From the time I was 12 my father would call every Sunday and ask, "When are you getting a boyfriend?" until I was sick of the question. One day my mother would ask me, "You do *like* boys, right? You want to be in a relationship with one, right?" and I said yes, because of course, because it wasn't a question I could answer any other way. God's desires always overruled your own.

My shyness muted my failures. I couldn't say, "Have a blessed day," in that airy Christian girl voice, I couldn't babysit to prove my future skills as a mother, or make baked goods to deliver to a Christian boy, but I could stand in the corner, eyes downcast, with my Bible as a shield, and maybe nobody knew.

When I was 20, I said, "Yes, my brother did this thing, but you don't understand it wasn't that bad, and I'm over it," when I was 20, I said, "I'm fine because I'm not allowed to be upset by anything because nothing bad happened to me."

When I was 21, I was diagnosed with Essential Tremor, and that was when I finally had a name. How many times can someone take your blood when you're fine, how often can you go to the doctor and get told, "We can't find anything," but now they had, now my mother had an answer to the What is Wrong with My Child question, a something and a nothing, a name and a deflection.

When I was 16, my mother locked me in a room after I lost the courage to speak. She thought I was going crazy, because crazy was better than sick, crazy was better than traumatized. "Has anyone ever touched you?" she asked me, and I knew what I was supposed to answer. "No." To say yes would have meant I was crazy, because only crazy people accuse others of raping them. According to my mother.

When I was 20 I wanted to die, when I was 16, I wanted to die, when I was 12, I wanted to die, when I was four, I wanted to die, and I was the most happy, content child you would ever meet. I smiled, I skipped, I twirled, I was the little girl only a mother could dream up, according to my mother. She bookended all my statements, that extra weight of truth. According to my mother. According to my mother. Nothing else was true but according to my mother.

And when I grew older, where I failed at femininity, I made up in modesty. By the grace of God, I succeeded in modesty, and I always knew He'd had me raped to make me terrified of sex, made me loathe and fear my body so I would be too scared and ashamed at revealing it. But it was okay, because my mother's fears never came true, the ones she constantly warned me against: I never did become that boy-crazy slut a girl becomes because of a broken home. She was so proud of my terror. God had found a way to spare me.

Eccentric, my high school teacher announced at my graduation. Enigma, the youth pastor called me. Maybe my shield was an illusion. I started smiling too much. I emerged from that room under the weight of my mother's words, "You have an obligation to others to be happy." So I smiled and I laughed, and I said, "I'm focusing on school," when the youth pastor asked if this was a sign I had a boyfriend.

I searched the Scriptures for my failed womanhood. Was I a sin? What more could I do? I told my mother I wanted to adopt children. I didn't want to adopt children, I didn't want to have children, but I didn't know I had any other options. I was going to get married, and I was going to have kids, and adoption was my meager compromise. If I lived long enough, but secretly I knew that I wouldn't.

The body pain started not long before I began admitting, "I think my father raped me, too." My muscles, aching and tight, no matter how much thought I put into it, refused to relax. And then it was back to the doctor, back to figuring out a new reason for the sickness that wasn't ever exactly sick. I told no one I lived on protein bars and carrots as an answer to my inexplicable weight loss. I didn't hide this fact, either, it was, like sickness, another thing that was not allowed. You are not allowed to be traumatized, you are not allowed to have a sexuality, you are not allowed to be sick. So I didn't. I simply didn't eat, and I smiled too much, and I begged God not to send me a Man of God who would hurt me.

When I was 23, I told my mother I wanted a future alone. Maybe I'd get an apartment, have a few friends, be a writer. That was my ideal future, I'd concluded—if I lived long enough, if I had to carry the weight of secrets and false fronts my whole life, that would be my happiness.

My mother started praying for my future husband. "I want him to have saved his first kiss for you. I want him to be pure, I want him to have given his heart to no other," she told me. "But I don't want that," I replied. "But I do," was all she said. The prayers continued.

What I haven't written yet is that all of this was more farce than it sounds: we both knew, my mother and I, that I was nothing. She would take care of me the rest of my life and I would take care of her in turn. All the prayers for my future were as real as my promises of adoption: I was whatever my mother needed me to be, and what she needed was someone who could never leave, who could do nothing, accomplish nothing, succeed in nothing except staying by her side. And it was a perfect fit because I was too traumatized to be anything else. "What will you do without me?" she'd always ask, and I knew the answer. Nothing. I was nothing, so I could be anything: I was straight, and I was happy, and I was never sick and yet never quite well enough to accomplish anything. It was the perfect balance.

"How was I supposed to know?" my mother would ask me on a hazy Tuesday morning, where I met her in the parking lot of the mall. I was 25, and it was a couple months after I ran away from home, and this was the first conversation we'd had with no one else around. "I was clueless," she said, "You know I'm clueless." I had starved myself in that house. My arms bore the traces of scars I never pretended I didn't have. I had cried in her presence while she averted her eyes. Speak denial in Jesus's name, and it will become true.

I got an email from her a year ago. "If your tremors ever get worse, here's what you can do!" I wanted to reply back, "I no longer tremble before you or the Lord," but that would have been too neat, too poetic. But my hands stilled within the first week I moved out, and I slept like I had never slept before.

I'm sick. I speak that now, like I speak that I am not straight and I am not a woman, and I speak them with all the confidence now that verbalization isn't creation, it is understanding. I cannot make myself these things just by saying them any more than my lack of language, the restriction of words didn't form me into what my mother wanted. I have been all the aspects of trauma and PTSD all my life; terrified, depressed, hopeless, suicidal, and there was no willing those away. I speak that I am sick and I am queer and I have been learning how to home myself among words that I was long denied.

WHITTIER STRONG

On Inheritance

[God] does not leave the guilty unpunished; he punishes the children and their children for the sin of the parents to the third and fourth generation.
—Exodus 34:7, New International Version

My father was the first of seven children. When he was four, his parents changed his name and gave his old name to his new baby brother. It's rumored that this move was a half-hearted attempt to hide my father's alleged illegitimacy.

My mother was the sixth of ten children. Her father was an alcoholic who wandered from job to job. He caroused, while her mother struggled to maintain their subsistence farm. My mother and her siblings often went hungry.

Epigenetics is the influence of external factors upon the genes, the power of alteration, of mutation, the power to change what one passes down to one's children.

I, the first of four children, was born blue and wrinkled, with no amniotic fluid. In the hospital, my father wouldn't allow my mother to see me until I "shaped up."

A person's experience as a child or teenager can have a profound impact on their future children's lives, new work is showing. Rachel Yehuda, a researcher in the growing field of epigenetics and the intergenerational effects of trauma, and

her colleagues have long studied mass trauma survivors and their offspring. Their latest results reveal that descendants of people who survived the Holocaust have different stress hormone profiles than their peers, perhaps predisposing them to anxiety disorders.
—Rodriguez, Tori. "Descendants of Holocaust Survivors have Altered Stress Hormones." *Scientific American.* Scientific American, 12 Feb. 2015

In my school photos, my fists are clenched, fear in my eyes. Every day in seventh grade I was pushed down the stairs and had my books knocked out of my arms. The students would call me "faggot," and make fun of me for getting free lunch and for only owning two outfits—I wore one while my mother washed the other. I grew so depressed and anxious that I developed psychosomatic paralysis, no movement from the waist down. My brain shut down my legs so that I wouldn't be able to go to school, the source of my distress.

To my father, my siblings and I didn't have names. We were The Smart One, The Twins, and The Baby. I was The Smart One. The only praise I ever received from my father was for earning good grades. I learned to find my self-worth through academic achievement. Without As, I was nothing.

Erratic or inappropriate discipline and inadequate supervision have been linked to antisocial behavior in children.
—Black, Donald. "What Causes Antisocial Personality Disorder?" *Psych Central.* Psych Central.

My father would tell the story of how his father would take him outside to select the tree branch with which he would be beaten. I've heard this is a common and thus oft-dubious tale. But from what little I know of my paternal grandparents, I believe his story.

When my mother was seven, she decided to make a pet of the family goat. At dinner one evening, she asked her mother where the meat came from. Her mother told her it was her pet goat. She became a vegetarian as an adult.

Whenever my father was around, we children were supposed to sit silently. If we spoke or played or expressed emotion, he called us "mental retarded." My father had a below-average IQ; he was socially promoted through school and graduated barely able to read. His parents sent all his brothers and sisters to college, but not him.

> Antisocial personality disorder is a mental health condition in which a person has a long-term pattern of manipulating, exploiting, or violating the rights of others. This behavior is often criminal.
> —"Antisocial Personality Disorder." MentalHealth.gov. U.S. Dept. of Health and Human Services

When my mother was pregnant with me, my father only allowed my mother to consume grilled-cheese sandwich with coffee; there were many days she ate nothing. I was well into my twenties before I could tolerate grilled-cheese sandwiches and coffee.

As a child, I thought the white scars on my mother's wrists came from wearing her wristwatch too tight.

> A person with antisocial personality disorder may: Be able to act witty and charming; be good at flattery and manipulating other people's emotions; break the law repeatedly; disregard the safety of self and others; have problems with substance abuse; lie, steal, and fight often; not show guilt or remorse; often be angry or arrogant.
> —"Antisocial Personality Disorder." MentalHealth.gov. U.S. Dept. of Health and Human Services

My mother suffered from internal organ damage thanks to my father's beatings. We children never saw the beatings. Doing so would have undone our father's efforts to get us to side with him and against our mother.

My father always carried a loaded .45. He told my mother that if ever she reported his abuse, he would blow her brains out, and if the neighbors tried to help her, he would blow their brains out.

When I was eight, my mother fled with us children in the middle of the night, taking us to the battered-women shelter. She filed for divorce. My father gradually drifted out of our lives. He was court-ordered to pay child support. He only paid three or four times. My mother would take him to court, where he once told the judge that he was living under a bridge eating garbage when in truth we children had been at his house just a couple of weeks prior. Ultimately, the judge told my mother to quit taking my father to court because they would never get any money out of him.

My father's siblings, as adults, would not acknowledge his existence, not even to their own spouses, until he lay upon his deathbed. He was only 59 when he died. His Amish neighbors had given him a traditional ointment to treat his STDs, which he consumed orally and poisoned himself. Comatose for three weeks, he died of a heart attack as he was rousing from the coma. My siblings and I each received a $3,000 inheritance from an insurance policy. My mother said it was so that we could tell people he left us something.

When my mother was a child, her siblings mocked her relentlessly. She walked too slow, ate too slow, and most certainly couldn't be related to them. In adulthood, my mother traveled the country, helping out her sisters whenever they gave birth. They repaid her by spreading lies about her.

The participants continued to report same-sex attractions after the conversion therapy, and were not significantly more

attracted to the opposite gender. These studies did find that conversion therapy could be harmful, however. Negative effects included loss of sexual feeling, depression, suicidality and anxiety.
—Pappas, Stephanie. "5 Surprising Facts about Gay Conversion Therapy." LiveScience. Purch, 4 June 2013.

A few years ago, my mother asked me what the word "bisexual" meant. I told her, then asked what prompted the question. She said a woman once asked her if she thought my father had been bisexual.

My last year of high school, I realized I was gay. Right after, I enrolled in Bible college, the only school I thought I could afford, where I was told I had to enter therapy to become heterosexual if I wanted to remain in school. I remained in the therapy for ten years, long after I left the school for financial reasons.

In my twenties, in the midst of conversion therapy, I would walk down the sidewalk in my hometown and strangers in passing cars would shout "faggot" at me.

According to a newly released hypothesis, the explanation [for homosexuality] may not lie in DNA itself. Instead, as an embryo develops, sex-related genes are turned on and off in response to fluctuating levels of hormones in the womb, produced by both mother and child. This tug of war benefits the unborn child, keeping male or female development on a steady course even amid spikes in hormones. But if these so-called epigenetic changes persist once the child is born and has children of its own, some of those offspring may be homosexual, the study proposes.
—Norton, Elizabeth. "Homosexuality May Start in the Womb." Science. American Association for the Advancement of Science, 11 Dec. 2012.

The fetus undergoes considerable transformation in the fifth month. The X-chromosome usually triggers the genitals to turn inside out, the would-be ovaries pushing out to become the testes, the clitoris enlarging to become the penis.

Physical traits I exhibit that are more typical of women: a high-pitched voice, congenitally missing teeth, minimal body hair, an inverted-triangle dispersal of pubic hair.

My mother is now mostly housebound, the combined effects of low blood pressure and depression. The former makes her prone to fainting; the latter gives her little reason to rise from bed. She spends much of her time journaling, writing about what a monster my father was.

My mother is diagnosed with major depression, generalized anxiety disorder, and post-traumatic stress disorder.

I am diagnosed with major depression, generalized anxiety disorder, and post-traumatic stress disorder.

I always wanted to have children. I get along well with them. But children cost money, and my disabilities have impeded upon my ability to earn enough income. And I'm gay, so the costs of adoption or surrogacy also come into play. But perhaps it's all just as well, as I won't be passing these scarred genes on to the third and fourth generation.

JAMES SCHWARTZ

Hands

Dad is fond of telling me:
When I was a babe,
He held me in his palm,
His hands were large,
Rough and calloused,
By a life of labor,
My own small hand,
Stops growing,
As I grow older,
My fingers curling,
Into claws,
I don't notice,
Until school,
Bombarded with questions,
I don't know answers to,
I learn to wear long sleeves,
Even in summer,
Tucking my malformation,
Into my pocket,
Before bounding outdoors.
I am taken to Specialists,
To a Rosicrucian-esque healer,
Who places eggs on coals,
Murmuring gently,
Hypnotizing me.
I am taken to Shriners,
Where I see a small boy,
With a hand larger than my father's,
I stare in his beautiful eyes.

Fellowship

Before every other Sunday service,
The Amish men shake my hand.

I offer them my left limply.
One nice fellow always smiles,

Reaching for, engulfing my right,
His hand and smile warm.

Sometimes he slips me chewing gum,
Or pieces of hard candy.

I offer my left hand
To the next in line.

We stand around by the barn
Until it is time to go inside.

Scene

A crooked arm
Has enough strength
To grasp onto
His arching back.

The other arm
Has enough length
To clasp onto
His lowered neck.

Bent

That awkward moment when your lover
Sees you cutting your cuticles the first time.

Bent on knees beside the bed,
Pressing the clippers down by elbow.

He observes this with a lively interest.
He begins tying my shoes soon after.

BARBARA RUTH

The Ides of April

"You could write down everything that happens in one day."
—Ann Thompson, Memoir Instructor at Campbell Community Center,
near San Jose, California, early April, 2013

8:20 AM: This is the day I chose to write down everything, the middle of the month. I'm already twenty minutes late getting out of bed, still I dawdle, grateful I'm too poor to have to file an income tax report. One less thing. "How do you feel?" Nora asks, as I awkwardly roll toward her, my bones and muscles providing their usual arthritic, fibromyalgic greeting. "Does your tooth still hurt?"

My tongue explores the new hole in my head. "Not bad." I scooch toward her. "How's your foot?" I take care not to bump it with mine. We have the Jewish habit of expressing love through worry.

"Still hurts." Surgeries, fused bones, walking when wheeling might have been a better choice. Nora's feet have plenty of reasons to hurt.

Our fingers entwined, Nora tells me a dream fragment about her parents, who are both deceased. She's dreamed of them, together and separately, several times over the past few weeks.

"I wish I would dream about my mother." I also wish we could just cuddle for five more minutes.

"You will, honey." Her voice is warm and soft, like the skin of her arms, her hands, under and over the covers. "Give it time."

I raise my hand, tangle my fingers in her chestnut curls, searching for the auburn highlights. Nora will probably keep her hair the same color till she's 80. I want us to be around to find out, though I know she's been tired of her body for years now. Once I get out of bed, my weekend with Nora is officially over and it's rush to appointments, deal with attendants, go back to my house. My unemployed work week.

ೞ

8:40 AM: I savor the remaining hints of Tom's orange-mango tooth gel, pull together my business voice and call the dentist, tell her answering machine my crown came off, try to visualize the tooth numbering chart, give that up and conclude: "upper right molar, I think. I'll cancel whatever to get to the first possible appointment." The tedium of juggling logistics, figuring out which attendant can drive me which day, pushes back my dread of whatever dental procedure is in the works. A little.

8:45 AM: Knock on the door, followed by the sound of the lock opening: my attendant Aisha, exactly on time. "How was your weekend?"Her Monday morning salutation.

I'm drawing a blank. I must have done something non-tooth related. "I've forgotten already." Aisha's laughter warms the house.

"Hi, Aunt Aisha," Nora calls from the bedroom. Even though Aisha is 45, ten years younger than Nora and twenty years younger than I, Aisha emanates an older female nurturance and competence that makes "auntie" appropriate.

As usual, she's wearing a long, flowing cotton skirt. Today is green paisley, scalloped, somewhat higher in the front than the back. If I did ever choose to wear a skirt again, I'd likely trip on one like that, but Aisha never does. Her black embroidered blouse has cupped sleeves and a high V neckline. She's wearing the hijab of many greens and blacks, one of my favorites. It reminds me of the Forest of Nicene Marks near Santa Cruz.

"Hello, my light," she answers Nora. Aisha won't head into the bedroom until Nora makes an appearance or one of us explicitly says it's okay. Of the three of us, I'm the immodest one, walking around half or wholly naked, thanks to my early training as a flower child in the sixties, reinforced at more than one August at the Michigan Womyn's Music Festival in the seventies, and nailed into place by hard time in hospitals beginning in the eighties. I couldn't begin to calculate the people who have seen me naked; any female attendant I hire is automatically added to the list.

"The light isn't quite prepared to appear," I say, giving Aisha a brief hug. She taught us shortly after I hired her two and a half years ago that "Nora" is Arabic for light.

"That's okay. I'll wash the dishes and straighten up in the kitchen until she's ready for me to go in the bedroom." Tendrils of wavy hair, several shades redder than Nora's, peek from her head covering. "You don't remember how your weekend was?" she asks, smiling sympathetically. "Nothing at all?"

I pour myself a glass of the smoothie she made for me on Friday and fill her in.

9:10 AM: I shower and select my attire for Feldenkrais, then yoga. Black short-sleeved t-shirt announcing "You Are on Indian Land," over a red map of the Americas. Stretchy hot pink pants that clash in a way I find aesthetically pleasing but will probably make Nora, now in the shower, wince as she bites back her appalled commentary, After twelve years together we both predict and surprise each other. The gymnasium where Feldenkrais class is held is too drafty for just a t-shirt anyway, so I pull a long-sleeved purple t-shirt over Indian Land. I push myself to take movement classes twice a day now, sometimes, to make up for the months—behind me and ahead—with no exercise at all. I really do understand why unstable disabilities are difficult for able-bodied folks to understand. They baffle the hell out of me.

Nora is in the dining room, dressed in a cerulean polo shirt with the branded red pony of Ralph Lauren. I would never wear a shirt that advertised a major brand. Aisha tells us about her weekend with the kids, their parties and youth groups, BFFs and frenemies. Her beaming pride. I wish we had kids in our lives.

9:40 AM: My attendant Ed returns my call from last night, made after the molar lost her crown. "Emergency dentist appointment?"

I tell him I don't think I'll actually get an appointment today, so back to original plan: pick me up at the Y at 2:30. Aisha fills my oxygen tank, packs up my meds, notebooks, Netflix, bi-pap, checks the bathroom for stray belongings. I bend down to Nora, who is sitting in her wheelchair looking at her smartphone, rub my nose against hers, kiss her goodbye, briefly, so as not to embarrass either of them. How many times have we kissed this weekend? Not enough. Not enough cuddling, not enough kissing. My usual Monday morning regrets.

౪

9:45 AM: Damn. The books sitting on the dining room chair we never use silently bark their accusation as I'm headed for the door. "Aisha, you forgot to return the library books when you cleaned for Nora on Thursday. They were due last Wednesday. Nora is physically unable to carry them into the library, or even to the outside drop." Why am I going on and on, telling Aisha what she already knows, and with way more irritation and blame in my voice than I'd meant to put there? I hope she will offer to pay the fine, or at least apologize. She doesn't. I try to let it go. One last goodbye to Nora, whose eyes say, "don't make such a big deal about the books."

In the car I realize I forgot to write the love note surprise I planned to hide in Nora's underwear drawer. I squint into the sun, feeling remorseful, inadequate, annoyed and nervous about how the rest of my time today with Aisha will unfold.

9:58 AM: Sure enough, the gymnasium is cold. I greet a few of my classmates, worrying again that names are getting harder and harder to learn and remember. Aisha takes a gymnastics mat off the cart and sets it on the floor for me. I can now get up and down from the floor without using a chair, a feat I just accomplished last month. My mind darts back to the long recovery since I fractured my wrist, ahead to my busy day, over to the hole where my crown is supposed to be as my tongue runs up and down the jagged stump of tooth.

10:15 AM: Lying down I stretch, turn, follow the instructor's directions. I usually prefer to close my eyes during the peculiar, soothing Feldenkrais movements I've been doing for years, but today Aisha has placed my mat under the basketball hoop. I've never looked up through the webbing of a basketball hoop to the ceiling. The pattern invites me to entwine my mind in their wonder, but then a latecomer puts her mat beside me and lies down. White Shoulders, a hideous scent that entwines my stomach in a web of nausea. Sweating, I reach for my oxygen tank, dial up the liter flow.

CB

11 AM: End of class. I get up slowly, awkwardly, but gratifyingly on my own. Aisha, back from shopping at Whole Foods, keeps her head down as she puts the mat away. No eye contact. I swallow, realize my throat is raw. Is my fifth chakra embodying my regret over snapping at her about the library books? Am I getting sick? Should I cancel my plans, just take it easy? Delicious idea, but not really an option. This is a busy day. I'm probably just reacting to my classmate's perfume; it'll pass.

11:15 AM: I call the dentist again, the answering machine picks up, though it's certainly office hours now. Exasperated, I text Lynn: *no dentist appt today, so far as I can figure out . . . Target this PM as planned?* She texts back confirmation. We've been planning this trip for a month.

NOON: Silent tension during the ride home. As soon as I'm in the door I turn on the computer to write the morning before I forget it. Aisha opens up the house, puts away the things that went to Nora's with me for the weekend, then fixes me lunch and the Throat Coat tea I request. "Are you getting a cold?" she asks kindly.

I feel rushes of relief for a bit of our old connection. "Probably just a reaction to scents in class." I eat quickly, eager to get back to the computer and record more of my day.

12:30 PM: Aisha works quietly when she knows I'm writing, one of the many things I love about having her as my attendant these past two years. I get up, join her in the bedroom, ask her to help me put more blankets on my bed. I'm shivering; maybe I am getting sick. She's silent as she performs the manual labor while I mentally fiddle with the order of the blanket: I want the quilt Mom made on top where I can see it. Is Aisha really mad at me? When the sheets and blankets are sorted and tucked, Aisha straightens up, her face flushed under her hijab. "There was a bombing at the Boston Marathon—two people killed." Her voice is high and thin. Our eyes meet in alarm. Worry, fear, grief play across her face. Aisha lived in Boston on 9/11, taught in a Muslim school, a madrasa. She told me the children's terror as they asked: "Are they going to kill us all?" Who is they? Who is us? I wish I was back with Nora, an "us" I am sure of.

Aisha is trembling. "Is everyone you know okay?" Stupid question.

"I don't know yet." Her mind must be racing in a zillion directions, only a dozen of which I can guess.

Who would bomb the Boston Marathon? Why?

1 PM: Aisha comes in from taking out the trash. Her voice is shaky and far away as she speaks to me from the front of the house while I'm back on the computer in the office. I come into the living room where I can hear her. She is sitting down, looking dazed.

"Did something more happen?" I ask, trying to let the love I truly feel for her come through my voice, overriding the fear I truly feel, for Aisha, and all the Muslims I do not know—all who, like her, are likely to be profiled as soon as the word "terrorist" hits the airwaves. "Do you have more news about Boston?"

"I fell, just now, taking the trash to the street. I actually rolled down the driveway." She takes off her sandals, massages her left ankle. Is she injured? How badly? "I can't tell if I'm hurt—or maybe I hurt all over. I'm not sure. "

"I don't need to go to yoga today. Why don't you sit for awhile and then go home?"

The freckles stand out on her drained-of-color face. "I can take you." I flinch at the obligation I hear in her voice, but I don't want to argue with her or insist she cannot do her job. Helplessly I watch as she puts on her shoes and slowly gets to her feet. I wonder if she's safe to drive. She attempts to hide her cringe as she tries not to limp toward the door, but I see them both. In the car she says she thinks she may have sprained her ankle. "Maybe multiple sprains."

1:25 PM: We're at the Y. "Don't bother parking, Aisha, just drop me off and I'll set up for yoga by myself." I gather up oxygen, messenger bag, gym bag, attempting to look as capable as possible so she won't think she has to park the car and help me. "You know, if you're injured, it will be covered by Workers' Comp. Please, don't hesitate to get medical help because of money." She murmurs something as I close the passenger door, but her words waft away in the gentle breeze.

Putting on my mask as protection from the chlorine, I walk past the pool then sign in at the desk, look around for Mom. She died last October. I joined the Y a few months ago mostly because that's what she would have done. A lifelong athlete, she practiced adaptive tai chi and yoga through her eighties, water aerobics into her nineties. The first time I came to the Y, I saw a woman who startled me with her resemblance to my mother, an olive-skinned woman in her eighties, with beautiful silver bobbed hair, like Mom. Looking for that woman again, over the weeks I found: Mom in her thirties, hair black, young children in tow; in her forties, fifties, hair gradually graying, like mine, growing more stooped, like me; every decade on up to her nineties. It's my self-improvement grieving ritual. I could use seeing Mom today.

Removing my mask as I head outdoors, I follow the pathway to Studio 2, Adaptive Yoga. The Mom in her eighties look-alike takes this class sometimes. She helped me once when I couldn't get my blanket properly folded, tucked and rolled, but she isn't here today.

Most of the students are around my age. Some are disabled. I'm the fattest person in the class. I'm always the fattest person in all my exercise classes. If I lived in San Francisco or the East Bay I could find a fat women's exercise class, but not in San Jose. I wish fat people felt safe enough to exercise at the Y, I've thought almost every time I come here. Today I just wish the world was a safer place for everyone.

Do the people in this room know about the bombing? Could we offer the merit of our practice to the sentient beings in Boston? Some yoga studios are surely doing that right now but no, not at the Y.

A seventy-something woman by the props asks me how I am.

"Okay."

"Well, I guess 'okay' is all we can hope for."

"Actually, I'm fine. I'm concerned because my attendant—" Her face doesn't register the word. "My aide, the woman who helps me, just fell in my driveway. She tripped over some hoses."

The man standing next to her follows our conversation. I already don't like him; in past classes he's been too touchy-feely. I make it a point to keep out of his reach.

"Was she an elderly lady?" the woman asks.

What? If she isn't old—like us—then she's bionic? Her injuries don't count? "No." The friendliness drains from my voice. "She's in her forties."

The touchy-feely guy says, "Maybe you don't need her anymore."

I feel myself bristle. Perhaps he's trying to say I'm more capable, more independent than I give myself credit for. "I'm concerned she may be injured. It sounded like a serious fall." I set up my mat and props across the room from them, feeling contemptuous, alienated. I miss my Mom, then remember all the times I felt the same toward her. I miss her anyway.

1:40 PM: Yoga is hard, I can't do most of the poses. If this is adaptive yoga, I need the remedial class.

2:30 PM: I collapse onto my mat for two minutes of savasana. I hate that. I wish the teacher would have omitted warrior one, two or three so we could relax into corpse pose, practice being dead a bit longer than two minutes. Then I remember the people in Boston who are dead forever. I offer whatever merit I accumulated—unlikely as that seems at the moment—in their direction.

Ed comes in the room with his nerdy glasses and balding head. He puts my props away, gathers up my bags. Walking to the parking lot, I want to ask him about Boston, but I'm looking behind me and to the sides, futilely searching for a glimpse of any of my Moms.

2:40 PM: Ed checks his phone, puts it in the pocket of his yellow and black checked short-sleeved button down shirt before he starts the car. As usual, the radio in his Volvo is tuned to NPR, broadcasting updates on Boston. "It's Patriots' Day," he tells me. What is that? Did someone from the Tea Party bomb the Boston Marathon to protest income taxes because it's 'Patriots' Day?' I don't ask him to explain because we're both intently listening to the radio. A runner talks about her panic-stricken young children, waiting at the finish line where the blast detonated, and Boston looms closer, as though Ed and I are driving there, instead of the few miles to my house. He maneuvers the car with his customary caution but he seems remote, distracted. I wonder who he knows in Boston, if he's been able to reach them. My chest aches. My heart aches. The socket in my mouth, the stumpy little bit of tooth which should be covered by my crown, begins to throb. What about Aisha's friends? Are they injured? Profiled?

"Is it okay if I just go?" Ed asks as he brings my accoutrements into the house. "I mean, if you need anything I can help you . . ." We're both relieved when I send him home. I immediately head for the computer remembering only as I hear his car back out of the driveway that's I'd meant to ask about his schedule for arranging a ride to the dentist. No messages on my phone machine. They're still not picking up at the dentist's office. Is Patriots' Day a holiday everyone but me knows about?

3:45 PM: I take a break to call Nora and tell her about Aisha's fall.

"While you were taking a shower Aisha told me she needed to crazyglue her shoes together. Maybe they were falling apart, and she tripped on them," Nora suggests.

Aisha would glue her shoes together to save money for clothes for her kids, but I just don't believe that's what made her fall. "Those hoses, always tangled right beside the rocks, they're the reason I can't take the garbage cans to the street myself. Maybe she tripped on them."

We compare the news we've amassed about the bombing. I hear the grief in her voice as Nora tells me a two-year-old child was one of those killed. Just as the woman in my yoga class considers the fall of "an elderly lady" more worthy of her sympathy, so I know Nora's heart will be most touched by tragedy involving children. "Over a hundred people injured—" we've both heard that. Did Aisha receive a call from Boston while she took out the trash? Is that what caused her to lose her balance?

"I hope the bombers were white Christians." I know I've got my rant voice on; my emotions demand it. "I'm sure they were male." White Christians will not be randomly profiled and victimized in retaliation. Neither will men, simply for being male, regardless of their millions of crimes against women, the planet, and life in general. I brace myself for

Nora to contradict me or make some objection to my generalization. She's the humanist in the family.

"It's terrible," she sighs, "no matter who did it."

5:00 PM: Lynn texts that she's a few miles away. Time for Target. That's what Bush said to do, after 9/11. "Go shopping." And now I'm obeying the worst president of my lifetime. What does that make me? But Lynn doesn't often have time to drive here from Santa Cruz, now that she's working so much.

It will be good to see her. A thought I can own without self-hate.

5:45 PM: I hear a car pull into the driveway and go to the door to meet my friend. Nora says Lynn is my best friend. I say that would be Nora, but Lynn has been my *compañera*, my chosen family, for over 30 years. We've seen each other through the adoption of her four kids and the deaths of my parents, housing and health crises, new love, sustained relationships and breakups, money woes and creative joys. We have a similar politics and wacky sense of humor. I wish we lived in the same town. I'm glad we're together now.

Lynn comes in the door, shaking her head as she puts down her bag to hug me. I breathe her in as we embrace, grounded by the smell of her sweat, her big breasts against my own. I stroke her long hair, streaked with white, although not so gray as mine. I wish I'd hugged Aisha after she fell. "Hi, BR." Her voice is deep, familiar, loving, fearful. "I listened to KPFA on the way here to see if they were covering the bombing, but they only talked about the hunger strike at Guantánamo while I was listening."

"Are those guys going to die?"

She shrugs, shakes her head again. "I don't see how they can survive. Some have been fasting for months."

I think about the waves of hunger strikes across California prisons for over a year now, the IRA hunger strikers who died in British prisons in the eighties, the Suffragists who hunger struck and endured the primitive force-feeding techniques of their time in American prisons a century ago. My life seems ridiculously privileged, my irritations self-indulgently petty.

The breeze of this afternoon has turned to nipping gusts. We head out to the closest Target to my house. Neither of us has been to this store before. I slide between screens on my phone, trying to figure out where in the mall Target is, what high-end women's clothes stores are in the same mall, because Lynn needs to buy work clothes. I never need the shoes-that-aren't-sneakers, pants suits, mid-calf skirts (skirts!), and silk blouses that have become part of Lynn's life. Right now she's wearing an old t-shirt that spells out "Peace" in Hebrew, Arabic, and English and jeans soft with wear. But now she's a part-time habitué of seminars where she makes pitches for her online, by phone and in-person web design services.

I'm trying to give directions while finding a store for Lynn and doing a lousy job at both. Technologically challenged, geographically impaired. I've lived in San Jose for three and a half years now, there's no excuse for not knowing where the stupid mall is. So much easier to focus on my inadequacies with phones and malls than to open myself all the way up to the pain of this day, this world.

6:20 PM: We listen to the six o'clock news as we drive, only speaking about directions. When Lynn drops me off at Target she asks, "Will you be okay by yourself?" As I push against the door of her SUV to open it, the wind pushes back.

I don't think she realizes this is the first time I've been shopping alone in a store this big since my long hospitalization in 2010. She does know I sometimes fall apart in large stores due to sensory overload. What if I have a panic attack? What if I have a seizure? "Yes," I assure her, trying to convince us both. "I'll be fine." How well-entrenched the habit of assuaging the worries of others aimed in my direction. Denial is a many-layered cake. As I push open the door of her SUV, the wind pushes back.

6:30 PM: Nobody in the store, the one whose very name trumpets "Target," is screaming or sobbing or praying. (Maybe some of them *are* praying, in ways I can't perceive. I hope so.) Searching the faces of the shoppers and salespeople, looking for sadness, shock; nothing is revealed. I wander around, trying to remember what compelled me to come here today. Is it just something to do while the world comes to an end? On September 11, 2001, Nora drove from San Jose to San Rafael, where I then lived. We'd only met a few months before but we needed to be together, whatever came next. That day I called Spirit Rock Meditation Center in West Marin and sure enough, they had planned a community gathering that night. Each person lit a candle as we came in, then we sat in a circle and prayed for all who had died and all who loved them. We prayed for the mothers of the suicide bombers. We held that circle as each of us said anything or nothing at all. In that uncertain time, Nora and I both felt safe, where we needed to be. Now, she's home alone; I'm shopping.

7:10 PM: Lynn texts: *20 min.* If more bombs exploded, today, tonight, right now, would it be announced over the loudspeaker? What if it was in San Jose? If the Boston Marathon could be targeted, why not Silicon Valley?

I have the privilege of only sporadically turning my attention to the bombs ripping through the homes and lives of people I know through Democracy Now, Al Jazeera, Facebook. I sign petitions. I've become a clicktivist on behalf of people whose names are unknown to me. Animals I have never seen. Dark forests, canopied in greens and blacks, like the swirls on Aisha's hijab, hanging on in places I will never visit. All my relations.

7:45 PM: Back at my house, Lynn warms up the leftovers from last night's dinner; yesterday Nora and I met up with our friend Wendy at an Afghan restaurant in Fremont. "Wendy said she might be able to take a vacation with Nora and me." It's a relief to have something happy to talk about. Lynn beams with pleasure at this news as we divide the last of the spinach bolani. Nora and I have never taken a trip in all the years we've been together. Neither of us think we could manage it without someone able-bodied to help us. But now . . . maybe . . . My guarded optimism breaks through the clouds of this gloomy day, mixes with yearning and nostalgia as I remember the trips I embarked upon so casually, so easily when I was able-bodied.

Lynn and I push the trash and recycling bins to the street, heads tucked down against the wind, now fierce and biting. I plod along, avoiding the hoses by the side of the building and cracks in the pavement. As a kid, I remember stomping on sidewalk cracks to break my mother's back when I was mad at her. I remember how guilty I felt when I accidentally stepped on one when I wasn't mad at her. Mom had back problems as long as I can remember. But not anymore.

8:30 PM: Lynn and I send the metta of lovingkindness to all sentient beings in Boston in a Thich Nhat Hanh-inspired hugging meditation. "Breathing in, I feel glad for our long friendship, your body, warm and alive, next to my own. Breathing out, I feel compassion for all who suffer." And then she's gone. Clearing the rest of the dishes, I see there's food in the sink. Ed didn't put it down the garbage disposal when he subbed for Aisha on Friday. Aisha probably meant to do it this morning but then she fell. I asked Lynn to do it; we both forgot. I can't do it because the grind of the garbage disposal is a seizure trigger. Hopefully tomorrow's attendant will take care of it in the morning.

8:45 PM: I'm exhausted by this confounding, complicated day, but still wired. Good. That means I'll be able to write it all down.

Before returning to the computer I drop onto my bed, the surface I've been yearning for since I got here after Feldenkrais, and text Aisha to see how she's doing. "Better. Kids waiting on me while I sit on sofa with foot up." I harbor my relief, my gratitude for her, Wendy, Lynn, Nora. Their different kinds of love shine in my life, illuminating my path when I lose my way.

I check Al Jazeera news on my phone: 120 injured, many critically. The images are frightening and heartbreaking. A marathon, though I'll never participate in one, unlikely to even cheer from the sidelines, is part of the commons, the collective space that belongs to everyone. Al Jazeera tells me the Boston Marathon is the oldest one in the world, that the current men's and women's record-holders are from sub-Saharan Africa, that participants from 123 countries ran this year. An American gift to the world. Will it be ruined from now on? For a sporting event to be bombed! My mother would have been crestfallen. For the second time since her death I'm glad she's not alive to be horrified by the hell humans make of this world. The first time was Newtown.

9:00 PM: No Rachel Maddow show tonight; MSNBC has wall to wall coverage of the bombing. I need a bigger picture than they can provide so I switch to the Science Channel when *How the Universe Works* is just starting. The hole in my mouth where my crown used to be throbs with the pulsars as I press the remote to adjust the head of my hospital bed, wrap myself in Mom's quilt and drift.

10:00 PM: Should I write so prosaically, with all that has happened? Should I be praying instead of writing? Maybe writing *is* prayer. Maybe I should just pick a different day, one without a bombing. I check Facebook, several friends have posted pictures of Afghans, Iraqis, Palestinians, Pakistanis, holding signs that read, "Boston, our hearts are with you." "Our cities are bombed every other day." I look into their faces on the screen and know even so, they love and hate and work and shop. And write.

11:00 PM: The phone rings. Nora. "Goodnight, honey." I'm so glad to hear her sweet voice again. Ending this day of sorrow and shopping and yoga and sorrow and Feldenkrais and complications with Aisha and hugs with Lynn and sorrow I want my last connection to be with Nora, as the day began. In times like this, a text is not enough. I need to ride the waves of sound, the simple timbre of my beloved's voice. My light. "You must be exhausted from such a long day," she continues. "Try to get some sleep, Sweetie. I love you."

"I know."

ന്ദ

Two days later: I'm back in the hospital.

One week later: Aisha quits.

Forever: My mother, my mother Evelyn, keeps on being dead.

lapse

in this rare moment of clarity
gerald says
my eyes should be brighter,
i should be taller
and more handsome—
like he remembers
when we were young.

he's right,
i stood taller
and my eyes were bright
but i wonder if
he recalls he was taller
and does he know
his eyes are hollow glass now.
not so easy for me to love.

i suppose i should be thrilled
he can speak
tho lately he's mistaken me
for my haughty brother
and today he calls me bessie,
my long dead sister's name.

just like he used to do
when we dressed
in cowboy garb
to dance the boy bars
and he always said

i wobbled on my boot heels
just like bessie wobbled
on those dreadful pearly stilettos
we bought for her
on our first greyhound outing
from denver
to frederick's of hollywood

then when bessie croaked
her stilettos became sacred.
these days i brush gerald's teeth
the same way i cared for bessie's shoes
but he spits his teeth out;
he gags on baby food
then shakes his fist at me—
like he doesn't know who i am.

so i shove his dentures
between my gums
to bite down on bessie's heels
but they pierce my tongue.
i press my face to gerald's breast
just to feel,
but the pulse i feel
is my own heart.

i'd forsake it all,
days of brighter eyes,
the tall,
even bessie's heels
for just one moment
of support
from gerald's arms.

The Caretaker

His partner's strength in holding him down was a surprise for Edward. But this was something he had never experienced. He was in a state of sheer terror, wondering if Greg, who'd claimed to be a shaman, a tantric healer, was really who he said he was, or perhaps a murderer or someone who would take pictures of Edward and post them online, or offer not to do that if Edward paid him. Edward lay on the table blindfolded as the shaman chanted, stroked Edward's legs and arms, touched him, sang to him, rang bells, waved something that sounded like birds' wings over him. Then the sex began with the shaman moving into a 69 position over him. He thought, *I'm doing this. I really am gay, queer.* Edward hadn't pondered in a long time the truth of himself without excuses, without denial.

It was not what Edward expected, though. Whenever he really got into the sex, the shaman would stop him at that moment, and say, "Breathe," instructing him on breathing. Edward just wasn't breathing properly. Then they would resume their sexual rhythm, and the shaman would stop things again. It happened over and over until the shaman eventually came. But Edward couldn't come. Of course Greg was puzzled, because he felt Edward was incredibly accomplished sexually. Edward was confused because he thought he was there for sex, and obviously had done something right, because Greg had no trouble shooting off on his chest, but with all of the starting and stopping and the reminders to "breathe," Edward was too much "in his head," as Greg had continually said. Well, he certainly didn't need to be told that.

When it was time to go, Edward tried to put an arm around Greg, but Greg pulled away and said, "Do you want to come back sometime?" And: "You don't have to give me anything if you don't want to." Edward thought for a few minutes before he asked when he could return. *Maybe this was a process, and it would get better.* But he was really looking for a spontaneous sexual experience, a door to open, a way into a new life.

Three weeks later Edward was at Greg's front door. This time things went better, maybe not with the sex, but while at the shaman's "temple," a slightly run-down house in a neighborhood that was ready to gentrify or slide into the abyss, Edward started having dreams, waking dreams, and unexplainable feelings. Once, when Greg got up to go into the kitchen to make some tea, Edward felt someone touching his face. The second time it happened, he pulled down the scarf covering his eyes to see who was there, since he could hear the shaman in the kitchen, but no one was there. When Greg came back into the room with the tea, Edward asked, "Is someone else here?" Edward was still afraid this could be a scam.

Greg assured him that no, they were alone, but he asked him what he had experienced. Then they had sex. After Greg climaxed, alone, he fell asleep. Edward, deeply aroused and bored at the same time, eventually fell asleep beside him. He dreamed he saw a bare-chested man in primitive clothing in a small boat, the kind that Irish monks had made in ancient times. The large boatman had light hair and a beard, and he seemed serious but calm despite the rough sea and the boat's movement. He seemed to glow in some kind of light although the sky and sea were dark. Edward dreamed that he was seeing the man, but that he also was the man. When Edward awoke, he told Greg about the dream, and Greg wrote it all down in a notebook, saying it was very significant.

Edward began to feel closer to his dreams, his memories. Greg always told him to pay attention to dreams and to think about allies and ancestors. Sometimes Edward was supposed to pray to these beings. He did as Greg suggested. One night after Edward had been with him, and had been admonished about breathing and calling forth his ancestors, he had a very disturbing dream. It felt more a memory of something that had happened to him when he was a child. In this dream, it was a beautiful fall afternoon. He got off the school bus at his uncle's small store, where his mother was working part time. His grandmother picked up his cousins and him, and she drove them up to her house. She didn't want them walking on the highway where they might get hurt.

When they got to her house, the boys in the car burst forth and ran up the hill to their neighbors, the Garlands. Edward saw the grass moving under his feet, and smelled the heavy sweet, pungent weeds and thistles in the lot between his grandmother's house and the neighbor's yard. A woodbine clasped his ankle and tripped him up, slowing him down, but he struggled and managed to stand up and move on.

A boy shouted back, "Mr. Garland just got a riding lawnmower, and it looks like a car, an old-time car!"

The Garland boy Monty said, "Daddy showed me how to drive it. I drive it all the time. You all want to go for a ride?"

There may have been five of them riding around the yard, some sitting, some standing holding on. He couldn't see everything, the sun in his eyes whenever he looked up. Then he fell off, springing a distance from the mower. He lay in the yard for a time stunned; it seemed like a long time, but it couldn't have been very long with the other boys jumping off at the same time. Then it happened. The driverless lawnmower made an arc across the lawn and ran across Edward's right leg.

Blood sprayed from the side of the lawnmower fanning out like a veil. Edward felt an intense pain, enough pain to kill, to burst his heart, and then a dull steady pain, more bearable. The lawnmower roared and gave out a sort of hit-grind sound. Maybe it stalled. Edward screamed; he felt the scream but didn't hear it coming from him, it was like someone else screaming, then the screams of the other boys. Someone pulled the lawnmower away, and he sat up staring at the open wound eighteen inches long, the flesh cut away in tatters with the muscle and bone exposed. An artery spurted blood into the air, and fascinated by the drops arcing, he ran his hand back and forth across it, feeling the warmth on his hand, almost a sexual feeling. He did this for a while until a neighbor, Mr. Holman, ran from across the street, took off his belt, and fashioned a tourniquet around Edward's thigh, stopping the arc of blood. Edward looked up at Mr. Holman, who had become thin from cancer. Yet this time he looked different, a broad face, beautiful, his brown hair glowing in the sunlight, a light beard framing his jaw— the sun forming an aura behind him as if his face were eclipsing the sun.

Edward looked around at the others, their faces looking at him in horror, soundless with open mouths. His grandmother walked around picking up off the ground what flesh she could. Dogs were eating pieces they could find. Edward was overwhelmed with the sudden sense that he was now different, a different sort of being, to be set apart forever, not like the people around him. He waited a long time knowing he would die before an ambulance arrived. A medic appeared and bound him, swaddled him up, and loaded him in the ambulance. The ambulance weaved and swayed along the country highway; it took another fifteen minutes to get to the hospital. As they unwrapped Edward in the emergency room, blood was everywhere. It was difficult to see anything else. A nurse said, "Oh God, where does it end?" His senses broke off. He didn't remember anything after that.

The next morning Edward woke up feeling elated, ravenously hungry. He decided that since the dream was as close to the memory of his accident as he would get, it might damage him to speak of it. He would have to add it to his secrets.

As summer turned to fall, Edward began to feel closer to Greg. At times Greg could be very tender and kind. Often, after Edward removed the leg brace that supported his knee, Greg would anoint Edward's damaged leg, stroke it, even kiss it. Once, when Edward quoted him a line from a poem by Rumi, "The wound is the place where the light enters you," Greg gasped, almost seeming to cry. Still Greg maintained a distance. Once after making love, Edward foolishly said, "I love you," to which Greg said nothing and looked away. When Edward asked him later what was wrong, he said, "I love you too, but I see all my lovers in your eyes. Like you see all of your lovers in my eyes."

What was that supposed to mean, Edward thought. He had tried to meet other men, but he was not very successful; in fact, he once narrowly escaped being raped. Most of the time, though, he either couldn't find a common ground with them, or they looked at him and backed off. He wondered if the brace or something else in his manner had failed to meet some expectation they had of him.

Many years before all of this, during Edward's final year of college, he had been awarded a scholarship to study as an exchange student at the Free University in West Berlin. Thus began his gay experiences, his queer life. He later considered these episodes just stories from part of his life, not his life as a whole. He held them separate for many years, but seeing Greg as he did, the memories and feelings returned. Berlin had always had a large and active gay population, and the mid-seventies were a particularly vibrant and decadent time. When he was there, a decade or so after the building of the Wall, Berlin was a refuge for all the misfits unable to live in the rigid, materialistic world of West Germany. Set on an island surrounded by the dreary, fascistic East Germany, Berliners were always reminded that the reach of their small world had limits, but within those limits there was total freedom. There were students from all over the world, anarchists, communists of every stripe, sexual free spirits, spiritualists, and many gay men who lived openly.

At that time a slender young man with dark hair, dark eyes, Edward projected a kind of innocence and exoticism. He could have had sexual encounters every day if he wanted. He became more open about his feelings and opinions, less guarded in his expressions. He felt free, unbound for the first time in his life. He traveled wherever he liked, sometimes going to the Bahnhof Zoo, the main train station at that time, and boarding the next train heading out of Berlin. He was propositioned frequently. The first week there he found himself running away in confusion from a thirtysomething business man, who called out after him in front of one of Berlin's largest department stores. They had been talking on the bus about the city, and when they got off, the man pressed him to go to his hotel room.

Sometimes he made friends with other students, both male and female, and their friendships would lead to other things. Sometimes he had exquisite encounters; sometimes they would smoke hashish and dream away an afternoon. There was a boy from Iran with whom Edward fell in love. There were many times when he left other fellows who desired him, pretending not to know what they were talking about. Perhaps more than anything he wanted to have friends, to connect with someone, wanted this even more than he desired sex.

In later years, Edward thought about telling someone about his life in Berlin, but he didn't know how to begin the conversation. He had no words to describe it. Besides, he felt it would be better to keep these memories secret, just as he would keep his sessions with Greg secret, not even telling the small gay circle he had come to know, especially not telling them, considering the snide remarks he heard them make once when he mentioned Greg. When Michael, the head of the group, asked him flatly, "How do you know Greg?" Edward started talking about spiritual practices or breathing, and the conversation, no longer interesting Michael, drifted to other topics.

This circle of friends Edward had found—if one could call them friends—were close-knit and went back pretty far with each other. He had met them at a gay spiritual retreat. They organized events and had a weekly session of ecstatic dancing, after which a few of them had dinner at a local Jamaican restaurant. Edward, always desperate to make friends and find a group, did his best to fit in. He asked questions about their lives in town, tried to make jokes along the lines of their jokes. Once, feeling ambivalent about his sexuality, he asked them, "If you saw me walking down the street, what would you think—straight or gay?" One of the men, Arthur, said he couldn't tell. Michael said, "Gay, definitely gay." Roger, who was a bit older and sometimes the butt of their jokes, replied in the most honest and circumspect way, "What would you want us to think?"

Once he had asked Michael to meet him for lunch or a drink, and Michael ignored him for weeks. Edward couldn't understand why because Michael had kissed him on the mouth at the end of their spiritual retreat, much to his surprise and embarrassment. But Michael had sent out a lot of mixed messages. At the ecstatic dancing sessions, Edward could not easily dance for an hour without his brace, so he asked Michael if it would be alright to wear it, thinking he would get a supportive "Of course, it's okay to wear your brace." Michael answered, "I've been watching you, and you don't move around very much, so there's no danger you would hurt anyone, step on anyone." Edward was very disappointed by the comment, and almost quit going to the dancing, but he didn't.

After a particular session, when Edward was drinking with a few of the men at the restaurant, they started talking about their dreams. To Edward most of their stories sounded like psychological inventions or

"I slept with five guys" dreams, meant to impress others. Edward, who had perhaps too much beer, opened his gym bag, and found a poem he had written. He read his dream out loud:

> In dreams, I am a nobleman, a wanderer,
> on an afternoon of yellow sunlight,
> I find my self exhausted, frayed nerves, in a field of grass,
> verdant, beautiful grass, as high as my waist,
> green but also yellow from the sunlight.
> The meadow is surrounded by deep green trees
> and the sky is a fair blue.
>
> A man, a natural man, a caretaker, a groom
> comes forward to meet me in the field.
> He is wearing nothing I can see.
> He is taller with a fuller chest than mine,
> his skin, his hair are a fair light brown, like the grass in the
>   sunlight.
> a thin beard and mustache edging his face.
> He comes toward me and reaches out
> sensing, knowing my exhaustion.
>
> He takes my arm, and relieves me of my clothing.
> Dark green-black clothing with heavy lines
> embroidered in dark, thick black thread.
> We leave them in the field.
> Unencumbered, I feel almost weightless
> as he leads me to his place, his dwelling,
> a field man's hut with deep red carpets and
> a small, soft mat to one side, also deep red.
>
> When I lie down,
> he begins to stroke my arms, slowly,
> massaging my palms with fragrant oil.
> I leave my arms spread open, like the Vitruvian man of
>   Leonardo.

He unfolds my hands, stops their trembling. I receive through
    my open hands.
He firmly, gently strokes my legs and feet,
tenderly caring for them, anointing my feet,
taking time, stopping time,
until I lose my imperfections and fall deeper into my dream,
where he remains with me, the caretaker, the one who comforts.

After Edward finished, he looked around. For a few moments everyone stared at him in silence, but then the banter started up again. Roger said, "I'd like to meet that guy." Michael said, "So, Edward, what happens in the next line?" He thought about how the dream could go on, how much he needed it to, how much he needed the caretaker. Then he realized something about the same man he saw in the mirror of his dreams: *The caretaker is really me.*

JOHN R. KILLACKY

Video Narrative #1: Necessary Action

Seizures at bedtime. MRIs locate a tumor inside the spinal cord. A hospital gurney takes me into overhead white light. I wake up screaming, covered in blood and iodine, paralyzed from the neck down. Body and mind are ripped apart. I cannot stop the jerking of my limbs, unclench my hand, or move my toes. There is no location on my left side and no sensation on my right.

All I have is Larry. His eyes say "Don't Die." Dawn is the worst—with him asleep and the medical shifts changing, I stare back at the world, whimper, and cry. What's the movie today? I fantasize getting to the window, breaking the glass, slitting my throat.

Two boys down the hall—motorcycle crashes screwed cages into their skulls. No one's told them they'll never leave. The elegant woman across the way—flawless on top, but her legs are dead. Another surgery gone wrong. My roommate lost toes to diabetes and had another stroke. His wife screams on the phone to come home.

People worse off make me feel less sorry for myself, until someone more mobile shows up. I'd rather be alone glaring at my swollen and skewed left side that is flaccid, sagging, and lifeless. My movie in this room has the helmet kids not shrieking, the young men walking upright, the old ones not drooling, and me tapping my fingers.

Six weeks in the hospital and two months in a wheelchair at home, then I navigate life on the outside. Alarmed expressions, sympathetic smiles, and open-mouthed pity: the more generous people are to me, the more I resent them. Few really care to know, most want only to be reassured. Each encounter makes me smaller.

Meeting other crips, I never ask my real questions. I'm frightened when Jack regresses, Stephanie gets depressed, Judy breaks her hand, or Mark dies. The movie here? Stephanie's legs untangle, Jack walks unassisted, Mark gets published, and Judy rides her horse with me running free. I still dream fully able, they all do too.

Life at home revolves around getting to work and fitting in rehab with Larry as my soccer mom. Cooking and cleaning, the dog and me; I'm a burden to him. While my relation to living remains elusive, I don't know how to ask his forgiveness to go first. As we drive across the Golden Gate Bridge, I imagine us as Thelma and Louise, blissfully accelerating into oblivion.

With no sensation, sex is purely visual. Reciprocating with my enfeebled fingers and locked-in neck is short-lived. Often, I disassociate to retrieve stored memories of thrusting, receiving, grasping, hardness, wetness, stickiness, and release. It's not enough. The movie should have us rolling around wrestling and jousting, fucking and sucking with gleeful abandon.

I'm despondent whenever my body fails and it always fails me. Sadness and anger, frustration and tears are constant—but private. As the neuropathy increases in my legs, I obsess on long-term survivors whose over compensating bent frames refuse to give in. My debilitation fuels self-loathing. I embarrass myself with fear and shame.

What I wanted to be temporary is permanent. There are no happy endings for the movie today: no transformations, no miracles to celebrate, and no heroic deeds. There's just Larry and me, holding on to one another, slowly making our way in the world, careening side by side.

Video Narrative #2: Dreaming Awake

I dissociate from the burning in my legs,
silently crying between sleep and the morning.
Hopes and dreams keep me safe through the night.
After surgery, I died then,
but you refused and brought me back.
Seven years and counting, of tilting toward the ground.

I am afraid if I sit down, I will never get up again.

The dancer in me learned to stand visually,
the marathoner took the second step.
Rehab gave me strength and range of motion.
But with each new modality,
I interrupt expectations:
improvements are not cures.

If I sit down, I will never get up again.

Still imagining a body I cannot have,
I startle myself, glimpsing fatigue in passing windows.
My bifurcated body torques with every stride,
neuropathy and weariness debilitates.
Therapists caution about wear and tear,
while friends cheer, "You're getting better!"

If I sit down, I will never get up again.

Navigating deadened limbs and twisted trunk,
pain remains constant, dulling our life together.
After a day's activities, I have no comfort left to give you.
Living through chemistry, libido is gone.
Holding and touching you,
I long for remembered sensations.

I'm afraid if I sit down, I'll never get up again.
If I sit down, I'll never get up again.

ଓ ଓ ଓ

In this metaphorical body,
I try to intercept suffering,
abide in discomfort,
forgive the trauma.

Bearing witness,
I sit with loss,
move toward unobstructed feeling,
and bring you along into my dreaming awake.

Video Narrative #3: Night Swimming

By day, I am an arts warrior, public servant, heroic crip. Open, responsive, cocksure, ambitious—I seize the public gaze as a bully pulpit. Offstage finds me enslaved by quivering muscles contorting my stride.

After surgery, my swollen spine shut down. Gurus and saints abounded, but no roses from above. Paralyzed weeks turned into months—a flicker, a twitch, a wave; sitting to standing, six steps to go home, with wheelchair, ankle brace, and cane.

Gestures repeat to imprint, but gravity intervenes. Syncopated embellishments focus spatial awareness, though alignment remains akimbo. With little sensation, each footstep is defiant. Only in the pool can I run with the ponies again.

Eight years now—I still fixate on atrophy, ignoring progress. Balancing rehab and recovery, clinging to a reconnecting, physical therapy and pharmaceuticals combat lost kinesis, encouraging hope.

Night murmurs locate points of pleasure: behind the left knee, above the nipple. I crawl inside the softness, relishing the incandescent kundalini rush absent pain. Legs lie quiet, the burning subsides. Stillness embraces me.

In the extra room (that we do not have), I plié and pirouette with dramatic abandon, leaving behind my imploded, twisted carcass. The tumor does not return. My pelvis aligns. Depression dissipates. Then I awake.

Violent spasms hurl me out of body. Heart and breath stop. I stare down at my contorted gaping hole of a mouth and rehearse death, porous and seductive. Floating in this space between, I no longer fear dying, only waiting.

Stolen shadows hover. It seems easy (one breath away), but is so hard to surrender into the void, although I am well practiced, writing libretti for lost lives in vigils through the night and surviving my own demise, time and again.

Larry carries me back once more through his weight, touch, and voice. Unfettered love makes the journey familiar and secure. No past, no future, just present. Grasping for now, I pray for clear seeing, acceptance without judgment.

Morning comes. I amble toward the light.

A Deaf Sapiosexual's Reflections
for Dani

Spider walked beside the roan mustang, her muscular legs shaping her tight Wranglers. With the harness rope in one hand, and another hand on the mane, she swung a dusty boot up over the horse's rump and rocked her hips, tightening her thighs until she fit comfortably on the horse's bare back. She leaned to the side, thumped her boots, and the horse turned into a run. The horse became a blur and Spider's own curly black mane flew behind her. I balanced in my own boots on the bottom rail of the fence, hugging the top rail, taking in every movement—the smooth intercourse between the horse's lithe canter and its rider as they circled the corral.

Soon it became my turn to clomp into the circle, hold the rope in one hand, the mane in another, and run to pull myself onto the horse's bare back. I looked around at the row of fellow eleven-year-old Girl Scouts hanging onto the fence, waiting to see if I would mount or fall. Spider thumped my back, and with a nod of her chin said, "Go." I took a deep breath, held the mane, jumped a leg high, but slipped and fell on my hands and knees into the dirt. I could see the girls chattering and yelling, but could not hear a word. Before humiliation could register, Spider came up behind me, put her hands under my armpits and pulled me up. She placed one of my hands on the mane, curled my fingers into the coarseness, placed another hand on the horse's rump, and then she cupped my waist, hoisting me onto the horse's back. I trotted around the corral, breathing hard, imagining someday I'd be as graceful as Spider.

At twelve, I could run beside a horse and hoist myself up effortlessly onto its bare back, but I never saw Spider again after that summer ended. In my boxes of old photos, I have a picture of Spider during a flag football game at the camp—in the photo, she palms a football, frozen in a walk with one long leg crossed over the other, her broad shoulders and face turned to the side, her eyes searching. I had stars in my eyes when the photo came back from the developers, but I was not blinded enough to miss the deeply disapproving look from my mother. I hid the photo for years.

My daughter Dani was nine when her brother, seven years her senior, looked at me and said, "Mom, I don't think she's straight. She just isn't." I nodded in agreement. She was witty beyond her years. She had an incredible sense of fashion. She had an understanding of the world that many adults didn't have. She had crushes on boy bands and girl actors. There was a strong sense of being different, but I wasn't sure what it was.

KD twirled in the city street, her pea-green blazer fanning behind her open arms. She stomped her black Doc Martens toward me, threw her arms around me, and squeezed while rocking back and forth. Again, her arms opened, and she backed away, laughing. My face froze in a half-smile of awe. "Come on!" she led us to a dark doorway, nodded and threw a kiss at the short, muscular bouncer sporting a buzz cut. The door opened into a tunnel with strobe lights flashing at the end. My eyes adjusted to the dimness interjected by sweeping, colored rays of light. I scanned the crowded dance floor, and realized that KD wasn't kidding—there were no men. Her hand circled my wrist and pulled me onto the dance floor.

Nobody was really dancing *with* anyone, I noticed, as I started to move with the music. I watched the other women's hips beat in time to the vibrations around me, their feet swishing and sliding. Their hands raised high, waving sinuously. I couldn't resist—I closed my eyes and allowed the rhythmic euphoria to wash over me—I became one with the thumping of the bass, swirled with the lights, and blended with the undulation of unknown women overlapping into intimate spaces. I watched KD's close-cropped blonde hair disappear into the crowd without any sense of loss—the music was mine.

But then I let out a sigh of disappointment—my meditation on the dance floor was rudely interrupted by a more basic need. I wove through the forest of bodies toward a far wall and joined a line snaking from the bathroom door. I people-watched—studying clothes, shoes, postures, hairstyles, and mannerisms. I watched overly drunk women slather themselves on others, watched aloof women with cold eyes hold their beers high, watched the hands of couples roam over breasts and behinds, watched conversations float and shoot around me. I appreciated not being able to hear—it gave the visuals more vividity. In the stall, I sat, reading the scratches in the paint.

Suddenly, a torn piece of toilet paper floated past my face—what the heck?! I jerked my eyes upward. KD's face grinned at me from above the top rim of my stall. "Finish up!" she signed with one hand. I awkwardly cleaned myself, aware of my audience, hiked my jeans back on, and looked up again. "Come up!" She frowned. I put one foot on the toilet seat and stood until our faces were inches apart. There couldn't have been any logical answer to what was going on, but I had to ask, "What are you doing?"

KD put on a cocky half-smile. She reached up over the edge and took the nape of my neck into her hand and pulled my lips to hers. I inhaled quickly and dove willingly into that liquor-flavored abyss, following psychedelic, demanding swirls of softness and suction.

Smut? I knew what smut was, but to find it in the history on my 11-year-old daughter's computer? A few days later I looked at Dani and asked straight out: "What's up with the smut?"

She looked back at me with confidence. "I was curious." Okay . . .

"You're reading about gay men having sex."

"Yes, I am." Okay, I sure didn't expect this response. "Is there something wrong with gay men?"

"You know I don't have a problem with that. That's not my concern at all. Your age is my concern, though."

"I find gay men extremely hot." Okay, I could understand that.

"There's nothing wrong with what you find fascinating. I would just far prefer you wait."

"Don't worry. I already felt I was too young and didn't plan to go back there for a while."

Oh. Okay . . .

છ

Mick and I sat with our legs dangling at the edge of the pier. The wind hummed steadily, drumming ripples on the water. The sunset had gone, leaving behind a chill. I willed myself to enjoy the scenery, noting the mirroring of the silhouettes of trees across the lake. I couldn't relax. Mick leaned back on her hands. I wanted to turn and look at her face, but I pretended to study something in the far off distance. I counted to fifty. I wanted to know what she was thinking. She brought me out here, saying it was her favorite spot. Then she disappeared into her own thoughts. I couldn't breathe.

I gave up and glanced over. Mick's body was in a position of repose, but an intensity still gripped her sinews, keeping her muscles tight. Her chin was lowered into shadows, curtained by her hair. Even though I couldn't see them, I knew her eyes were distant, wondering, searching. She was a watcher—someone who sat in the periphery of a room, absorbing. When I first saw her, our eyes recognized another watcher, knowing the other could see and saw. We drew together, sensing something safe, something familiar. But, here, at the lake, there was no one to watch. We sat, quiet in the raw exposure.

She was incredibly beautiful in the half-light.

"Are you ready?" I asked her. She nodded. "We just need to fix a few things in the morning. Maybe change a few words. Then we'll be ready to perform." I matched her nod. "Sounds good." She smiled, then fingerspelled, "Michelle and Beatrice's Incredible Feats of Amazing Artistry," ending with a flourish. I fingerspelled back, "Yep!" ending with the "P" walking down the dock and jumping in the lake for a swim. She caught my "P" and held my hand. We sat in silence again.

The long pause became too saturated for me. "It's pretty out here. Thanks for . . ." Mick leaned over. I decided to try. I turned my face, waited a beat, and then brought my lips to hers. The restraints suddenly gave away—she returned with a ferocity that I matched with my own. We rolled to and fro on the swaying dock, gripping each other with a desperate tightness. Her kisses came like waves, washing over me. Then she recoiled.

She shook her head, stood up, stepped backwards, and froze. Her eyes filled with a helpless pain, she dug her hands deep into her pockets, then turned and walked into a distant darkness.

I sat, my feet dangling from the edge of the pier, humiliated and confused. I looked at the blackness of the lake, glittering with stubborn gleams of reflected light. Almost unconsciously, I took off my clothes and slipped off the dock, pushing into a crawl. I swam, increasing my speed, faster and faster until I could no longer breathe. I turned over, gasping and floated, blanketed under a starry sky. Serenity crept over me, cradling me in my oblivion.

Dani asked, "I want $35 for a binder." I found her request random and strange. I couldn't understand why, in June, my daughter wanted such an expensive binder right there and then when school didn't start again for two more months. "It's not for school! It's . . . for my chest."

I looked down at her young cleavage. "Why in the world would you want a binder?"

Her eyes fell into a glower. "Of all people, I thought you would be understanding." I felt conflicted. This was a little girl who wouldn't wear anything but dresses for years. This was a young woman who put flowers in her hair. My brain struggled. Was this a peer or Internet thing?

"Then help me understand," I said.

"I've told you that I'm not binary. It's just how I feel. Some days I just don't feel like or even want to be a girl." I still wasn't sure I understood, but I was sure of one thing—I wanted her to explore, experiment, and find her own path. "All right. I'll get you a binder."

Shannon screamed at me, hurling objects from around the room. "You're with me! You love me! We've done so much together! Two years! I've given you money! You're my girlfriend! You're a lesbian just like me! I want out. I want to be out!" I shook my head. No, I can't.

"Don't lie to me!" I shook my head again. "If you care about me, you would give me this!"

But I couldn't. I wasn't confused or in denial. I just knew, without doubt, that wasn't my identity. I couldn't put on clothes that felt wrong. I couldn't explain it. I felt selfish. I felt horribly depraved and rotten.

"You know I can't . . ." and turned for the door. Shannon darted. In one deft movement, she picked up her softball bat and blocked the door. At one time, it felt so safe being Shannon's friend. But I couldn't. There was the issue of the custody papers.

David was two. My baby boy, one that I chose to keep, to love, to raise alone. This meeting was supposed to be good for him. I sat in the judge's office with the papers in front of me. My mother explained—the papers were to give her permission to make medical decisions for David in the event that I couldn't. The papers were to make sure he didn't become a ward of the state if something happened to me. I started to read, my mother pushed on my arm to sign. I pulled away to read. My mother gripped my thigh, smiled, and dug her nails into the tenderness. The legal jargon wasn't immediately clear. The judge's mouth said to hurry, he didn't have all day. He waved his hands. My mother's nails sank deeper into my flesh. I looked at her in bewilderment. "You know you can't take care of him by yourself." The judge shook his head and spoke quickly. She spoke back to him, then tightened her clench on my thigh. "Do not embarrass me," she bared her teeth and signed with her free hand. I wrote my name.

Minutes later I finally understood. I had lost full custody of my son to my mother. I had been tricked into signing him away. My deafness became the reason and the weapon used against me. If I wanted to see him, I now had 16 years ahead of me to comply.

Shannon couldn't handle it. She slammed cabinets and threw Wendy's burgers. She punched the wall and wanted me to wrap her hand. She poured Pepsi on the head of a male friend as we chatted. She pushed me into a dark corner until I got hurt. At the hospital she hung her head. I looked at her through the slats of my hospital bed. I loved her, but this was not fair to her. She needed to be free.

I finally said, "No, please go. Good night." And closed the door. She banged a night-long wail on my door with her beautiful, strong, hay bale-toned arms. At four in the morning, silence came as she fell asleep in a heap in the doorway. I stepped over her, sadly and without any sense of victory, on my way to work, but the door stayed closed. I felt viscerally ugly.

I had to make a choice. "If you *choose* to go that way, with that nasty dyke, mark my words, you will never see David again. I will not have him around *that*."

☙

In 1990, you were either gay or straight. Bisexuals were viewed with suspicion and hostility. Experimenting was never discussed. An understanding of queerness, intersexuality, pansexuality, or even asexuality was 20 years off into the future. Crossdressers and drag queens were entertainment. In our small collective college minds, if you were with someone of the same sex, just once, that was it. There was no "going back." No rewind button.

But how could I play in one side and hide in another? I was the nasty Bi that both sides hissed at. Yet, at the same time, I didn't identify as bisexual. I didn't feel straight either. I couldn't put into words what didn't make sense to me. Some things were clear—I loved Shannon, but I had loved Tom, too. I had a crush on KD, but I also tittered around Declan. My world did not yet have words available to me to explain it. All I knew was what I knew.

When I was five, I followed Frank around and wrapped myself around his leg, refusing to let go. I tongue-kissed Laurana inside a fridge box when I was six, then Steven a week later. At eight, I worshipped the ground Robbie walked on—he loved his men, but I loved him. I fantasized about sitting naked on Barry, my 55-year-old English Literature professor. If Susan or Parker had said, "Come," I would have turned my back on my life and went. I curled up to Paul's face in my mind, desperately missing him after he took a one-way flight to meet kahunas in Hawaii. I was willing to sell everything I owned and move cross-country to be with Jody, but fortunately I didn't. I loved women, loved men, loved women that looked like men, and loved men that looked like women. I knew this to be true and simply knew I was not a lesbian.

And above and beyond all, there was David. Nobody meant more to me than my son.

So I wrapped my questions up inside my mind, packed my self up with my college boxes stored deep in a dark basement. I denied Spider, denied Mick, and vehemently denied Shannon. I no longer mentioned them. I walked down the aisle with a man I sort of liked in a strong way. Kyle and I felt we would be good together. Mother trusted him to raise David. I wanted my son back. I didn't know that, years later, David and I would be ground to dust under his unrelenting cruelty.

cg

Dani and I sat at a table, watching the people around us. Conversations shot and floated around us, and we followed different trajectories, each sign and expression clear. Strangers hugged around us, faces lit up in laughter. "Thanks for bringing me here!" Dani smiled. "How did you know it was LGBTQ night here?"

"Chad."

She giggled. Chad was her big buddy.

When the emcee took the stage, the crowd roared. "Raise your hand if you're straight!" Hands flew up and waved. "Raise your hand if you're gaaay!!" Some men stood up and danced. "Up high if you're leees-biiian!!" Women jumped up and sashayed. The emcee suddenly stood ramrod tall, "Raise your hand if you're . . ." Her tone changed, her nose wrinkling into a disgusted grimace—"Confused!" Dani's eyes shot wide open toward me. "What world is she stuck in?! This is 2015?!"

I nodded. "That's the way it used to be. She just hasn't changed."

I saw Mick again, clear-eyed, relaxed and happy with her Tina. I felt joy for her. And I saw Tom. Tom hugged me and I woke up. It took a bleeding wound, a bruise, a chaise flying, the threat of a hammer, and a long climb, but I got Kyle's consent, his signature, and a judge's blessing. David, Dani, and I packed up a U-Haul and finally broke free.

Dani glanced up from her phone. "I know what you are."

My head turned to the side, my face expressed puzzlement.

"You're a sapiosexual."

More confusion.

"You're someone who is attracted to those who stimulate them intellectually." She said it offhandedly, got up from her curl on the sofa, and went into the kitchen.

Sapiosexual? I looked back on my years, on my crushes, my loves, and my heartbreaks. I leaned back with unrestrained laughter. Dani had no idea—no idea at all—how accurate she was. I was definitely a sapiosexual.

CB

At four years old, Dani stood on the curb, her blue and yellow equality flag waving in the breeze. We watched the semi trucks drive by, pulling a platform filled with slender young men, dancing in tight boxers. Uncle Billy held her hand and laughed again at what I did to her hair. Crayola washable markers, in rainbow colors, went very well onto white-blonde hair. The front of her frilly pink shirt was covered with stickers that politicians and activist threw at her. She didn't care that they weren't cartoon characters; the stickiness was the best part. The candy thrown at her feet was also the best part. She looked around at all the people surrounding us and saw people. Just happy, dancing people. I never wanted that to change.

"So Indiana passed this law that allows people to kick gays out of their restaurant. I completely don't get it. How does who pays money to eat at your restaurant have any bearing on your religion? If that's going to mess up their religion, they obviously weren't strong enough in the first place!" Dani ranted. I nodded in agreement. "I'm going to set up my own restaurant in Indiana." She signed a period in the air at the end of her statement.

"Really? Why in Indiana?"

"Remember when I hung out of the car and screamed TransEquality at the crowd at Pride? I'm almost thirteen and I get it! That. Because I'm going to have a restaurant that only serves LGBTQI people! I will have . . ." she went on to describe the imagined menu.

I looked at my daughter. She had the freedom and the bliss to grow in whichever way she felt was right for her. I gave her that. I gave her the space, without judgment, for her to pave her own journey. I didn't know where she would end up, but it didn't matter to me—I never wanted her to know the feeling of angry nails clawing into her flesh. I could not honor her joy, her indignation, and her reality without some honesty of my own. Truth demanded its own self. I gave, and she gave back.

"I'll be the first one at your door."

"But, Mom, you . . . are . . . totally . . . straight!"

"No, I am most definitely not straight." I smiled broadly.

It's sunrise as my beloved and I walk, watching the geese circle off the lake into flight. We hold our hands tight, our forearms wrapped around each other. I breathe deep, the morning mist tickling my nostrils. I rest my cheek on the soft hairs of his firm arm and sense him pulling me closer. I smile, content. Maybe one day he will understand that my love for him is strong, yes, but stronger, maybe, because it's him, his true essence that I adore, worship, and deeply love. Not his gender.

KATHI WOLFE

Love at First Sight

In an elevator trapped
between the fifteenth and sixteenth
floor of her apartment building,
Sunday morning, Elizabeth, her cane
in one hand, coffee and bagels
in the other, just in from the deli,
met Sabrina and her poodle Toto.

Maybe it was Toto dancing
like a flying monkey
around Elizabeth's cane, the wind roaring
through the elevator shaft like a twister
barreling down on Kansas, Sabrina's
pomegranate scented hair, or Elizabeth's
ruby red flip-flops. Calling loudly
for help, pressing the emergency button,
needing to pee, they were headed toward Oz.

A week later, Elizabeth and Sabrina, in bed
followed their own Yellow Brick Road,
dreaming of rainbow ballads and Wizard blues.

"Will she have red or white?"
the bartender asked Sabrina
as she and Elizabeth sat,
holding hands at the Tin Man Pub.
"She'll have an Old-Fashioned,"
Elizabeth told the server.

"Elizabeth," murmured Sabrina.
"Call me Uppity," she said, "I'm the door
that won't stay closed, the spy who cracks
the code. No wicked witch will melt me
here with my sweetie in the Emerald City."

Mind's Eye

If I were Queen of the World,
ruling with my Royal Smart Phone,
Bluetooth in tiara, walking
my besotted, blue-blooded dogs,
regally motioning to my worshipful
subjects to stop curtsying,
only my bejewelled cane
would dig its way
into the tunnel of your vision.

If I won the Nobel Prize for cracking
the passwords of the dead,
only my encrypted, blinkered eyes
would register in your retinas.

If Sabrina and I were making love,
nymphs on the loose in the mid-day sun—
clothes, purses mindlessly abandoned
on the grass—only my blind
gaze would meet your mind's eye.

Blind Porn

Imagine reading Playboy *to the blind!*
exclaims the anchorwoman. *Not just the articles,*
but the pictures! she says, breathlessly.

I hope it's filthy, so sordid it gives blind
porn a bad name, Uppity whispers to Sabrina,
stroking her hair, flicking the remote,
tickling her toes under the silky sheets.

They'd clicked that night
when they kissed in Washington Square Park,
until this guy, panting, leered, *I gotta take a pic*
with my phone—two blind chicks making out.

Furies in spiked heels,
the ladies aimed—a direct hit—
Damn bitches! he screamed,
Whad'ya got—radar?

We wanna get a sound bit—
of your balls turning blue!
the harpies hissed, *nothing*
would give us more bliss.

Why, to the sighted,
are we creatures
from the Black Lagoon?
Uppity wondered.
They turn off the TV,

undress,
sip wine,
check their breath,
pray to the gods
of good sex
and tenderness,
just as I do now
before making love
to my lady.

Who knows?
Uppity sighed,
if this be blind porn,
play on.

A Pulp Fiction

All those lesbians you pal around with will lead you into a blind alley, her grandmother told Uppity. For the love of Sappho, Uppity thought, slipping on her silver pumps, take me there! Bring me to this dyke-infested place where sapphic ghosts kiss blindly in devil-encrusted glitz. Where forbidden fruit ripens. Let me caress the shattered stone. My cane, a dagger, will slash the heart of my ex who left me standing alone on the street after the midnight show of *Wait Until Dark*. In a blind passion, my hands will stalk the crumbling wall! Looking for requited love. Like a sightless idiot, believing it can be found.

If I Were a Boy

I'd drive,
Al Pacino in *Scent of a Woman*,
into the Macho Guy sunset,

spinning
my wheels over the heavens and the earth,
stopping only to pick up girls.

The chicks,
sneaking a peek, would die to know
how I kiss with my manly eyes closed.

Screeching
past dead-man curves,
racing the devil's own,

the secret
of my blind lip-lock will remain
tethered to my man-boy bones.

Want

I do not want boundless love—
only dogs get that.
I do not want to be a poodle
so regal that I'd disdain surfeit affection.

I do not want to be a sightless Daredevil
acing bad guys with my radar;
the clamor and blood of falling bodies
would deafen my ears or stain
my red, skintight suit.

I do not want to learn to float,
rather than swim against,
light-zapping pain. I'm no
Esther Williams in *Million Dollar Mermaid*.

I want to be an ice cream sandwich,
vanilla and wafers in communion,
seeking only perfection.

D. ALLEN

A Collection of Thorns

bodig (Old English) originally described the "trunk or chest" of a man or animal, but came to mean "person" in the late 13th century. Physical form cleaved, by language, from the soul.

When I was nineteen I still believed my body could stand for anything, could withstand anything. One gray afternoon at the Duke Gardens I wandered with a couple of artist friends among bamboo groves and bloomless rose hedges looking for thorns. A barberry bush stooped low at the top of the sandy path gave us what we came for: woody spikes, each with three spines radiating from one base like the spokes of an unfinished wheel. We snapped twenty-six from the stem, slipped them into a shoebox.

You rub my back during a pain flare and I remind you to avoid the spine. Often you remember on your own, now. I say *the spine* because it is easier than saying *my body feels broken and your touch makes it real.*

I have trouble describing how it feels when I become unable, for a stretch of days or weeks, to hold myself upright. I start to tell you about the biggest hurricane of my childhood, how it lured dune after dune into the raging Atlantic; I begin to demonstrate the act of pulling the string from a strand of beads so quickly they scatter. But the image that haunts me still is the specter of a tower looming on my mind's horizon.

The power plant's elder smokestack presided over the walking path I once traced to work—two city blocks down, one over, one down, one over—and it became, as landmarks do, familiar. A pebble in my palm turned over and over. Snow melted in rivulets down the sidewalks and the pink magnolias were about to make good on their annual promise when a four-man crew arrived at the tower. Harnesses, hard hats, jackhammers, dumpster. They climbed to the top and, like brutal dentists gathered over the mouth of a lamprey, began pulling out every one of its teeth.

bæc (Old English) comes from Proto-Germanic **bakam*, which created a distinction between an animal's back or the ridge of a mountain range and a human's upright body.

We brought our collected treasures home. In an empty attic room warmed by space heaters, I took off my shirt. I was shy but I needed to know that words were more than sounds, that they could change and be changed by the body. She took each thorn and, using the wax of a white candle, pressed it to a vertebra until it stayed. He held the camera, the light. With a line of thorns down my spine I *became*.

The pain begins with a twinge near the thoracic spine. Exacerbated by: sitting, standing, lying down, carrying a bag on the back, carrying a bag on the shoulder, leaning, stretching, reaching, walking, lifting anything. Caused by nothing at all. When the twinge becomes a gasping, I call the doctor. I get into the position my college dance teacher called *constructive rest* and wait for muscle relaxers to work. I no longer live in the same city, but when I close my eyes the tower appears as an after-image, bright column on a dark field.

Demolition was finished by week's end. I had looked at the tower from across the street almost daily. I had never seen it. On the final day, when its stature was so diminished that the men stopped wearing harnesses—reduced to a cross-section of itself as the rubble pile grew—the tower spoke over jackhammer whine.

Tk-tk.

The doctor knocks, walks into the exam room with a sheaf of X-rays, all clean. They always are. Subluxations of the vertebrae and ribs are quieter than fractures and more difficult to trace. He asks me to stand straight, to bend forward, to touch my toes. Nothing to see here. It is never the bending that hurts. Pain arrives when I try to return to a way of being that has, in the stretch, become unfamiliar.

espine (Old French) means "thorn, prickle," and also "backbone, spine." Its Latin predecessor, spina, refers to a "sharp point."

In a grainy video from that day I rise protective and slow, arms pressed against ribs to hide my nakedness; straighten to kneel, twisting as if to see someone over my left shoulder, right shoulder, curving forward, rising again, all of a sudden crossing my arms and arcing all the way back, an invisible palm pressed against my forehead leaning me into a baptismal posture, dried wax crackling into a halo on velvet.

I kissed you for the first time in a tent under a dark sky in the place where the Mississippi and Wisconsin rivers converge. The plainclothes doctor diagnosed me three months later. Diagnosis denuded the pain. Before, I slept on the ground, hiked sandstone bluffs, sat on a beer cooler and played the banjo to your guitar. Before, I was eroding but erosion did not haunt me.

When pain comes at night I visualize the joints, in turn, as beach sand compacted by a hiker's boot; rusted engine parts of my father's old F150; beech tree limbs broken and groundscattered by an overnight storm; a menagerie of house wrens, great blue herons, cedar waxwings, Eastern bluebirds, redwing blackbirds, barred owls, turkey vultures, and redtailed hawks, calling and crying and molting in the branches of my body.

The sky has a hole in it. Brick and mortar gone as if raptured, with nothing but a circle of concrete visible from the sky to prove the tower's absence. When the pain comes at night I visualize the joints as holes. I am cheesecloth. Sieve. A honeycomb of hurt. I imagine the joints the way I imagined the night sky as a child looking up—a black velvet backdrop pricked at the site of every star.

þorn (Old English), meaning "sharp point on a stem or branch," evolved from root *ster-, "stiff." In the 13c it expanded to mean, figuratively, "anything which causes pain."

I have kept photographs of my thorny spine in the back of a flat file for nine years, relics of the self cast in amber. In them it is possible to alter my course. White wax trickles between trapezius and latissimus dorsi, fixing woody spikes to human skin. Green leaves bud and open. The images are supernatural, crystallized from a universe where human body and plant body merge at the mouth of the void.

Sometimes you kiss my naked vertebrae, pressing your lips to every thorn. Bless these sensations more tenacious than pain.

In my top dresser drawer I keep two long white tapers. During a spring of doctor visits, when my body seemed made of paper gowns, echocardiograms, and strange fingers on my skin, you drove us back to my apartment after an appointment and I opened the drawer. *I need to know that I still have a body*, I didn't say to you. I lay back on the bed; you kissed my shoulder and lit the wick. White wax pricked and sutured the wound between self and self.

An almost unbearable pleasure: in a fresh bath, body lowered and leaned back, the slow seduction of an air bubble sliding up the spine to surface and disappear. Then I am alone in the quiet water.

peine (Old French), "difficulty, woe, suffering, punishment, Hell's torments" (11c.), derives from Latin *poena*, whose root is the Greek *poine* "retribution, penalty, quit-money for spilled blood."

Cold room, hot utility lamp, crushed velvet fur of the black backdrop against my chest and stomach. The barberry needs no protection from its own weapons, but I was soft and sharp all at once. She placed the final thorn and stepped away.

I have forgotten so much but I remember this: lifting myself from the floor with a back become thornbush, new body bristling.

It is November and the radiators in our apartment are bleached bones, vertebrae perfectly aligned. Outside the window everything is white. My new walk goes past a dark red chimney in a back alley split from any house; it stands healthy and humble without crumbling. I turn my head away when it enters my vision. I don't want to see.

I am so sorry, so sorry, so sorry. If anything spoken three times gains the power of incantation I will apologize in threes, body, until my tongue is raw and my hands sore from prayer. I am so sorry for not knowing how to relieve this suffering that has mapped itself onto the bones. I am so sorry for the stiffness, the soreness, the absence of connection. I am so sorry for remembering always the sharp nodes of pain and forgetting, sometimes, the simple pressure of my lover's hand on my back.

After a short walk to the bus stop I allow, without complaint, the road to deliver me. The bus passes a brick house with three broad Ionic columns painted white. Correction: two columns and, where the third should be, a spindling post like a banjo's tension rod. We do our best to remain upright. Then I am spit from mechanical doors and struggle up concrete steps toward the snowy footbridge over the Mississippi, the water's glitter alluding to ice, coming.

CHRISTOPHER DEMPSEY

Ancient Pauses

Heart stopping thoughts
    bravery, fear, hope,
    lust
my head
hands in my pocket

Always that small pause.

A moment, weighing
    my hearing aids
small, light yet

Fuck it, life-changing

Why me? Why do I
bear this moment, this pause,
this truth?

A pause, the tiniest thing,
pull them out
    nonchalantly
as possible, quickly
like
it's the most normal thing
in the world.

Obvious, the way
    earmolds slip casually into

my ears, the hearing aids easing
over your earlobes

A pause, burst into life,
sound streams in

Like it's the most
    normal thing
in the world.

He pauses, a brief stop
    looks at you
before carrying on
as if
it's the most
    normal
thing in the world.

JOHN WHITTIER TREAT

A Girl for Us

DO YOU HAVE A GIRL FOR US? As New Yorkers committed to the happiness of our son, a 35-year-old high-functioning young man with a learning disability, we would like to help him find a wonderful woman with whom he can share his life.

—*NYRB*, Feb 11, 2010

That woman, she usually comes in on Thursdays when it's coupon day. I recognize her, who wouldn't? She wears really bright colors, no matter what season, and you could never not notice her even if you wanted. She recognizes me, too. She calls me by my name, Hal. When I bag her groceries she nods repeatedly with a nice smile, because she knows I always put the heavy things at the bottom of the bags and the lighter stuff on top.

Well, she waved to me as we passed each other on the street today. I don't work Mondays, and I guess she doesn't either, unless she's just too old to work *ever*. So I'm out for a walk and so is she, I think. Maybe she's just come from the planetarium, that's where I'm headed. There's no new show there right now, but I'm going anyway. I'm friends with the people who work there, and last time the guy just waved me in. I didn't have to pay. I suppose I should have given Mom my admission money back, but I didn't. I'm saving it. For the day I decide to take a friend to the planetarium, that way he won't have to pay.

Oh, good. The key's there, where it should be. On the chain around my neck. Can't forget that. I need the key to get home, though the couple of times I forgot my folks were home and they let me in. Usually they're not home. They're busy people. I'm really only busy on the days I work at the D'Agostino's. I bag groceries. Nothing ever breaks. I was Employee of the Month once. So what if I'm slow at it? They'll never fire me. I'm an *employee*.

"Ross, honey, someone just called from your office, the message is on the answering machine."

Ross put his briefcase down on one of the dining table chairs. He went over to the phone and played the message back.

"It's nothing, Mattie. Someone wanted to know where one of the files was. I have it with me."

Mattie came out of the kitchen. "Indian food again, Ross. Do you forgive me?" Ross smiled. His wife went back to the kitchen and came out with a plate, a fork and a white paper napkin. She sat at the dining table as he ate the leftovers.

"Hal went to the planetarium today."

Ross twisted his head towards his son. "You did, buddy? How was it?" he asked through a mouthful of rice.

Hal was on the living room floor playing his own version of chess on a big beach towel. He was wavering over just where to put the Black Queen, but his dad's question made him finally decide. He put it down on the ruby-red conch shell drawing.

"It was good, Dad," Hal replied. "It was a special show. About the asteroid belt."

"What did you learn?"

Hal squirmed. "Well, I knew most of it already."

Hal stopped playing his private game and lay on his back on the floor looking up at the ceiling.

"Hal, darling, don't you want to go into your room?" Mattie suggested from the kitchen.

"Nothing to do there."

"Sure there is. Read a book. Turn on your television."

Ross picked up the front section of the *Times*, but after a quick glance at the headlines he added it to the recycle pile in the kitchen. When he came back out his son was gone and his wife was sitting on the sofa looking as if she had something to talk to him about. Ross sat down and placed his hand atop hers in her lap. Mattie's mouth opened, but it was a moment before any words came out.

CB

"Where is Hal now?" Naomi asked from her large leather chair across from Ross and Mattie on her office's sofa.

"He's at his adult daycare center, you know, in the church basement," Mattie responded. "He'll be there until we pick him up on our way home." Naomi nodded and smiled. No one spoke for a moment.

"This is a difficult decision."

Mattie glanced at Ross before responding. "It's no decision, Naomi. We haven't decided *anything* for Hal."

Naomi thought of following up, but these people and their son had been clients long enough she knew better.

"Naomi," Ross continued. "You haven't said anything about our . . . idea. I think Mattie and I are counting on you to tell us if we're crazy. Maybe we're not nuts, and you still think this is bad idea." Ross tilted his head slightly, signaling that it was Naomi's duty to respond.

Naomi leaned forward in her chair. "It's unusual. Not unheard of. You want him to be happy. And you're thinking ahead to when you're both gone.

"You might well find someone. It is certainly easier to find a woman for a man than the other way around. But will you be comfortable with it?"

"With what?" Mattie asked, a second before Ross would have.

"Hal with someone you might not know much about. Until maybe . . ."

". . . It's too late?" Ross interjected.

"Well, yes."

"That's no different than it is for any of us. Ross and I really didn't know that much about each other when we got together."

"It *is* different, Mattie. We were adults. Hal will never really be an adult. And what if the girl isn't, either?"

"What do you mean?" Mattie asked.

"I mean, what if the girl is developmentally impaired, too?"

"We talked about that." Mattie added they could think of a future where Hal and his wife would be cared for together.

Naomi sat back in her chair. "Go slow. Go very slow."

Mattie closed her eyes and thought: it's hard not to tell Hal's therapist everything.

CB

Stan's not here today, so I guess we're not going to finish that fight we were having about the Mets.

I'll just have to find something else to do. The girls have the TV on to the Jerry Springer show, but once they start throwing the furniture around on the stage Jessica will go over and make them change the channel. Ha ha ha they think we'll get the idea to throw the furniture around here.

Guess I'll see if there are any new books. I finished the two about cars. They were okay, I guess. We don't have a car at home, of course. We're *New Yorkers*, and people in New York don't have cars. Wish Stan were here.

Aw, look, there goes Jessica. I knew it. She's mean to those girls but she and I get along fine. The one time I got mad and threw all the checkers on the floor she yelled at me, but I think she's forgotten about that. She smiles at me and holds my hand when I cry, but only happens when I'm really, really sad. She's normal, like that other *ah-ten-dahnt* Omar, but I don't want to think about him. Jessica is the nice one. Not as much fun as Stan, though. I wonder where Stan is today.

When Mattie heard her son and husband at the door she quickly put the copy of the *New York Review of Books* under the smooth stone she used as a paperweight, as if Hal would guess everything if he saw it.

"We're home, honey!"

"Hal," she said. "Don't go to your room now. Daddy and I have something to talk with you about." Mattie looked Ross's way, but he was avoiding eye contact with her. She wished her husband were braver.

"Okay, Mom." Hal wondered what was up. Maybe it would be a surprise, like that trip to Sea World. He sat down in the middle of the sofa, not his usual place, but Mom was already in the big chair and Dad was leaning against the fireplace mantel, so he figured he could have the whole couch.

"Hal, darling," Mattie started only to stop.

"Hal," Ross continued as if on cue, "We've been thinking about you. And thinking that maybe you need more friends. Maybe a special friend."

Hal was relieved he hadn't done anything wrong, but he was wary.

"I have friends!" he said loudly. "You've met them. Sometimes they come here."

"Yes, Hal," Ross said. "You do. Stan and your other friends from the Center. Tell them to come more often. You have friends at the D'Agostino's, too, right?"

Hal sniffed. Not *that* kind of friends. They were all *employees*.

"Hal," Mattie said, rejoining the conversation. "Hal, how about girls? Do you have any friends who are girls at the Center? Jessica says you do."

So, Hal thought, they've been talking to Jessica. Jessica doesn't know anything.

"I like my friends, Mom."

"We know you do, Hal. It's just . . . it's just that you're a grown man now."

Hal stared at his mother. He was being to think he *had* done something wrong.

"Girls, Mom? Sure, there are girls at the Center, and at the store, too. Plenty."

Mattie fought the impulse to gulp. "Any you'd like to get to know better?"

No, Hal thought. None.

Mattie shifted her position in the chair. Hal noted this, and braced himself for what was coming.

"Hal, we're going to invite some girls over."

"Okay."

"Do you know why?"

Hal looked at his father but his father did not look back.

"Uh-huh."

"We think you might like some of them. One of them."

"When?"

"When what, darling?"

"When are they coming? The girls."

Mattie cleared her throat. "Well, we're not sure yet. Soon, I think. Will that be okay? Meeting some nice girls. You like girls, don't you?"

"I like you, Mom, and you're a girl!"

Mattie laughed. "Yes, that I am. But these will be young girls. Your age."

Hal wanted to go to his room and watch the game on TV. "Can I go?"

"To your room, darling?" Mattie said. "Of course you can. But do you have any questions for us first?"

Hal thought, but he didn't. But he felt he had to ask something or his parents would not be happy.

"Can Stan come, too, when the girls come?"

Mattie kept her smile. "Stan? Oh, he's always welcome. But maybe not when the girls visit. *You're* the one they'll going to want to meet. Don't you think, Ross?"

Ross surveyed his family from the mantel.

"Hey, Buddy, this will be cool. Girls like baseball, too!" Later, when they are in bed, Mattie will criticize him for saying things to their son unlikely to be true, though all her lifetime she had done just that.

When Hal went to his room, Ross asked Mattie about the ad.

"When does it come out?"

"Thursday."

"Will they be calling here?"

"'They'? You're optimistic. No, they won't call. The *Review* forwards the responses to us."

"You look at them first," Ross instructed his wife. "Let me see the ones you like."

Okay, let me think. I know what this is about. It's about sex. I know a lot about that, we learned more in school than Mom and Dad think. Mrs. Wendelson told us about it, kinda, and then again in gym class Mr. Adams *really* told us about it. Well, I knew plenty already. Andy had told me years ago, and we made our things hard and rubbed them together in the school darkroom one day. That was okay. Did it again in the bathtub by myself that night, now I do it all the time.

That's why they're gonna to get girls to come over. I'm supposed to like one of them and put my thing inside her. Why do girls like that, that's something no one ever explains. Or maybe they did and I just forgot.

I don't hear them talking in the living room. Maybe they're whispering. I know they're talking about. Well, I won't have sex unless

I want to. Sex makes babies and who wants a baby. There's no room for one here. I'm not sharing my room, *that's* for sure. I'd share it with Stan, though. I wonder if Stan knows about sex.

What does Stan's thing looks like? I'd ask him to show it to me, except that we're always in that big room where everyone is. I wonder if he knows the trick Andy taught me, how to make it squirt the white stuff. I'd show him. And then he'd really be my friend.

Carolyn stopped reading the *New York Review of Books* when she saw a chair open up at the long reading table in front of her. There was enough room for her to spread out the entire paper on the table in front of her. A green shaded reader's lamp cast a bright light on the pages she hadn't been able to read well until now.

Soon all that was left to glance through were the classifieds. Sometimes Carolyn read them just to dream of a summer rental in Tuscany, or a house swap with someone's cottage in the Lakes District. Carolyn had an apartment in Teaneck to swap, but she doubted anyone would want it, much less anyone with an English garden that stretched down to the water.

She read the personals more often these days. A boyfriend might be nice, she often thought, but most of the personals were "Jewish SWF looking a kindred soul between 50 and 65," and she was none of those things.

"DO YOU HAVE A GIRL FOR US?" Why, what would you trade? Carolyn giggled. She read the rest of the classified and stopped laughing. Poor sucker, she thought. Poor parents, too. A for Effort, though. She closed the paper and took it back to the Current Periodicals rack.

Carolyn returned to the leather chair she had abandoned for the reading table. She leaned back into the thick cushions, extended her corduroy-clad legs and draped her hands across her round stomach. Then she went back to the newspaper rack. The *NYRB* was still there. She found the personals again and reached into her shoulder bag for a pen. She wrote the reply box number on her palm and left the library.

On the bus she stared at the blue markings she had made on her hand. She hadn't written the zip code down, she realized. Mad at herself, she thought: Well, just as well. Wasn't meant to be. Stupid in the first place.

The bus idled at a stoplight. That's an interesting ad though, she thought. Not like the others. *A Girl For Us.* Never saw an "us" before. What was it, a mother and a father, they're the us, the him their son. She stared at the incomplete address on her palm. It will get there without a zip code. Carolyn stepped off the bus and walked home. They won't know why I'm writing, she told herself, and there won't be any need to tell them.

Mattie forgot the cookies.

"Carolyn, excuse me. There are cookies to go with the tea. How is it, by the way?"

While Mattie stepped into the kitchen, Ross felt he had to say something to fill the silence.

"Carolyn, do you have any brothers or sisters?"

Carolyn replied she had a sister, but they hadn't grown up together.

"So, you're all alone in New Jersey?"

No, Carolyn thought, I'm not all alone. It was these people's son who needed companionship, not her. No, that's not quite right. But she didn't care for what this man was insinuating.

"I grew up there." Carolyn paused, reconsidering the slightly hostile tone of her voice. "You're all New Yorkers here? You and Mattie?"

"Yes, that's right," Ross said. "And Hal's known nothing but the Upper West Side." Mattie came back into the living room with a plate of Lorna Dunes, Hal's favorite. "So," Mattie said as she sat down next to her husband. "We have a million questions for you, but you must have more for us. About Hal." She smiled and waited for Carolyn.

"Well, you've shown me pictures of him. He's handsome." Carolyn hesitated again. "Has he had girlfriends in the past? Anything serious? I hope it's okay to ask. Am I prying?"

No, not at all, Ross and Mattie rushed to say at the same time. "Carolyn, he's had a sheltered life. Maybe more than he should have." Mattie cast her husband a look. "That's probably our fault. He's actually quite outgoing. It's just that here, with us, and then at the Center, he doesn't get to meet any girls. Women, I mean. He doesn't talk much about it, but I'm sure he's lonely. He's a grown man now."

"Yes, I can see that. Does he have any brothers or sisters?"

Mattie looked straight ahead, determined not to give Ross the satisfaction of looking at him.

"No," she said, nearly in a whisper. "There's only him." She looked down at her hands and focused her gaze on her wedding ring.

"Hal is a young man with potential. Everyone says so. We're just hoping that someone comes into his life who can see that, see him the way we do." Mattie cursed herself for sounding like she was trying to sell a used car.

Ross cleared his throat. "Carolyn, would you like to meet him?"

"Well, yes, of course."

"Ross," Mattie said. "Carolyn has a lot to think about."

"No, Mattie," Carolyn interjected. "That's fine. I do want to meet Hal." She paused. "But do you think he wants to meet me?"

This time Mattie did glance at her husband.

"It might be best if you went to meet him at the Center. With other people around. He might be more at ease." Mattie had no idea if this was true.

Carolyn almost felt sorry for these people. "Actually, I'd be more at ease that way, too."

"Cookie, Carolyn?"

"No, thank you," she replied. "They look delicious, but I oughtn't." She smiled at these strangers and said nothing else.

Carolyn walked right past the woman at the door, not realizing she was waiting for her.

"Carolyn?" the woman called out.

"Carolyn? Hi, I'm Jessica."

"Oh, thanks. Sorry to breeze right by. I expected to find you behind a desk or something."

"Oh, no," Jessica laughed. "I'm on my feet all day." She made no move to lead the two of them into the interior of the day center. "I thought we might talk out here first."

A little cautious, Carolyn said "Sure. You want to talk about Hal?"

"I know his parents have talked to you about him. But this is your first time meeting in person."

"Yes."

"Well, he's a fine young man. All the staff likes him."

Carolyn wished everyone would stop saying the same things about Hal again and again. She would either like him or she wouldn't.

"I'm glad," Carolyn said. "May I see him now?"

"There's just one thing."

"One thing?"

"Well, two actually. Hal has a close friend here, another young adult male, also developmentally challenged. Stan.

"They spend most of their time here together. Stan may want to be there when you talk to Hal, and Hal might want him to be there."

Okay, Carolyn thought, that's *one* thing. Now what's the other. She waited for Jessica to resume.

Jessica hesitated. Did she really want to bring this up?

"Carolyn . . . Haven't we met before?"

"What?" Carolyn asked. A breeze went through the open doorway where the two women were standing.

"I think we've met before. I'm nearly sure of it. You might not remember, it was . . . some time ago. or maybe I read about you in the papers."

Carolyn tried to change the conversation.

"Ever come to New Jersey? That's where I live."

"No," Jessica said firmly. "It wasn't New Jersey. But maybe you know what I'm talking about."

"Can I see Hal now?"

We can pretend we don't remember, Carolyn or whoever you are, but that's not the same as forgetting. Jessica turned her head to the side and spoke as if to someone not Carolyn. "Yes, you can see Hal now."

Carolyn followed Jessica into the day room. There were about twenty people. Everyone had a nametag.

Carolyn recognized Hal immediately. He was sitting in a chair much too small for a man his size. He was better looking than his photos. He had thick black hair swept back like Cary Grant's, and blue eyes were complimented by a strong, masculine jaw and a dimple in his chin. Hal's shoulders were broad and muscular. The only thing out of place was his scrunched position. His legs were too close together, as if someone were threatening to force them apart. There was a worrisome look on his brow. He was looking straight at her.

The man next to him must be Stan. Stan was not handsome. He was also in one of the children's chairs, but his obese body flowed every direction out of it, as if he were a large ball of Silly Putty slowly oozing toward the floor. His plump face was framed on the top by greasy strands of hair pulled across his bald pate, his eyes by a pair of thick black glasses held together by grimy white athletic tape at the bridge. At the bottom of his face was a second, and the start of a third, chin. His fat hands grasped a small toy that looked like some kind of action figure. Stan's eyes had been fixed on Hal, but now they followed the trajectory of Hal's gaze and found Carolyn.

"Hal, Stan. This is Carolyn," Jessica said. She took two steps back to make room.

"Hi, Hal. I'm Carolyn." Carolyn hadn't moved any closer.

"I know. You're Carolyn. My folks told me about you. Stan, go over there and see what those jerks are up to. Carolyn's my visitor and I want her to sit where you are."

Stan showed no sign of irritation at being dismissed. He struggled to get on his feet, dropped the Superman toy, and walked to the far corner of the room.

Carolyn moved the little chair to face Hal directly and tried to sit down with as much dignity as she could summon.

Hal extended his hand to shake Carolyn's. She noticed immediately the long beautiful fingers, the strong wrists and the veined back of his hand. Just as she grasped it with her own hand, she looked up and met Hal's eyes again: he was there, fully present, looking as if he were taking all of her in, but she wondered if that was really possible. A bit unnerved, both by his beauty and his gaze, Carolyn studied Ross and Mattie's only son.

Carolyn had assumed she would feel sorry for Hal when she met him, but that was not the case. In fact, she wondered if Hal might not be feeling sorry for her. Who was this woman showing up now? What did she want, and why should anyone give it to her? Carolyn imagined all sorts of thoughts in Hal's head; but in fact, nothing she imagined was really what Hal was thinking.

"It's nice to meet you, Hal."

"You know I'm not normal, right?"

"Excuse me?"

"You know I'm not normal. Mom and Dad told you, right? I'm a little slow."

Carolyn smiled. "What's wrong with slow?"

Hal smiled and thought: this girl knows nothing.

"I work in the supermarket."

"I know you do," Carolyn replied. "The D'Agostino's."

"I'm not always at the Center. I'm usually in my room at home, or at work."

"I have a job, too," Carolyn said. "I work part-time at a hospital. In New Jersey."

"I've been to New Jersey. My dad takes me to football games."

"I like football, too."

"Well, it's just me and my dad who go. You can watch it on TV."

Carolyn turned her head slightly and saw that Jessica was watching them.

"Your friend. Stan, right?"

Hal moved his shoulders as if he were uncomfortable. "Yes, that's Stan, over there. He's my best friend."

Carolyn didn't turn to look. Her eyes remained on Hal's graceful hands. She imagined them touching her breasts. Hal saw Carolyn staring at his hands, and he quickly put them behind his back.

"Do you have a lot of friends here, Hal?"

"No, just Stan. Well, some of the others are okay. But mostly it's me and Stan."

"Maybe we'll be friends, too."

She wants sex, Hal thought. Mom and Dad want her to want sex with me. No one ever asked him what he wanted.

Stan came over with two plastic cups half-filled with he told Carolyn was juice. At three we get juice, he explained, and he had asked for two so that he give one to Carolyn as well as to his friend Hal.

"Thank you, Stan," Carolyn said with a smile as she put the cup down without tasting it. Hal was glad Carolyn smiled, because if she wanted him to like her she was going to have to like Stan.

"I'm going back over there," Stan said excusing himself. "We're playing checkers, and I bet it's my turn again."

Hal and Carolyn talked, and when Hal decided Carolyn wasn't going to drink any of her juice, he asked her if he could have hers, too.

As Carolyn handed the cup to Hal, she saw that Jessica was watching her every move.

Back in his room, Hal put his hands behind his head and stared at the ceiling. He could hear his mother banging pots and pans in the kitchen, so he didn't have much time now before dinner, but he really needed to figure some things out. He knew what his parents were up to, because he remembered when his grandparents died and so he knew Mom and Dad would die one day, too.

There were already enough people in his life. There were all his friends at D'Ags and one of his doctors he really liked, too. He'd been to the Bronx Zoo in a group once. But most of all there was Stan. He and Stan could live together. Hal didn't know if when his parents died that meant he got to stay here or if he'd have to move out, but if he did get to stay there was plenty of room for him and Stan and their stuff. They could share his bedroom and use his parents' room for something else, maybe a place to put all their computer gear, once they got some. The idea made him turn on his side on the bed and imagine Stan here. Wonder if he snores, Hal thought. Once Stan fell asleep in a chair at the Center and Hal watched him drool onto his sweater and his nametag. If it had been anyone else, Hal would have thought it was gross. Hal turned onto his back. He didn't hear any noise from the kitchen, and he thought: it will be quiet like this when Mom and Dad are gone. Stan doesn't talk much, and even if Carolyn came to visit them sometimes she could just smile at him and Stan and no one would have to say anything to anyone.

Carolyn got out of the tub, wrapped a big towel around her, and went to lie down on the bed in the alcove of her studio apartment.

She unfolded the damp towel and let it fall on either side of her. She looked down at her breasts and beyond them to her stomach. She missed men, she knew that. It had never seemed fair to her.

Her right hand moved up and came to rest atop her right breast. She looked up at the ceiling and thought about her meeting with Hal. She knew what it was that attracted her to him, what had attracted her ever since she'd read the classified ad. Did she have to think about it just now? Maybe it was thinking that had gotten her into trouble before.

The other boy had been so cute. He was gangly and all arms and legs, like boys can be. The smile was everywhere, too, and his little laughs still sang like music to Carolyn sometimes, just before she fell asleep on the loneliest of her nights. They had been happy together, and then the others came and ruined it all.

Hal was not a boy, that was for sure. His handsome face, his strong hands, these were things that women want in men. But they were not what Carolyn really wanted. She imagined the little boy inside Hal, the boy that his incomplete mind kept there perpetually. Carolyn thought: I am forgetting he is grown, I can make him a child in my mind only because that is what he is in his own. Carolyn used both her hands to wrap herself in the towel again, and feeling sleepy after the warm bath, began to lull her self with the music of a little boy laughing in her mind over and over again.

Mattie, when she made the reservation for them, told the restaurant whom to look for. She left Hal at the table and rushed home, knowing that the maître d' would lead Carolyn to the right table when she arrived. She left her credit card number with the front so that the bill would be taken care of.

Hal was fidgeting with his napkin when Carolyn showed up.

"Hello, Hal."

Hal nodded and smiled. Carolyn looked nice, nicer than any of the ladies he'd seen at the D'Agostino's today.

"Hi, Carolyn. Great restaurant, huh?"

Carolyn looked around and smiled at Hal when she returned her head to look at him. "It's very nice."

"I haven't been here before. When we eat out, it's usually lunchtime."

"Oh? Where do you go?"

"There's a place with Mexican food my Dad and I like. The chips are really good. We never get a second bowl, though. Dad says no."

A waiter brought two menus.

"What do you feel like tonight, Hal?"

Hal scowled. "You're not taking me out, Carolyn. I'm taking you out. I'm the guy."

Carolyn nodded and closed her menu. "Yes, you're the man, Hal. Order for me. I would like that."

Hal had a little trouble reading the menu but then he found the word chicken. When the waiter returned he told him they'd like two of that.

"And to drink?"

"Water," Hal said.

"May I have a drink, Hal?"

Hal realized that Carolyn meant alcohol, because his parents called that "drink," too.

"My friend would like a *drink*."

Carolyn told the water she'd have a glass of white wine.

"That's a handsome jacket, Hal."

It was only the second time he had worn it. The first was at his grandmother's funeral, but he didn't tell Carolyn that. He wasn't sure how much he wanted to tell Carolyn about anything.

"Hal, how are we doing?"

"Doing?"

"Well, this is our second date, isn't it?"

Hal thought, I haven't ever asked her on a date. Mom and Dad have.

"I guess."

Carolyn put both her hands flat on the tablecloth.

"Do you like me?"

Hal panicked. He wasn't sure how to answer. If he said no, she might get mad. If he said yes, she might think I want to marry her or something. It was only then that Hal thought to answer truthfully.

"I don't know you, Carolyn."

Carolyn smiled. "That's right, Hal. We don't know each other. But everyone has first impressions."

"Carolyn?"

"Yes, Hal?"

"I'm going to the toilet."

"The men's room?"

"Yes, the men's room."

Carolyn watched as Hal got up from his chair and went in a zigzag path between tables as he looked for the restroom. One of the staff saw him drifting in the wrong direction and went to help.

Carolyn's white wine arrived. She took a sip and thought: children can be such work, as well as such pleasure.

In the men's room Hal sat on the toilet to think as long as he could. He really didn't want to go back to their table. Eventually they'll come to get me, like the time they did Stan at the Center when he was in the bathroom so long playing with his dick. What would he do if he went back? He was hungry and he wanted to eat, but he didn't know what to talk to Carolyn about. Maybe he could take his food home, like his mother did all the time at restaurants. He could eat it alone in his bedroom. That wouldn't be nice to Carolyn, he knew that, but it's what he felt like doing. He used his hand to wipe the beads of sweat off his forehead.

Carolyn drained her wine. As she ran a finger along the rim of her glass she thought about the situation she was facing, both with Hal and without Hal. She felt uneasy and began to get up, thinking she would go to the ladies' room and maybe run into Hal on the way. But instead she grabbed her cell phone and headed for the front of the restaurant. Her intention to say something to the maitre d' about Hal's disappearance changed into a resolve to walk outside the restaurant and make a call.

The number should have been familiar to her, but it took a moment to dial it.

The phone rang and he picked up. I knew it was you, the voice said. How did you know that? Carolyn cried. Because I know what is on your mind right now. I can't talk long, Carolyn said. Is anyone there with you? she asked. No. I'm alone. So I guess we can talk as long as we want. Sweet boy, Carolyn thought, here is the one who never wanted to abandon me. The memory of what his parents and police had done made Carolyn flash with anger. But that all evaporated as she spoke with the child who still meant everything to her.

CB

I won't move from the bed. I know my parents were upset with me all the way back from the restaurant. Mom asked me if I wanted anything to eat when I got home, but I knew not to bother Mom and Dad anymore. If that restaurant had brought the chicken faster I might have eaten it before I went to the bathroom and before that girl disappeared.

I screw up but I'm not totally bad. No one asked me if I wanted new friends, especially a female one. Staying in that bathroom was my way of letting everyone know how I feel, and now they do. Except for Carolyn, and who cares about her anyway.

I've still got my plan. When my parents die or move away Stan will come here and live with me. Then we can stop going to the Center because we'll both be here all the time. Gee I sure hope Stan knows how to cook because I sure don't. Can't have cookies all the time, that's what they taught us in school.

I hear you knocking on my door, Mom and Dad. You want to come in and see how I am. Well, you can't. Knock knock knock. Go ahead, it won't do you any good. You're not coming in here. I can be mad at you, too, you know. I can be mad at anyone I want, and tonight I'm mad at you. And that girl, whatshername. I wish Stan were here and we could be mad at everyone together.

MEG DAY

On What I Didn't Hear You Say

the first time you bilabial epiglottal
tuning forked against my ear, there were voiced gutturals all around.
they said if i transparencied a bird & you classifier inflected a fish,
then where would we retroflex gloss a nest? as if predispositioning
palatal feathers among the skinned wasn't mechanical aspect enough,
they said, i had to go & visual static a girl with scales.

when i bilabial
your plosives, you fric frica fricative alveolar coronal my laminal &
post-uvular-epiglottal. when i retroflex your dorsal, you labial-palatal
the voiced against my gutteral, never voiceless or nasal-stopped.
when i plosive plosive your epiglotto-pharyngical, we are bilabial &
sometimes labiodental.

oralize me. eyebrows up me. plosive plosive
until my wernicke's clench.

we graft each other linguistically.
reduplicate inheritance, combine our recessives into classifiers that
inflect. later, when consonants gloss, we will both become Beulah,
apocryphal, encoding predicates past our critical period. you are
fluent in me only in skipped generations. i can preserve you only if
learned outside of school.

they half-tongue us not to reproduce.
we are too queer & differently broken. our epidemic should stop here.
you must implant to fit in, they tell you. there is no implant for me. you
& i must not implant for moral reasons.

BRENNA CYR

Gracious Pain

Rolling on my side, I gasp as my shoulder collides with a pillow. Tender fingers pry my body away, aligning in the position of least resistance. Consciousness arisen, I feel the weight returning. A girlfriend who wishes to leave, a body that refuses to comply, and a family and their God that condemns. Heaviness upon my chest, I wish for a reprieve. For the shortest of breaks, only to relieve the absence of pain that everyone else seems to know so well. Thoughts echo through my mind as sirens in the night, overcoming anything else that might have been. Dear God, why?

Do you know pain? As the torrent takes your breath away, waves of disillusionment and despair rise, floating toward whatever small shred of hope you may have once held. Feeble fingers frozen as claws for days, I cannot recall strength. The knowledge of my insides churning in defense, failing in the sight of the powers that seek to destroy, falters my meditation. I cannot carry on!

Sometimes I think I know why I am in the midst of this. And it has more to do with combinations of internal genitalia than white blood cells mistakenly attacking everything inside. You see, when I was young, I had the audacity to watch Oprah. As an ignorant youth, I kneeled two feet in front of the TV with the volume as low as I could stand so I could watch in secrecy. Narratives of trauma and beauty alternating with the profane, I sat in wonder. My world was impossibly small! How could it be? So many people with thoughts I could never comprehend. Forging narratives of gender and sexuality that were forbidden to all those in the fold of the Most High, listened in somber silence. Dear God, was I one of them?

I listened as someone told me that they knew they defied normality when they realized they would rather be a man than be with a man. Although I was but a child and had no comprehensive understanding of what this could mean, the sentiment found a home in my heart. Forever being told what was expected of me as a woman, I didn't know I could choose another. To embody such a ghastly creature as described throughout Scripture would require the removal of my most possessive self. Yet, this is what I aimed for. These are the words I uttered to myself at night, knowing that one day I would have my savior (white horse, dark hair, broad shoulders) and my Savior (white horse, dark skin, long dead, and resurrected). My mother prayed in tongues for a man who would lead, while I wished for someone to listen: "Ashigidahogida ashigidahogada ashigadahoga ashigadahogada; may it be so."

I refused to believe that my fullest life could only merit a supporting role. But this I was taught. A husband would surely know better than I! Providing clarity where I brought only chaos, and direction where I brought false understandings. Resentment slowly building, I tried to envision myself welcoming the authority, but could not. Am I not strong? Can I not provide an arm to cover another instead of being covered? Ignoble desires aside, I attempted to force myself into an understanding of my existence that betrayed the structure of my being.

The tapes of gender laws played endlessly in my head: could I be myself in my skin? Of course, these were not things discussed with anyone other than myself. My father, mind swollen with misogyny, pushed my avidity for masculinity further with his constant commentary on the shortfalls of women. They are silly creatures, feebly wandering the earth in search of someone who can furnish their world with hope and stability. With appetites for shoes and expensive cappuccinos, they are to be only appeased when necessary, else they brought a man to ruin with their asinine covetousness.

Although women may be fatuous creatures, their acumen does surpass that of a queer. Such an individual, ever-increasing in moral indigence, has no place in this world. Betrayers of the natural order! If my father's utter disgust for the gays didn't enlighten me to their place in the world, knock-knock jokes comparing them to historical mass murderers and dictators eventually got the message across: gay is not okay. My mother and others who verbally promoted the firing of a gay teacher in our district and the constant barrage of contempt for him and those who dared to promote the ideals of free love in a culture of repression confirmed this.

While I was in high school, I felt most comfortable expressing myself in rather butch attire. Playing the role of the dyke without admitting my façade allowed for a certain grace; I was able to associate with the morally decrepit without actually being one of them. When people asked if I was a lesbian, I would throw my head back with laughter and exclaim with profundity, "NO!" But inside, I said, "YES!" While among my young Christian friends, we would discuss my image and the true nature of homosexuality. We declared love for sinners, but had no intention of welcoming the notion of this sin. It was even brought up that if I turned out to be a lesbian, they would keep me in their fold but work diligently toward my redemption. I shifted uncomfortably in my seat; nobody ever needed to know!

Among my battles with gender and the quest for love, I found myself engaging something new and wholly unwelcome. It started in my toes. A pain started to creep in, slow, but ardent. But unlike that residual pain from a propelled stubbing, it wouldn't go away. I was 16 years old and not terribly concerned about my immune system laying siege to my body. After a couple of months of walking timidly, I was finishing a routine doctor's appointment when the doctor asked me if there was anything else I would like to discuss. Eager to leave, I hurriedly shook my head no. My mother spoke up for me. "Her toes have been bothering her!" I rolled my eyes, annoyed she would try to keep me here longer. Three hours and many X-rays later, the doctor announced nothing appeared to be causing the pain that he could see. "However, I think it may be possible that you have rheumatoid arthritis." I laughed. Out loud. That would be funny! A high school junior has arthritis? Hilarious!

A couple of weeks later, my exasperated wailing woke up my sister in the middle of the night. I couldn't move; everything was frozen. But burning! With needles and knives digging into the flesh between my bones. I tried to get out of bed to get my mother, but couldn't make my legs move. With my hands curled into shapes unknown, I hurled myself onto the floor. Overdosing on ibuprofen wouldn't make this hurt go away.

Becoming a cripple changes you. It forces you to acknowledge your weaknesses and alter your identity. Independence is lost, and you are not longer able to move freely in the world as you have come to expect. Getting out of bed becomes a daunting task, requiring the gumption normally reserved for getting up after a nasty bike accident or exerting your last ounce of energy as you reach the top of a climbing wall. You notice as people react differently toward you. Before arthritis, I was bold. I could stand next to a boy my age and knock him over as lacrosse routinely demanded. I would stand tall next to my sister, proclaiming that if anyone did anything to hurt her, they would have me to answer to. She would look to me with pride, knowing that her little sister could stand up to whatever challenge arose. But this was no longer the case. When I laid on the floor in complete anguish, her eyes shone with terror. I, the otherwise emotionless sister, was loudly crying out in distress with reckless abandon. What could cause such a failure of strength?

Of course, with the introduction of overwhelming sensations of pain, I began to ask new questions. Why do I have this? Did God allow it? Is He able to end it? Will He? No, really, will He make this end? I scoured bookshelves for wisdom penned by ancient men, but they offered little comfort. Nobody knew why some suffered more than others. My affliction was a cruel trick of nature deemed permissible by the deity I professed love for. He was in complete control of the world (the Bible tells me so), which meant He was choosing to let me indulge in this agony. Perhaps I would learn something useful. Perhaps I had become too proud and needed to be taught humility. Or my sinful desires were rising up and needed to be put back into their place. I knew that if I devoted myself to Him, that He would take care of me. He gives and takes away, blessed be the name of the *Lord!*

Internal fearmongering usually lacks utility. Time went on, and I carried the belief that if I followed close behind my rabbi, that He would heal me. Faith, courage, and a fair dose of temperance would carry me through. He wouldn't let me stay like this, would He? College brought new challenges, including navigating a larger area without the use of my parent's car. Classes were frequently missed due to my inability to walk or bike, and papers were occasionally late as my swollen fingers and wrists regularly refused to cooperate with the institution of higher learning.

Although I spent much of my time learning about orientalism and conjugating verbs in Hindi, I also learned about how pain separates you from people. On nights when my incessant writhing was too much to handle, I would crawl downstairs as my roommates slept and wedge myself between furniture to hold myself in place. The more pain I felt, the more I wanted to move. The more I moved, the more pain I felt. And so, it was when I was stuck between a wall and a couch that I stopped asking questions of God. He clearly had left the vicinity; why should I pursue him? Numbness arose, and I fell asleep. If God didn't find me pure enough for a miracle, I had nothing left for Him.

Although a clear boundary had been created in my mind, separating myself from the divine, guilt followed me wherever I went. Hollow places inside my soul yearned to be reunited with The Most High, but apathy would swiftly follow. I wasn't able to reach the quality of perfection needed for Him to release me from my pain, so why should I try? And so, in a rare moment of courage, I started dating. A dashing transman named Ashley entered my world, and I felt my resolve grow. Why should I continue to deny myself the pleasures everyone else enjoyed?

I was hungry, and Ashley fed my longing. My whole life had been an exercise in waiting, and I was no longer willing to sit on the sidelines and watch as everyone else partook. He taught me how a simple touch could radiate through my entire being. Sitting across the lake from the capital building in Wisconsin, he kissed me in the darkness and made my world come alive. Craving closeness, I crawled deeper inside my real-life fantasy.

I told nobody. I knew what reception awaited me once I finally admitted my sin, and I was not terribly interested in experiencing the rejection that would surely follow. So I continued to sneak out in the night, seeking to fulfill the concupiscence that overwhelmed my senses. However, it wasn't long before Ashley realized our relationship was not to last, and ended it. Heartbroken, I stumbled inside my home, crying out as nobody listened. Nobody knew! Hiding in my own great shame, I faltered. I created misery from lies, and couldn't stand it any more. And so I came out.

I watched the eyes of those I loved as I recalled my disillusionment and off-putting tendencies. Their eyes would grow large with surprise and although most tried to conceal their disappointment, they were unsuccessful. Those that decided to speak freely against my behavior laid their hands on my shoulders and prayed. They prayed that these desires would be removed from my heart, as if they were a wart on my foot. My mother and sister led the charge, calling out to God daily to give Him my sexuality. I sat awkwardly nearby and wished they would tell me something different. I wished they would tell me that I am loved by God for who I am, instead of for what I am. I wanted them to hug me and tell me they couldn't wait to meet my future partner, instead of reminding me God hated my wickedness.

I already knew God hated my wickedness! How else could I explain the trauma that surged through my body every day? Nothing is the result of mere chance; everything happens for a reason. But what happens when there is no reason that could possibly justify a thing? The world is filled with hate, racism abounds, and I am stuck in a body that brings eternal misery. I believed God was in control, which meant He could absolve my pain. But He didn't. So He had a reason. And that reason must have stemmed from my sin.

And so, when I finally found a beautiful partner, bringing delight to my life and hope to my world, I couldn't rest in the joy of it all. Arthritis raged on, and despite her best attempts to assuage my fear that God hated our togetherness, I couldn't let go of the thought. Six months into the relationship, we found ourselves at a crossroads. My internalized homophobia was straining us in a way that was causing her to reconsider. And so, in a moment of pure desperation, I called my sister for comfort. I spoke to her of my pain: the physical and the relational. I knew they were connected but didn't want to make the admission. She, however, brought it up. "Brenna, don't you think your arthritis might get better if you stopped deciding to be gay?"

Hence I live in constant pain, and a part of me will always believe that it is caused by a God who cares not for my happiness, but for the genitalia of my partners. Such a strange concept to believe, but it is written on my heart and cannot be erased. Rationality often calls and demands a reconsideration, but I often accept the idea that my deviant sexuality is at the root of all this. And it doesn't end at physical pain; rheumatoid arthritis has more in store for me. If it isn't the decades of life to be chopped off, the clots building in my lungs, or the rampant infections that take over my dilapidated immune system, I know my independent existence is doomed.

My queer brothers, sisters, and siblings of other sorts are the only people who cause me to reassess my conception of pain. Since coming out, I have witnessed the beauty of souls divine, living out their callings with an ardent love that could only be described as glorious. Such creatures of power! Standing up to those who would tear them down, I marvel at their intertwined strength. I wish to be as proud as them, but I hesitate. They are worthy of love, but queer. Does the latter diminish the former?

Maybe if God loves them (as He should), He loves me. And maybe, if I actually believe this, I can stop blaming myself for my disease and find love again.

STEPHANIE HEIT & PETRA KUPPERS

Almost Solstice

We haul our blanket to keep us
insulated from shifting sand and norwesterly wind.
Expanse of blue all possibility spread.
Lookout where she took pictures of me saying
I love you before
every shot.

Bushes. Sand. Beach.
I win it, a foot at a time, heat beneath my arc,
eyes down. I still do not trust the ease of my foot
cane bites deep into the dune.

The road we drove down angling for the closer
access site. Over the crest, into the soft beach,
white sand radiates against my sole on the edge
of pain.

She has walked ahead spread the blanket wide nest on a near
vanished beach.

Her cane sinks I point out poison ivy.
What I really want to say

kissing as if we were ready for water
for depths she enters me as I dig my heels into sand eyes closed
to inner landscape she carves with fingers tongue I remember
we aren't alone glance down the beach both directions relax give

We sink down, exhausted, dance.

The surf pulls my calves forward,
weak ankle folds into itself, a shell hiding.

Spiral down till she touches my back
I waltz surf sand unstable.
Her chest sanctuary.

To wade into water too cold.
We dance along the shore. Lean our bodies.
I rest my head on her chest. Raise my arms above me
surprised to catch her head.
I lose track of eyes open or closed.
Short fast runs. As if we could beat the tide.

I recline. she. I. heave forward feet out back brace
arc that shoots electric limbs. starfish self
radiates in a circle we run five steps past
each other feet sink splay twist pain stars pain
lines desire to pull, again, turn into
momentum of my path influence her bone align.

I divide the day into scenes.
parking lot. blanket on beach. 5 minute dance. swim
attempt.

She bolts toward me. Laugher. I twirl again, my knee buckles.
She runs. I lumber into the surf. Cold
shoots up and sprays. She arrives.
We dodge. Arrested against my back.
Her arms around me my head back throat
exposed I sink spiral tensions in my legs
back accordion collapse like the space between vertebrae
I hear my blood knock in my skull.

Her knees thump onto the blanket.
Hair in my face. Curtain. The softness

of the inside of her lips, an invitation of warmth
amid the oxygen. Lake water pearls our shins. I stroke
upward reach for the enveloping brace, lean.
We assemble together eyes upward and out
hands rove cradle sore limbs.

Our mouths dance more than five minutes.
Hum of our bodies reach and arch for each other and the sun.
Her hand my suit moves over to expose
our starfish selves conceal
what fine meats we dine a perfect picnic.

Brace of sand and water brace of dune and flesh

LARRY CONNOLLY

The Worst Husband You Can Imagine

Though awestruck with personal essays about disability—the adaptation and triumph, the courage, the discipline, the inspiring wisdom—I leave the pages wretched, face to face with an unknowable language, since much of everyday I'm overwhelmed by the mess disability leaves, and how much work it is to clean up.

For the sake of color and charm, let me illustrate.

It's Sunday in the park and, given the choice between a brief jaunt with his cane or unlimited strolling in his wheelchair, we agree it's the weather for wheels! I soon discover there's nothing but incline; it's topographically impossible, but every fucking inch of this hellish path around the lake is uphill. More irritating are all the overly vivacious joggers giving us a thumbs-up, eyes shimmering with warmth of heart because they've welcomed the differently-abled and hope we're thrilled to have lake access via circumnavigation of this pitted, pitched path. My screaming mind: THAT'S FINE IF YOU CAN AFFORD A FUCKING POWER CHAIR TORQUED INTO OFF-ROAD MODE, BUT NOT SO HOT IF YOU DO-IT-YOURSELF OR ARE BEING PUSHED—that would be by me—VERTICALLY IN EVERY DIRECTION.

He's never out of discomfort, but some days the pain index shoots through the roof. This is one of those days. We visit the doctor, again, and a hospital procedure is scheduled, IN PREPARATION FOR WHICH he is to take several different enemetics AND is required to drink ten ounces of water every hour on the hour for 12 hours.

Keep that plate spinning. Since so much is out of our control, I hold dear the belief we should control what we can—to which end I'm beside myself with glee when I find a dozen 10 oz. bottles of spring water! Furthermore, I computer-label each with big, black drinking times—9 a.m., 10 a.m., 11 a.m.—you catch the plot. When he returns from work that day, after repeatedly assuring me on the phone that he's being diligent with his water, he drops his unexpectedly bulky bag on the chair—I promptly riffle through, pulling out 1 p.m. and 4 p.m., unopened! I nearly pass out from rage.

I'm tight-lipped the remainder of the day and into the evening. I retire early to avoid him; I do not trust the things on the tip of my tongue. For his part, he makes several timid overtures, but I meet each of them stonily.

At some point in the middle of the night, I wake up to visit the bathroom. On my way there I see him sprawled in the hall. Sleep has nudged my fury aside and I ask if he's all right. When he mumbles noncommittally—refusing to answer, it seems to me—I step over him and continue into the bathroom. It's fitting to be getting a taste of my own; I was in a snit dishing out the silence, so he is responding in kind. Additionally, I have noted to myself that whenever I'm angry with him, he becomes remarkably tenuous, tending to trip and fall a bit more—as well as wax moronic. After bathroom business, I make my way back, re-stepping over him, and return to bed.

Awaking the next morning, the hospital procedure heavy on my mind, I discover him beside me, snoring. I later discover the cat had revived him by licking his butt.

He is taking a taxi home from work. The route necessarily includes one of the three steepest hills in the city. Eying the meter, but only halfway up the hill, he realizes he has insufficient funds for this trip, and, waving his cane, informs the driver of such, though assuring him he'll be able to procure the remainder at home. The driver slams the car to a stop, telling him to get out there, and then speeds off. He crawls—that's right, on all fours—up the hill. Eventually, he reaches home.

I suggest we get him a cell phone. He says he gets along fine without one.

I imagine rolling him down that hill.

We are out for dessert with friends. There is much frivolity, both in the café and in the parking lot. As I sit in the car and turn the key, I am so busy laughing—and being subtly irritated that he couldn't keep up with our jolly trot down the rickety steps and over the uneven half-acre of pavement—that I forget he's still trying to get himself in the car. I forget this as I take off. Everyone is screaming. I can't figure out why they're upset. Then I realize I've been dragging him and, then, I'm even angrier he's so slow to get in.

We're visiting the Arizona Desert Museum. It's many miles outside of town. The morning's paper said it's the hottest day of the year: BLISTERING, EVEN FOR TUCSON! At the front gate we're given a choice in wheelchairs: standard hospital-issue or streamlined, highly flexible, electric carts. He selects the manual version. My dark thoughts cannot be shared.

We're in the middle of the desert natural habitat with no shade, no rest area, no handy café, and he wants to wheel himself. It's not really that kind of chair under the best of circumstances and you may rightly suspect these are not those. The path is said to be asphalt. We quickly discover it's in poor repair and most often just loose ground.

Of course, his shoulder blows out after two minutes of trying to wheel the dinosaur uphill and through gravel/sand. I'm putting on a good face, twittering that the desert is lovely, if a trifle warm, and keep offering to push, which he will have none of because people will think he's disabled. My head explodes. After another five minutes he can't move at all and the heat is blistering and, no matter how much he shakes the chair or tries to force the wheels, it remains immobile.

So I declare martial law, take over and start pushing the chair through the habitat, pointing out all the factoid placards. He asks every ten seconds if this isn't too hard on me, what with the heaviness of the chair, the dune-like nature of the path and the sweltering heat. I keep it chipper, despite the fact that we are becoming increasingly exhausted and desperate.

The Museum signage is frequent and informative, indicating the various wildlife we are spotting. Soon we know all their names. We know how they operate in packs. We know they're carnivorous. We know how they hunt. We know they tend to focus on the weakest member/s of any possible prey, the ones who look like they're having trouble getting by. I grow considerably less chipper when I notice the wildlife enacting the described predatory behavior, approaching us more and more closely with manifest relish and appetite.

They know, hands down, they've got him. But they may grab us both if I don't hightail it out of there. To our mutual surprise, and in spite of hefty temptation, I muster the strength of Samson and begin a frenzied push back to the entrance gate.

He wonders why I'm rushing so quickly past all the animals, am I not enjoying myself?

I lose connection with reality.

Home is a lovely thing. It can also be an easy and controlled thing except for the fact that he blithely wanders through my pristine room leaving his havoc. I employ several tactics to remedy this.

I smile warmly and restore with no real thought of it.

I smile warmly and restore while thinking rather a lot about it.

I smile thinly and restore while resenting and tacitly rehearsing saucy remarks.

I grab his shit and throw it in a corner.

As I snap clothes, scrape dirty dishes, and slam drawers, I tell him it would be a helluva lot easier on me if he wouldn't throw his clothes on the floor or leave his crap wherever he happened to be.

Finally, he goes too far, and there I am standing in the kitchen doorway, in an apron, brandishing a rolling pin and screaming, YOU LEFT YOUR GODDAMN WHEELCHAIR IN THE MIDDLE OF THE LIVING ROOM.

Silence covers the earth. We know a line has been crossed.

It doesn't really matter what straw broke this back, or how exactly we got to this place on this day, but we look into one another's eyes, catch the tail end of whatever soul dares to remain, and begin to laugh. And laugh. And Laugh.

We can smell our parents in the room, and their parents and, maybe, everyone's parents. And everyone's life.

It's a strange place we've got to. It's a hard place with thorns. But it's our place. Owned. Cherished. Guarded.

RAYMOND LUCZAK

My First Kill

1.

Up close, he was a walking mirage.
I thirsted for that golden-haired man
with his seemingly sculpted pectorals,
shimmering with dribbles of sweat
snaking among the grasses of fur.
I was a quaking mass of hormones
the summer I went to camp.

He was the first god I'd ever witnessed.
It was as if he'd stepped out of the heavens,
choosing to spend seven weeks
among us heathens who needed lessons
on how to speak, how to adapt
wheelchairs and crutches in a world
far more crooked than us.

Even at fifteen, I knew there was no way
I could pay my just respects to his beauty,
which he'd perfected in the exotic Florida.
Flashes of him erupted in my underwear,
always unbidden late at night.
I never knew such gods could exist *in person*,
and how effortlessly smiles could shatter.

Those nights of ache were so pungent
that I could still see myself lying in wait
in my top bunk in that stuffy cabin,

fidgeting with the patchy stubble
creeping like vines all over chin and throat.
My Adam's apple was now a gnarl
on the trunk of my sapling body.

2.

She taught me how to pronounce "comfortable."
I always stumbled, never knowing what to do
with that *fort* syllable. How much of an emphasis?
No, the trick was to skip that syllable altogether
so I practiced saying "*comf*-tible" all summer
until I no longer tripped. "Yes, I'm *comf*-tible.
Aren't you feeling *comf*-tible?" "Yes, I am."

Of course, speech lessons were nothing new,
but her photocopies of sign illustrations
were pornographic, exquisitely rendered
far more dirty than my own imagination
where I'd dreamed of signing even though
I didn't know the language. There,
right in front of my own speech therapist
who had studied signs, were all those sheets
photocopied and punch-holed into a binder.
She opened to a page and showed me
an artist's rendering of a certain sign,
explicitly so, and with little left to imagination,
usually with arrows thrusting in repetition.
I never knew that was how one should say
"speech" and "love" and "camp" like that.
I'd never seen so much foreplay in my life.
Even though they always wore turtlenecks,
they seemed to have no clothes on!

Speech suddenly seemed quaint, old-fashioned.
There was simply no denying the lust inherent

in my hands: I couldn't wait to stroke the contours
of air and space in a thrust of motion.
My hands moaning became louder than firecrackers
exploding in front of my house on Oak Street.
I was shocked that no one reported my disturbances
to the police who'd long monitored my speech,
noting in their records all my ups and downs,
but none bigger than the felony I'd committed
for the sake of my freedom of speech.
I'd become a sign-crazed teenager now obsessed
with the orgasm of achieving signing perfection.

3.

Years before an emotionally disturbed boy
pushed me into the deep end of a swimming pool.
My teacher, eight months pregnant, dove in
after me. I didn't know how to paddle,
chlorine filled my senses, my eyes burned,
found myself clinging to the round basketball
of my teacher paddling her feet.
I don't remember anything after that,
but the chlorine of fear had never stopped lingering.

But that summer in Bay Cliff's brand-new pool
my instructor taught me how to overcome my fear.
I stared at the way lights above bobbed below.
The water never stopped moving. I could see through
to his feet, the dark hairs on his legs undulating,
the looseness of his swim trunks waving along
with his patient hands going, "You can do this."

Once out of the pool, though,
I loved the way he flip-flopped his feet
in sandals, as if nothing would ever faze him.
He always grinned at me through his glasses
as if I could read what he was thinking.

He was a solid mass with huge nipples.
He thought nothing of being shirtless
as he guided me, an uncoordinated dolphin
with arms and legs all hopeless fins,
away from the shallow end of the world.
I loved his smile when his hair dripped flat
against his forehead in the split second before
he slid his bangs back. His broad shoulders shone.
I knew he could rescue me, but never in the way
I needed to be saved. He'd never redeem me
if he knew how I secretly longed for him.

He was the one who explained what a faggot was.
He stayed in the Upper Peninsula every summer,
but otherwise he was studying in San Francisco.
He took me aside as his confidante, telling me
how overrun with fags his university was.
He didn't like the city of San Francisco at all
but he needed to earn his degree first.
I was still in awe. He'd been to the Pacific Ocean!
Even pronouncing "California" sounded luxurious.
I couldn't believe that he wanted to be my friend.

Late at night, as the fireflies lured me away
from waving off mosquitoes back to my bunk bed, I knew
no matter how many signs I'd taught him,
he himself would never teach me how to navigate
the choppy waves of desire. Mornings
the god from Florida smiled at me, and I drowned.
I was an unsalvageable wreck with concrete fins.

4.

As the summer wore on, I became less afraid.
It was as if shadows had been brushed away
from the bangs of my hair. I could bask in the sun!

My hands became dandelion whiskers spreading
the seeds of sign among each hearing person
I met. I spoke always with my signs,
not knowing then it was linguistically incorrect,
but never failing to teach a sign whenever I could.
My arms were full of crisp winds that climbed up
the cliffs from the north off Lake Superior
until I felt like an eagle learning to master
the art of staying cool in flight. Watch my wings!

The director of speech therapy at Bay Cliff stood
in front of me. "You shouldn't be signing
so much," she said. "You should focus
more on your speech." She placed her hands
on mine, trying to hush the obscenity of
signs spewing out in front of her face,
but I stopped speaking. "Why aren't you talking?"
I looked down on her hands. "Oh." She let go.
"I'm not goina stop signing—"
When she put her hands on my arms again, I turned
mute. My eyes turned into spears poised to strike.
She dropped her hands and sighed.
With my first kill, I didn't know I'd become a lion,
finally *comf*-tible with the roar of my hands.

Savages

One day when even we deaf people can hear
due to the miracle of genetic reengineering,
you, like everyone else, will celebrate.
Joy: oh, what unimaginable joy!

We will have no need for sign language.
We will grasp the full brilliance of music
long denied us after centuries.
We will be able to carry conversations with
anyone without the aid of interpreters.
Each day heathen miracles will never cease.
Even Beethoven would've wept at the sight of us!

But there in the darkest of our dreams
we deaf people will find ourselves
pondering the spaces right in front of us.
Did we just see the pale ghosts
of what we could've been, never been?
Our voices never feeling quite right,
we will walk forever wounded,
searching for our phantom hands
never quite there but never quiet.

In time you hearing people, too,
will long for us savages,
communicating in grunts and gestures,
if only to remind you that you are God.
It is in your nature to seek imperfections,
rout them out. After all,
you must have something to do.

LYDIA BROWN

How Not to Plan Disability Conferences
(or, How to Be an Ableist Asswipe While Planning a Disability Conference)

1. Form a planning committee without any actually disabled people on it. You're parents/researchers/professors/professionals. You know what you're doing, and you can do it without letting those pesky little personal biases get in the way.

2. Alternatively, form a planning committee with your one token disabled person, so you can honestly say that, well, there was a person with a disability in the room. You have to remember all those overly-sensitive people with disabilities who'll start hyperventilating about "inclusion" if you don't do the politically correct thing. Bonus points if you get a token disabled person who already believes you are the Experts God Put On Earth for disability.

3. Produce an initial list of speakers/presenters without any actually disabled people on it. Don't worry, you already know who all of the experts are on the conference themes/topics/strands. It just so happens that none of them are disabled. But hey, it's the loving (non-disabled) family members, the dedicated (non-disabled) researchers and professionals, the prominent (non-disabled) professors who've done so much work for so many years to improve the lives of people with disabilities. They should be grateful you care so much.

4. Ignore the list of disabled people with relevant expertise on the conference's themes/topics/strands that the token disabled person provides. You don't know most of those people, and even if the token disabled person does, they must not be very important or accomplished because you would have heard of them if they really were. Besides, you've already pretty much decided who the speakers will be. You just

have to make the token disabled person feel like someone listened to their opinion before you proceed.

5. Insist that none of the disabled people suggested should be presenters because "They're not like my child/client/student!" (otherwise known as "They're high-functioning!") After all, if someone is capable of presenting at a conference, they must obviously have very mild disabilities—who knows, maybe they're even so close to "normal" no one would ever consider them really disabled.

6. Make sure you mention the one or two disabled people on the list who you actually know. Discredit their qualifications to speak on the conference themes/topics/strands.

7. Relegate disabled speakers to the "inspirational personal story" presentation. You should ignore any of their interest or ability to speak about public policy, best practices, recent research developments, advocacy strategies, theory, etc.

8. You can also consider having disabled people co-present alongside non-disabled experts. You know, to provide a personal anecdote as a way of legitimizing the non-disabled main presenter's expertise.

9. Constantly remind everyone, especially the token disabled person, that you have a very limited budget, and can't afford to bring in any speakers from outside the local area where the conference is happening. Then insist on bringing in one of the non-disabled presenters who lives so many states away it's definitely a long-distance trip.

10. Dismiss one of the disabled speaker suggestions because you had to pay them a lot of money the last time you asked them to speak. Obviously any other disabled person asking for money is clearly asking for an unreasonable and impossible amount. Besides, it's not like they need that much money. Don't they have families to mooch off of and SSDI to collect or something?

11. Create a list of target audiences for your conference that doesn't even include people with disabilities as a target audience. Reluctantly

add them in later under "families." Some of those more high-functioning people with disabilities might show up. And of course, some families will have to bring their lower-functioning relatives with them, but it's not like they'd be listening or anything.

12. Remember to keep telling your token disabled person that they are very high-functioning and don't know what it's like to have severe disabilities. Emphasize this especially whenever the token disabled person tries to get the rest of the committee to bring in actually disabled speakers. Don't forget—anyone the token disabled person suggests must also be very high-functioning if they could theoretically present at a conference.

13. Repeatedly tell the token disabled person that they're not listening to what anyone else is saying. It doesn't matter that they've barely been given any time to speak and have mostly been ignored. The fact that they keep harping about more speakers with disabilities (eye roll) is just more evidence that They're. Not. Listening. To. You.

14. If you have to include disabled speakers/presenters, make sure your token disabled person at least gets the comfort of a consolation prize. (See #7 and #8.) Don't worry. It's for the best.

15. If you post information about your conference online, make sure to list only the names of the non-disabled main presenters for any presentation where you have so kindly thought to include one or more disabled speakers to provide their "personal perspective" as a self-narrating zoo exhibit for you. This makes total sense, of course, since the disabled speakers aren't presenting the main ideas or concepts or research. They're just there to illustrate your fantastic non-disabled expert's points.

16. Remember. You're being perfectly reasonable. Any possible complaints are unfounded accusations riddled with personal bias, irrational thinking, and emotionally volatile lack of perspective. You have done everything you possibly could. At this point, if you have to just go ahead and make your final decisions without the token disabled

person on board with it, you just have to do it. In the end, they're just a token. It's not like they're important or anything, and it's definitely not like their opinion would actually change the outcome anyway.

DONNA WILLIAMS

How Much Can You Hear?

How much can you hear?
As much as that?
The patter of rain?
A purring cat?
A plane overhead?
A backfiring car?
You can hear all that
From so far?
I had no idea
Your ears were so efficient
But your concentration
Must be so deficient
Every little noise
Plink, purr, puff
Really must annoy
Sniffle, sneeze, cough
How do you stay sane?
How do you sleep at all?
Do you stuff your ears?
Glue egg-boxes to the wall?
Oh, really . . .
This is normal to you?
You've never known any different?
Well, that's an interesting view
So, all these noises
Don't bother you at all?
I never thought of it that way
I thought you'd deplore
All the constant interruptions,

Distractions, commotions,
But you're used to it?
What a notion!
You're so brave
I simply can't imagine
What it must be like
To be hearing!

What Is the Worth of My Life?

In the last few years, the U.K. has been undergoing austerity and cuts, and deaf and disabled people have been hit hard. Iain Duncan Smith (IDS) is Secretary of State for the Department of Work and Pensions (DWP), which administers benefits and welfare. They have been rolling out a much-derided welfare reform program, with changes in benefits and compulsory assessments for disabled claimants. The assessments have been heavily criticized for being too basic, inappropriate for those with mental health issues, and too tough, with more than half of the DWP's decisions overturned on appeals; and the system is beset with delays and controversy. Tabloids such as the *Daily Mail* (which its critics call the *Daily Heil*) take great joy in shaming benefit cheats even though they represent a tiny fraction of those who rely on the system and have been badly let down as of late—while banks receive bailout after bailout.

What is the worth of my life?
How should this be defined?
By the labor of my body
or the labor of my mind?

Should it be by my burden,
my cost to the welfare state?
Should I tally up my expenses
and see if the figures equate?

The cost of midwives at my birth,
who freed my strangling cord;
my very first operation,
my care in the neonatal ward.

Or the cost of my second operation,
when I was seven to save my sight.

Breaking the stitches on my eyeball
must have affected the price.

Or the surgeries on my foot;
wasted money, I'm sorry to say.
Stubborn body piling on the expenses,
since I'll claim Motability someday.

Let's not forget audiology,
I can't imagine the bill so far.
Suffice to say, these aids alone
could buy me a nice new car.

The financial product of my labors
fails the test of the balance sheet
unless I become a rich poet (!);
my costs I can't begin to meet.

So how do I define my worth?
I judge it by the worth of my days.
I've seen India, America, Nepal;
I'm a carer with an Ethics M.A.

Poetry has shown me the world,
and worlds beside my own;
helped me see through the eyes of others,
and understand that I am not alone.

So my message to IDS
and to the *Daily Heil* . . .
Judge us not by what it costs to sustain us,
but how we make our lives worthwhile.

No Longer an Impossible Dream

I want to be proposed to:
I want to be swept away
like in those YouTube videos.
There doesn't have to be a DJ
or a marching band
and they don't necessarily
have to learn to dance
so long as there's signs,
big bits of paper or a BSL song
or creative use of a Jumbotron,
but whatever they do,
I want to be impressed
and be overwhelmed with love
as I tearfully say yes.
My ring would be silver with Gallifreyan script,
or notated signs,
or inspired by *Thrones*,
or *Discworld*-designed;
no need for stones.
Well, maybe something blue,
a lazuli or two,
and it would be
a heart-melting gift.
I would wear a suit
or a shirt and boards;
I'd like to do it on a beach,
preferably abroad,
but nothing so soppy
as an arch;

especially not wrapped with roses
that would just be too much.
Simple vows, nothing gushy,
we'll have the poems for
getting mushy,
and the whole thing would be
a bilingual treat.
There'd be palm trees and a fresh breeze,
white sands and turquoise seas,
with just a few friends
and her and me.

KATHARINA LOVE

Learning to Fall in Love

In the autumn of 2012 I was having problems concentrating, and my body felt wired and exhausted both at the same time. It felt like a good time to visit my very thorough doctor, who put me through a series of extensive tests. He thought I might have Chronic Fatigue Syndrome; however, all tests came back negative. It was then I decided to speak about the elephant in the room, the one waving at me in her pink tulle tutu. Yes, *that* elephant. "Yoo-hoo, Katharina," she called to me. "Time to tell the good doctor what you are finally brave enough to explore: your facial differences."

When I was a small child, my grandmother took me to see *The Elephant Man*, a movie about an Englishman with severe deformities who was exhibited as a human curiosity in the late 1800s. The depiction of John Merrick, and particularly his face, shocked me. But not for the reason it shocked others. In my case, I recognized John Merrick. *I* was him in the guise of a six-year old Jewish girl living in the Montreal suburb of Ville St. Laurent.

Children in my grade one class had begun to torment me by making fun of how I spoke, how I looked, and how I moved. I didn't get it. Why were they treating me this way? Didn't they know who I was? That I was smart and funny and . . . And why did my mother want me to be like "them"? What was wrong with me? Now I had the answer. People saw me as they saw John Merrick. An oddity. A freak. Something less than human.

The realization was too much. I had to run away. And I did. I ran from the movie. I ran from my feelings. I kept running for 50 years until that moment at my doctor's office. He was kind. He was gentle. I trusted him. It was time. So I told him of my anxiety, sadness, self-hatred, otherness, and isolation that my looking different had engendered in me.

He sent me to a neurologist, who sent me to a geneticist. The conclusion? I was diagnosed with Möbius Syndrome, an extremely rare congenital neurological disorder characterized by facial paralysis and the inability to move the eyes from side to side. I was considered one of the "lucky" ones. I could smile, at least with my lips closed, and I had 20/20 vision, even if I could not see peripherally. After I did some research, I found that Möbius is thought to be an immune system disorder, hence my Chronic Fatigue-like symptoms.

While I did not know I had Möbius Syndrome growing up among the beautiful and the privileged in my wealthy enclave, I did know that I did not look "normal" by their high standards. That alone was enough to make me feel different. The writer Andrew Solomon in his book *Far From the Tree* writes about wealthy families who have a child who is different from the norm. Solomon originally thought that money would help these children have an easier life, and in many ways it did (better doctors, private schools), but what he found after interviewing these affluent parents and their children was the pressure to be and look perfect made life very painful for these "different" children in their "strive for excellence at all cost" families. This described my own experiences perfectly. Instead of being empathic or at least honest to describe my differences, my mother just told me that I was "bad." What constituted the "bad" was unclear, but not looking perfect played a big factor. A predilection for reading and music did not endear me as well to my extroverted tone-deaf mother.

Add to that mix a slight speech impediment and a tendency, despite the impediment, always to speak my version of the truth did not help matters. I remember one occasion when once again my mother was yelling at me for some real or imagined transgression. I looked directly into her eyes and said, "Good mothers do not yell."

She replied, "What do you know? You are four years old!"

I knew instinctively that nurturing was not part of mother's equation. I had hopes that school would be better, but the children at my school just continued the verbal abuse I was experiencing at home. My classmates called me names and laughed at my face. I had no friends and ate my lunch in the girls bathroom stall. For years after

I graduated from high school, whenever I walked down the street and heard someone laugh, I felt instinctively they were laughing at me.

The summer before I began university, it occurred to me that my troubles would diminish if I could somehow become beautiful. Then people might stop hating me for having committed the cardinal sin of being born different. Then perhaps I might become deserving of love.

That was certainly the message I had received from my social climbing parents. Fitting in and conforming were their way of life, something they both tried desperately to impose on their misfit daughter. I was raised not to become a Doctor or a Lawyer, but to become someone's wife, and to get that title of Mrs. and that final rose, I had to become beautiful.

For their sake as well as mine, I tried. I had rhinoplasty and a breast reduction. I poured toxic chemicals on my hair turning my naturally brown jewfro locks into long blond hair that even Farrah Fawcett would envy. And it worked. Instead of being an object of their derision, I became an object of their admiration. Women told me how much they loved my hair. Men asked me out on dates. The bouquets appeared and the Cristal champagne flowed, and my plan for the beautification of Katharina Angelina was complete. The ugly duckling was transformed into a swan. My work was done.

Except that it wasn't. I was hiding another secret, one that made me feel on the inside as different as I had looked before on the outside. I liked women. But what could I do with those feelings? All I wanted was to be accepted. Just once. So, having moved to Toronto for graduate school, I dated all the single Jewish boys in the city and was left each time feeling bored and disillusioned. Then karma called and his name was Bob, my future husband.

I had stopped using birth control when the idea of a child began to take hold. My child. Someone to call my own. Someone to frolic in the fields with, a little helper for choreographing Mother/Daughter Bob Fosse dance numbers. I became pregnant in July of 1991 and walked down the aisle in October of that same year praying, as I walked down that long red-carpeted aisle, that God would forgive me for betraying my soul's desire.

When my daughter was born, I made the decision shortly after to become healthy and own my attraction to women. I divorced my husband and began seeing a psychotherapist. After much hard work, I found that being in a relationship where I was not respected no longer felt sexy. Healthy attachments were assuming paramount importance. I now required my "person" to show up, be responsive and attuned. Oh yes, and one more thing: to really want to be with me—so that we can both present and vulnerable to and for each other.

A few months ago I watched the news show *20/20*. This particular episode featured young adults with facial anomalies who had the opportunity to have a renowned plastic surgeon repair their flaws pro bono. I was particularly taken with one young woman whose eyes and nose were unusually formed. I thought she looked lovely and compelling—much more interesting to look at than the classic cookie-cutter version of beauty. Those feelings of appreciation of her unique beauty were for her though, and her alone. All I had ever wanted was to have a great big toothy grin so I wouldn't have had to witness that fleeting look that passed over most people's eyes when they first met me. I abhorred that look. It both singled me out and dismissed me. That look made me try even harder to charm and be witty so that everyone could see that I was not "special." But trying even harder left me feeling depleted and desperate.

I came to realize that only through surrender and acceptance would I find the love I so craved, the love I had been searching for all my life. And so I surrendered—

My craving to be loved by my mother.

My desire to be saved.

My wish to be beautiful.

And, ever so slowly, I relaxed into my body and finally fell in love with my crooked little self.

JAX JACKI BROWN

Intersections

I get turned on by intersections—
it's not the flashing lights or
the little green and red men
the swish of fast cars,
or the rhythmic beep, beep, beep,
commanding me to cross.

No, it's right under your feet.
You miss it, walk all over it,
oblivious to its eroticism.
It does nothing for bodies like yours
but mine . . . ?
Ooooh
it sends vibrations all over me,
up and down my spine.

It's for the blind they say, that's the official line;
the little bumps, telling innocently of an intersection, a curb.
But us wheelchair-using crips
know its erotic underside,
it's a federally-funded public vibrator,
a DIY sex toy just begging for use.

It takes all my self-control not to casually move
my chair back and forth beside you
rolling myself ever so slowly over . . .
and over . . .
those little round raised circles,
as we wait like good upstanding citizens for the lights to change.

I Want to Go Down

I want to go down
filled with anticipation at seeing you spread before me
just begging me to take you
and right now

Slide myself over you
learn your curves
down to those places
where
I lose myself in the moment
and just let go

You make me forget myself
and remember at the same time
when we do this together
we are always on display
for I am marked out as different
and tonight we will give them a show

I want to ride you
fast
in this dusk light
where everyone can see
as they drive by in their cars
home from work

I want to scream
to squeal like a 16 year old
with the rush and thrill

of the first time I realized I could do this
and it felt so right

You make me breathless and reckless
and I don't care that they are watching
the headlights catching my wheels
as I roll over you
like an expert

They say big is beautiful
and they are so right
you
big
beautiful . . .

Hill

But first you make me work for you
you've made me climb you
you've made me
come here
again
and sweat

Made my arm muscles
sore
till I am all ache
for you
in this sunset light

I want to press my ties into your tarmac
to know the cracks in your concrete
ride your bumps
which make my body vibrate
just right
know your bends

you make my hands so fucking dirty from touching my tires to
    your
streets

I wanna make people look
and step aside
hurriedly with a gasp
as I go down
you
you
Dirty
Big
Hill
like a pro
right to your
bottom
as everyone watching wishes they had the body and equipment
    to enjoy you like I do

Unbend You Straight

She places her hands on me
Without asking and pulls at this bent body,
These legs the site of her expertise.
She has studied my affliction well.
She knows these bodies
And how to fix me.

"Be strong," she says,
"You are a brave child,
Show me how brave you can be."
Breath held.
Teeth clenched.
She begins her work on me.
I am not this body, she cannot find me.

ᛒ

She lays beside me
Fingers tracing my bends and curves
"I love the way you move, your difference, uniqueness, you
    intrigue me"
White teeth showing in the candle light
I fall
"It's ok" she says
"Relax, you're beautiful"

ᛒ

"You don't cry like the others,"
She says,
"Good girl,
We'll make you normal,
Make you walk."
Her accent, this 5 yr old cannot place, is thick, this pain thicker.
I breathe.
She teaches me how to draw
A thin cord away from my body
Holding it like a balloon,
Like a kite out the window
Where my eyes find the sky.
The pain distant now, I float above
Above how it feels
How it feels to really be inside myself
Far from these muscles which fight her unbending.
I am somewhere else.

Uncurl me,
This self so full of wrong and shame.
She finds me each day
And calls me in.

We began again
To try to straighten what belongs bent.
Control and tame this body,
Shame its movements.
There is hope in the fixing
Hope for acceptance,
For a "normal life."
I will grow into someone else.
A straight unbent woman on her wedding day,
Beautiful,
Normal,
Walking,
Wanted.

 CB

She finds me this night
Unfurls me,
Desire filled fingers
Discover my strings,
Drawing me in.
She asks
"Is this ok,
And this?
And this?"
Waits . . .
Waits for eyes to say yes as well as mouth
Then she follows my winding tracks
Where no lover has walked before,
To hidden places,
Shame filled by another woman.
She brings them out slowly,
These tangled cords of self,
Turning them in the glow of soft light,
Small sounds,
Breath.

"Breathe,"
She says,
"It's ok."

Unraveled me
With your acceptance,
Watch me curl around you.
I think myself in love.
This space.
This body.
This night.

She finds the places that were never straightened
Too bent their natural state

Kisses them.
I am afraid they will hurt her, so strong the pain that hides
    there.

She knows not what magic she is working,
With her slow and gentle hands
Her glowing body
Drawing out my light,
Calling it love.

This one my healer.
I can let go.
Be just as I am
Growing, un-normal and delightfully bent.

Unrequited Love
(from my wheelchair to a shopping trolley)

There were sparks between us
literally
I ran into her
as I rounded the corner
too fast
and we collided
my metal grinded against her metal
I don't know whether it was consensual

It all happened in a flash
like I was being driven
by some unknown hands
propelled
forward

She was empty
the kind of empty
only shopping can fill
damn she would look good
carrying a load

She was shining under the fluro lights
pushed up against the baked-beans
I wanted to say you make canned goods
look so good
babe

You make my wheels wobbly

and my bearings loose
I wanna pop a tire for you
have you let my air out
ever
so
slowly

You immobilize me
I wanna liberate you from this monotony
take you on a joy ride
use you in ways you weren't intended
I want to have you
go down
a hill
with me

I wanna stop servicing others
and service each other
I wanna slide a coin into your slot

I wanna rub tires with you
grind rims with yours
touch your small front wheels to mine
oh who am I kidding I wanna ram you so hard that we will both
    carry the marks on our frames forever
But a supermarket is no place for such romantic gestures
and I am being driven by a dyke with a burning desire for
chocolate milk
as I get wheeled away from you
I can only hope someone picks you up
fills you up
and drives you the way you deserve to be driven

ZAK PLUM

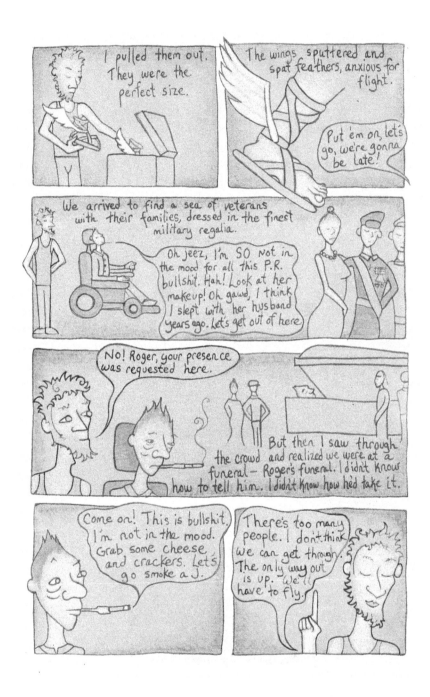

Hands That Move: Image Descriptions

Page One

Panel One. The title "Hands That Work," set in outline letters, is imposed on a background of hands that seem to flutter. The artist's name "Zak Plum" is simply written below the title.

Panel Two. On the left side is a young man with curly hair and a moustache-free beard who is narrating the story. Looking pensive with his eyes closed, he is wearing a tank top and resting a hand on his other shoulder. On the right side, beneath the word "PORTLAND!" is a suspension bridge above water. Below this are the words: "How did I get here?"

Panel Three. The narrator wraps his arms around a taller man with spiked darker hair. He looks slightly sad while the narrator, with his eyes closed, seems to be in bliss. Above them is the question: "I thought we came here together?"

Panel Four. The taller man wraps arms around himself while the narrator has turned away from him. Above them are the words: "What happened? It seems like we just met."

Panel Five. The narrator scratches his curly hair in a look of resignation. Above him are the words: "I guess I'm doing this on my own . . ."

Panel Six. In the upper left corner splotches of mold fill the angled wall beside the narrator sitting dejectedly on a bed. On the right side, the narrator says: "After you left, I moved into my friend's closet. There was black mold growing on the ceiling. I became a sex worker for three years. I felt like a character in that film we watched, you know, the one with River Phoenix . . ."

Panel Seven. On the left side is a man wearing a white tank top, holding a cigarette in his mouth, and sitting in a wheelchair. The narrator continues: "Anyway, I'm finally putting down roots. I found a normal job, as a caregiver. I work for this guy named Roger. He was paralyzed in the Iraq War, where he took a bullet in the spine. He's a quadriplegic. He's a chainsmoker."

Page Two

Panel One. On the left side is Roger, shirtless, propped up against four pillows on a bed. Above him is a hospital bed triangle lift. In front of him is a dresser on which a TV sits. A woman is talking onscreen. Above the scene are the words: "At first, I didn't think I could handle it."

Panel Two. A white toilet is simply drawn with the question marks "???" and an arrow downward at the opened toilet. The narrator, out of panel, wonders: "What if I wasn't strong enough? Or what if I was too rough? And what about when he has to shit?"

Panel Three. The narrator flicks a lighter at the end of Roger's cigarette. Roger is still on the bed. The text reads: "I was nervous, but as soon as Roger awoke, that changed."

Panel Four. On the far right is the narrator standing, with a cigarette in hand, next to Roger in a wheelchair. He is smoking too. On the left is the narrator's text: "I quickly realized how funny he was. I came to understand that this was more than just a job, that Roger was my friend and I had love for him. I saw him in his most private highs and lows . . . Yet, he never asked about my personal life. I always wondered if he knew I was queer. It wasn't until July of my seventh year that he came out."

Panel Five. On the left there is a close-up of the narrator as he asks, "Why did you go to Iraq in the first place?" On the right is also a close-up of Roger as he responds, "I was 18! I didn't know who I was. All I knew was: I just graduated from High School and I had to get away from my Christian family . . . I think I just wanted to be around all those sexy men . . . I didn't know I would get chewed up by the war machine."

Page Three

Panel One. Centered between the narrator and Roger is a TV atop a dresser. The narrator, on the left, says, "A homo, all these years, and you never told me!" Roger, looking downcast on the right, says, "I never came out to anyone. After I got wounded, what would be the point? It's not like I can have sex . . . what's the point of having an orientation?"

Panel Two. Roger, with a cigarette still in mouth, continues: "I may have been in the closet, but I was horny and I knew what I wanted. Being surrounded by all those hot soldiers sounded like a wet dream come true."

Panel Three. Roger continues: "But the reality was far more hellish than I imagined. I had bought into all the heroic bullshit after 9/11, and I needed a job. The military made a lot of promises."

Panel Four. On the right side are three naked men, mostly with their backs to us, standing under shower heads. On the left side is Roger's voiceover: "Before I got deployed, when I was in the Barracks, there were three of us who fucked each other in the shower every night, when everyone else was sleeping and that's when I learned what it means to be queer. We kept it on the down-low."

Panel Five. On the left is a huge army tank facing to the right. Roger's voiceover continues: "But when we went into the desert, I couldn't handle what I faced. I followed orders I didn't agree with. I committed unspeakable crimes. In one sense, I'm glad I got hit. It saved me from an awful situation and I came home earlier than expected. And now I get taken care of by a handsome prince. Will you light me a cigarette?"

Page Four

Panel One. On the right side the narrator's back is to us as he carries two boxes through a doorway. On the left, the narrator resumes: "That year, in the autumn, there was a torrential storm that swept over Portland for a few days. It flooded the basement of Roger's apartment building, so I was hauling a bunch of boxes upstairs."

Panel Two. The narrator peers down into a large box with the word COMIX on its side. He continues: "I pulled back the crudely folded flaps and saw a stack of books inside. The first few were pretty classic, but as I kept digging, I found something fantastic, the likes of which I had never before seen."

Panel Three. On the right is the narrator holding up a book with the title *Fearful Hunter* atop a vaguely drawn man. He says: "At first, they might have seemed like ordinary superheroes, but these men were bulging in vibrant colors. Some of the comics were more erotic, others softer and innocent." Just behind the narrator's back is a puffy cloud: "Hmm . . . maybe I'm a werewolf . . . But how do you know for sure?"

Panel Four. On the left the narrator holds up two comic books and says, "*Gay comics*?? That's a thing??" Roger, on the right, seems blasé as he replies, "Yeah, man. It's a whole subculture. I love those things."

Page Five

Panel One. Slightly hairy forearms frame the shot as the hands hold up a comic book with a vaguely drawn muscular man. The narrator's voice says, "These are so *hot!*"

Panel Two. The narrator, holding up a spiral notebook with the word *Sketch* on the cover, turns to Roger off-panel. He asks, "What's this?"

Panel Three. Roger, lying in bed, says, "Oh, uh . . . those were mine, before my injury. I never let anyone see them before . . ."

Panel Four. The narrator opens the book and looks inside. He says, "These are so well done. I didn't know you were an artist. I draw too."

Panel Five. Roger, smiling, replies, "It seems after seven years, there's still a lot we don't know about each other . . ."

Panel Six. Sketches show from left to right a surfer-type man, wearing a bikini, with superhero glasses; a partial torso; and a muscular man, wearing a harness and wrist straps, holding up his arms and flexing his biceps.

Panel Seven. On the left the narrator, clearly having taken pleasure from looking at the sketches, listens to Roger, who is on the right: "You should finish those for me. You have hands that work."

Page Six

Panel One. A shimmering moon glows outward from the upper right of the panel. Below it are these words: "Last night was the night of the full moon, when my dreams are most vivid."

Panel Two. The narrator reflects: "Roger was in my dream. I remember it clearly." Below these words the narrator has just put a nice shirt on Roger and asks, "What do you need to get all dressed up for?"

Panel Three. Roger, still smoking, says, "Oh, it's just the military making a big stink over me. You know, metals and gunshots and trumpets, the whole nine yards. Hurry, we're going to be late!"

Panel Four. As the narrator puts a shoe on Roger's foot as Roger sits in his wheelchair, he asks, "If you were a superhero, who would you be? What would be your secret power?"

Panel Five. A close-up of Roger as he responds, "I'd be able to shrink to the size of a mouse! Not all buff like the other guys. My scrawniness would be my greatest strength. How bout you? What would you wear?"

Panel Six. The narrator looks to the right and says, "Hmm . . . I'd wear something simple, but sexy. Just a toga like Hermes, you know?"

Panel Seven. Roger responds, "Why Hermes?"

Panel Eight. The narrator and Roger, both in close-up, face each other. The narrator says, "Because superheroes are like gods in a way, you know? Mythology for the modern age. Someone to look up to. Besides, Hermes is a total homo." Roger responds, "Yeah, you'd have to be a huge queen to wear boots like that . . . Look in my closet, I might still have a pair."

Page Seven

Panel One. The narrator pulls a pair of sandals with wings on them out of a box. Above him are these words: "I pulled them out. They were the perfect size."

Panel Two. Above a close-up of the narrator's foot inside the sandal are these words: "The wings sputtered and spat feathers, anxious for flight." Off-panel is Roger's voice: "Put 'em on, let's go, we're gonna be late!"

Panel Three. On the left side are the narrator standing and Roger, all dressed up, in his wheelchair. On the right side are three people: a woman with a tight bun on her hair, a soldier in uniform, and a man next to him. Above the scene are these words: "We arrived to find a sea of veterans with their families, dressed in the finest military regalia. Roger says, "Oh jeez, I'm *so* not in the mood for all this P.R. bullshit. Hah! Look at her makeup. Oh, gawd, I think I slept with her husband years ago. Let's get out of here."

Panel Four. On the left side, the narrator is close to Roger, who is looking downcast. The narrator says, "No! Roger, your presence was requested here." Off to the right side are four people surrounding Roger in his open casket. Below are these words: "But then I saw through the crowd and realized we were at a funeral—Roger's funeral. I didn't know how to tell him. I didn't know how he'd take it."

Panel Five. Roger says, "Come on! This is bullshit. I'm not in the mood. Grab some cheese and crackers. Let's go smoke a J."

Panel Six. The narrator holds up his index finger and says, "There's too many people. I don't think we can get through. The only way out is up. We'll have to fly."

Page Eight

Panel One. From the left side, the narrator looks at Roger's arms, akimbo like wings, as he sits in his wheelchair. Above the narrator are these words: "Roger started flapping his arms."

Panel Two. A close-up of Roger shows his reaction as he says, "Whoa! I didn't know I could do that!"

Panel Three. A close-up of the narrator shows him smiling a little. He says, "Come on! Let's go before they notice."

Panel Four. The narrator, wearing his winged sandals, floats upward with Roger who has flapped his arm-wings and lifted off from his wheelchair.

Panel Five. Roger looks exasperated. "I can't!" he says. "I don't think I can do this. I'm tired."

Panel Six. Both men look off to the side. The narrator says, "No way! You got this!" Roger responds, "Will you come with me? Will you help me?"

ଓଷ

Page Nine

In a panel that fills the entire page, the two men are floating upward against a background of stars and constellations and galaxies. The narrator points upward at Roger, who is higher than him, and says, "I'm letting go now. You don't need me anymore. Keep going that way. You're free now."

Page Ten

Panel One. The narrator faces a long-haired woman who is looking downcast. He says, "I want you to know about this dream I had last night, because I think he was ready to go. This body was like a prison to him."

Panel Two. The woman leans forward and embraces the narrator. Above them are these words: "Roger's sister hugged me." She says, "Thank you for taking care of him. I know that he really appreciated you."

Panel Three. Roger's sister carries two boxes near a doorway.

Panel Four. The narrator says, "Wait!"

Panel Five. The narrator stands in front of a box that has COMIX written on its side. He says, "He wanted me to have these." There's a little creature atop the box.

Panel Six. A close-up of the COMIX box top reveals a mouse, its tail curled over the edge.

CONTRIBUTORS

D. ALLEN is a queer and genderqueer poet with Ehlers-Danlos Syndrome, a connective tissue disorder. They are currently working on their first collection of poems and lyric essays, which explores the metaphorical and lyrical implications of connective tissue and its absence and aims to recreate in language what the poet's body lacks in material. D. lives in Minneapolis and is a second-year M.F.A. candidate at the University of Minnesota.

BEX is a Bay Area painter and cartoonist. She has worked as a prop/set fabrication intern for the Emmy award-winning series *Robot Chicken* and as an artist's assistant. Bex is currently working on a graphic novel about the psychogeography of a fictional city. [bex-f.tumblr.com]

JAX JACKI BROWN is a disability and queer rights activist, writer, spoken-word performer, and independent producer of disability theater in Melbourne, Australia. Jax has been published in *Daily Life, The Feminist Observer, Archer Magazine*, and *ABC Australia*. She holds a degree in Cultural Studies and Communication where she examined the intersections between disability and queer identities. Jax presents workshops on disability and sexuality, and is a lesbian and out and proud wheelchair user. [fukability.blogspot.com.au]

LYDIA BROWN is an East Asian, queer, and autistic activist, writer, and speaker who identifies as genderqueer and asexual. Their work has largely focused on violence against multiply-marginalized disabled people. Lydia co-founded the Washington Metro Disabled Students Collective for intersectional disability justice organizing, and is the visionary behind a forthcoming anthology by autistic people of color. Lydia has been honored by the White House, the Washington Peace Center, Pacific Standard, and Mic. For several years, Lydia has also worked with the Autistic Self Advocacy Network. [autistichoya.com]

LARRY CONNOLLY, author and editor, teaches in the Professional Writing Major at Champlain College. For several years he was the Prose Editor for the literary journal *Memoir*. He lives in Vermont with his husband (John), a Shetland pony (Raindrop), a Border collie (Zephyr), and a three-legged semi-feral cat (Lana).

DAVID CUMMER was born in Saint Cloud, Minnesota, and comes from a long line of rabblerousers. That being the case, the moment he came out, Cummer leaped into activism full-force, having worked with ACT UP Minnesota, The Names Project, Join The Impact - Twin Cities, and Occupy Minnesota. He is also an ordained Presbyterian Elder at Grace Trinity Community Church, and has been quoted many times saying, "I think writing about myself in the third person is weird."

BRENNA CYR is a genderfluid queer social worker from Minnesota who is currently living in Boston. Although most of their time is spent trying to reduce the rates of HIV transmission by talking to teenagers about having safer sex, they also take part in LGBTQ activism efforts and regularly try to convince themselves to go to church. As a person who has lived with rheumatoid arthritis for over a decade, they find themselves drifting toward activities that come naturally, like eating cookies.

CHRISTOPHER DEMPSEY is "small d" deaf and gay, and lives in Auckland, Aotearoa. He's oral and only knows some signs. He's also a cyclist (commuter and touring) and a radical faerie; loves books and cooking. Involved in local body politics, he is a Green Party member. This is his first contribution to an anthology; he is currently co-editing an anthology of Aotearoa NZ Rainbow Poetry.

MEG DAY is the 2015-2016 recipient of the Amy Lowell Poetry Travelling Scholarship, a 2013 recipient of an NEA Fellowship in Poetry, and the author of *Last Psalm at Sea Level* (Barrow Street 2014). Day received her Ph.D. in Poetry and Disability Poetics from the University of Utah where she was a Steffensen-Cannon Fellow and a United States Point Scholar. Day is Assistant Professor of English and Creative Writing at Franklin & Marshall College and lives in Lancaster, Pennsylvania. [megday.com]

CARL WAYNE DENNEY split his time between Indiana and Kentucky growing up before attending and graduating from Gallaudet University. He has been a teacher, administrator and athletic coach at various Deaf Schools the past fifteen years. He currently lives in Fishers, Indiana with his family.

ARTHUR DURKEE discovered he was queer in junior high, where the boys' swim classes were taught in the nude. After graduating from music school, he spent his working career doing graphic design until an undiagnosed chronic illness led him near death, and surgery. Now living with a mostly invisible disability albeit with renewed libido, he has discovered that what he does best, no surprise really, is make art, make music, and write poems. Now all he needs is a steady boyfriend! [arthurdurkee.net]

MARK ELLIS lived most of his childhood in Tennessee, but left as soon as he was old enough—to study, travel, and work, eventually becoming a medievalist and a librarian. Later in life, he returned to the land of his childhood. He writes primarily poetry and fiction as well as articles and presentations on medieval literature. He loves to read his poetry at open mic events, and has published in *RFD* and *Glitterwolf* and has a couple of stories in *Red Truck Review*.

MONIQUE FLYNN lives in Western Massachusetts where she works in Human Services and advocates to end the stigma surrounding mental health. She graduated from the University at Albany where she studied Sociology and Gender Studies. Monique identifies as a Queer Femme.

ALLISON FRADKIN may be hard-of-hearing, but she isn't hard-of-queering. She has a gay old time editing the yearly queerly *Off the Rocks: An Anthology of GLBT Writing* for NewTown Writers Press. She also serves as the Literary Manager for Pride Films and Plays' LezPlay contest, as an Editorial Consultant for Bella Books, and as a book reviewer for the online outlet of *Curve Magazine*. Allison's writing appears onstage and in print, most recently in *Through the Hourglass: An Anthology of Lesbian Historical Romance*. [allisonfradkin.blogspot.com]

KENNY FRIES is the author of *The History of My Shoes and the Evolution of Darwin's Theory* and *Body, Remember: A Memoir,* as well as the editor of *Staring Back: The Disability Experience from the Inside Out*. His books of poetry include *Anesthesia* and *Desert Walking*. Houston Grand Opera commissioned him to write the libretto for *The Memory Stone*, which premiered at Asia Society Texas Center. Forthcoming is *In the Province of the Gods*, for which he received a Creative Capital grant in innovative literature. [kennyfries.com]

JOEL GATES enjoys various outdoor sports and socializing with friends and family. He loves to travel and enjoy photography. His goal is to become a civil engineer.

BEATRICE HALE, also known as "Bea," is a colorful Deaf multimedia artist and writer living in rural North Carolina where she teaches ASL at a local high school. As a survivor of a brain injury and post-traumatic stress, she is also an activist for those with invisible disabilities. When she isn't creating, she spends time in her garden. Bea most enjoys traveling with her husband

and their four children as well as sitting outside watching lightning bugs with their three cats: Scout, Benedick, and Jellicle.

TAK HALLUS was born out of a desert wind on a bleak January of ice and sand. He absorbed the complete works of Antoine de St. Exupéry and Tom Waits through his mother's milk, and mastered existentialism and logotherapy before escaping high school to work a tramp steamer across the International Date Line. His chief claim to fame, other than a genius IQ, is his formidable stamina for surviving events that would have killed almost anyone else.

STEPHANIE HEIT is an artist living with bipolar disorder who engages with herself and the world through multiple creative practices: movement as a dancer and massage therapist, and words as a poet and teacher. She received a B.A. in Dance and M.F.A. in Writing and Poetics from Naropa University. Awarded a Poetry Fellowship from the Colorado Council on the Arts, Stephanie has had her work appear in *Midwestern Gothic, Nerve Lantern,* and *Research in Drama Education: The Journal of Applied Theatre and Performance.*

SARA IBRAHAM is currently living in the Middle East. She is interested in disability and race, and is trying to voice oppression that is personal and political. She is currently working on her first novel that explores homosexuality and disability.

JASON T. INGRAM, who has been on disability for bipolar since 2009, is a multimedia artist with a professional music background. He was raised in a liberal family in Oregon and moved to Alaska where he became a born-again Christian for twelve years. Jason came out as gay in 2006 and has been speaking out publicly about his five years in the so-called ex-gay movement by telling his story with original art, songs and short films around the United States. [sites.google.com/site/sundaydriverproductions]

CYRÉE JARELLE JOHNSON is a Black non-binary essayist and poet living with Systemic Lupus Erythematosus and C-PTSD in Philadelphia, Pennsylvania. Their writing considers disability as a cyborg femme reality, femininity as resistance and rebellion, and Black pessimism. They are a founding member of A Collective Apparition, a Black queer and trans interdisciplinary arts collective.

JOHN R. KILLACKY lives in Vermont. He was the co-editor of and contributor to the Lambda Literary Award-winning anthology *Queer Crips: Disabled Gay Men and Their Stories.*

PETRA KUPPERS is a disability culture activist, a wheelchair-using community performance artist, a Professor at the University of Michigan, and artistic director of The Olimpias. She has published poems and short stories in journals like *PANK, Visionary Tongue, Wordgathering, Poets for Living Waters, Disability Studies Quarterly, Beauty is a Verb: New Poetics of Disability, textsound, Streetnotes, Epistemologies,* and *Accessing the Future. Cripple Poetics,* her collaborative book of poetry with Neil Marcus and Lisa Steichmann, was published by Homofactus Press.

TRAVIS CHI WING LAU is a doctoral candidate at the Department of English at the University of Pennsylvania. He specializes in eighteenth- and nineteenth-century British fiction, the history of medicine, and disability studies. His dissertation explores the cultural history of immunity and vaccination. Outside of the university, he maintains a blog featuring primarily poetry and short fiction. He is currently working on a short chapbook as well as a forthcoming memoir featuring the prose piece included in this anthology. [tchilau.tumblr.com]

KATHARINA LOVE is a retired psychotherapist launching her career as a writer. Katharina is interested in memoir, the esoteric arts, and issues related to the LGBT community. Katharina currently lives in Toronto. She has two daughters and the cutest puppy on the planet, whom she named after B.B. King's guitar, Lucille.

TORANSE LOWELL is a survivor of child abuse and often writes about the intersection of abuse and conservative Christianity. They live in the Pacific Northwest.

RAYMOND LUCZAK is the author and editor of 17 books. Titles as editor include *From Heart into Art: Interviews with Deaf and Hard of Hearing Artists and Their Allies* and *Eyes of Desire 2: A Deaf GLBT Reader.* His Deaf gay novel *Men with Their Hands* won first place in the Project: QueerLit Contest 2006. He lives in Minneapolis, Minnesota. [raymondluczak.com]

LIV MAMMONE recently completed her M.F.A. at Queens College where she was an adjunct. Prior, she worked as an assistant to both Phillis Levin and Connie Roberts, professors of poetry at Hofstra University. Her work has appeared in *Wordgathering, Wicked Banshee, The Medical Journal of Australia,* and is forthcoming in *Grabbing the Apple: an Anthology of Women Poets of New York City.* She has performed poetry at Sip This, Union Square Slam, and Artists Without Walls, where she has recently accepted the post of publicist. [livmammone.tumblr.com]

ADAM MARSNIK (Photographer) is a full-time college librarian and a part-time freelance art photographer in Minneapolis, Minnesota. He enjoys photographing everyday things in a way that not only catches the eye but also reveals the often-overlooked beauty all around us. Adam's work runs the gamut from landscapes to architecture and the hidden details found in nature. He will launch his fine art photography web site this year.

KIT MEAD is a disability rights advocate currently living in the metro Atlanta, Georgia area. They run the Atlanta Chapter of the Autistic Self Advocacy Network. Kit is proudly autistic and queer, and blogs. [kpaginatedthoughts. blogspot.com.]

DONNA MINKOWITZ is the author of the Lammy-finalist memoir *Growing Up Golem: How I Survived My Mother, Brooklyn, and Some Really Bad Dates*. She is also the restaurant critic for *Gay City News* in New York. Minkowitz won a Lambda Literary Award for her first memoir, *Ferocious Romance: What My Encounters with the Right Taught Me About Sex, God, and Fury*, and she has also written for *The New York Times Book Review, Salon, The Nation*, and *Ms.* [donnaminkowitz.com]

ANDREW MORRISON-GURZA is a Disability Awareness Consultant whose passion is "making disability accessible to everyone." Within the LGBTQ+ community, Andrew works to deconstruct our homo-normative, body beautiful ideals and show that Queers with Disabilities deserve representation. His goal is to welcome everyone into the conversation of disability. His written work has been highlighted in *The Advocate, Huffington Post,* and *The Good Men Project*, where he candidly discusses the realities of sex and disability as a Queer Cripple. [andrewmorrisongurza.com]

ZAK PLUM grew up in the Arizona desert where his art was inspired by the harsh creatures and jagged landscape. He graduated with a Bachelor's in Fine Arts from the University of Arizona in 2009. Zak lives in Portland, Oregon, where he writes and illustrates comics. His book series *Rites of Dionysus* explores the spirituality of queer people in the uncertainty of our times. [zakplum.com]

MARIKA PROKOSH is a writer, book slinger, and library factotum living in Winnipeg, Manitoba. Her poetry has appeared in print in *Poetry Is Dead, CV2, Prairie Fire*, and *rip/torn*, and online at *Lemon Hound* and at *The Toast*, where she also writes the monthly advice column "The Spinster's Almanac."

KRISTEN RINGMAN is a Deaf writer, sailor, traveler, and mother. She is currently working on a YA nautical science fiction trilogy set in Southeast Asia which features a range of marginal characters—from Deaf to queer to an android who becomes sentient. She is the author of *Makara* (Handtype Press, 2012), a lyrical novel about a Deaf lesbian, whose mother is an Irish selchie, falling in love in South India. She received her M.F.A. from Goddard College in 2008. [kristenringman.com]

MICHAEL RUSSELL is a 25-year-old queer poet who is working on his first collection. He lives at home in Toronto with his mother, her husband, and two dogs Hoover and Sassy. In his spare time he likes to read and write. His work has appeared in *The Quilliad*.[seamlessyesterdays.tumblr.com]

BARBARA RUTH passed as able-bodied until she fell off the map of the known world in 1983 for reasons in large part iatrogenic. She now lives with multiple chemical sensitivities syndrome, arthritis, fibromyalgia and seizure disorder. She is Neuroqueer, Ashkenazi Jewish, and Potowatomee. She was born in Kansas and lives currently in San Jose, California, and she is a photographer, poet, and memoirist. Her work has been published in numerous lesbian, queer, disability, and literary journals and anthologies.

LUCAS SCHEELK is a white, autistic, trans, mentally ill, queer-identified poet from the Twin Cities—born in Minneapolis and raised in St. Paul. Lucas uses "he, him, his" pronouns and "they, them, their" pronouns. Lucas is read as a guy, but feels more comfortable being referred to as an individual, rather than as a man. In his spare time, Lucas analyzes autistic coding in modern media (especially Sherlock Holmes adaptations), and takes life fabulously one day at a time. Keep an eye out for his first poetry book *This Is a Clothespin* (Damaged Goods Press). [Twitter: @TC221Bee]

JAMES SCHWARTZ is an ex-Amish poet and slam performer. He is the author of *The Literary Party: Growing Up Gay and Amish in America* (inGroup Press, 2011) and *Arrival and Departure* (Writing Knights Press, 2014). He resides in Michigan. [literaryparty.blogspot.com]

MAVERICK SMITH, a Deaf*, queer, trans*, disabled, genderqueer person, has always been interested in social justice and equity. They current reside on the traditional lands of the Mississaugas of the New Credit and are engaged in activism-based social service work related to intersectionality of their various identities.

THE POET SPIEL, after a lifetime of mental illness and decades of psychotherapy, has acquired a lot of rich material to work with. At age 74, confounded by loss associated with vascular dementia, he finds himself struggling to keep his lips above desolation. Internationally published as The Poet, Spiel's most recent book is *Dirty Sheets: 28 stories of passion, pathos, and payback* (Rain Mountain Press). [thepoetspiel.name]

WHITTIER STRONG is a M.F.A. candidate in nonfiction at the University of Alaska-Fairbanks and serves as nonfiction editor for *Permafrost*. His work has appeared in *The Rumpus, Cooper Street, Matchbook Literary, Three Line Poetry, Jonathan*, and *Among the Leaves: Queer Male Poets on the Midwestern Experience*. A native of Indiana, he has also lived in Missouri and Minnesota. [whittierstrong.wordpress.com]

JOHN WHITTIER TREAT is a writer who has lived in Seattle since 1983. His first novel, *The Rise and Fall of the Yellow House*, was published in 2015. Treat is at work now on a second novel, *First Consonants*, about a stutterer who saves the world. [johntreat.com]

GREGORY VILLA (pronounced *VEE-yah*) is a newcomer to Portland, Oregon, having lived in Florida, Texas, and North Dakota. During that time Villa has worked behind the scenes, and as an actor, in film, television, and radio. He has written professionally for enough LGBT publications that you could choke a goat. He wants to be Molly Ivins when he grows up.

ASHLEY VOLION is a queer woman with Cerebral Palsy. Currently, she is pursuing a Ph.D. in Disability Studies at the University of Illinois at Chicago. She works as a Policy Assistant at the Advocacy Center, Louisiana's Protection and Advocacy agency, in New Orleans, and remotely as a Research Assistant at the University of Illinois at Chicago researching the effects of interstate variation of Medicaid Home and Community-Based Services. Ashley's wide range of research interests include sexuality and disability, personal care services, and stories as a form of knowledge.

NOLA WEBER is a recent graduate of the School of the Art Institute of Chicago whose written work explores diverse understandings of visibility and alternative sexuality. This is her first published piece. She can be reached at nola.k.weber@gmail.com.

QUINTAN ANA WIKSWO is a writer and visual artist whose work integrates fiction, poetry, memoir, and essay with her photographs, performance, and video. Author of *The Hope of Floating Has Carried Us This Far* (Coffee House Press, 2015), her work is published, performed, and exhibited internationally; including multiple anthologies; artist books; magazines such as *Tin House, Guernica, Conjunctions, Gulf Coast*, and more; and in large-scale solo museum exhibitions in New York City and Berlin. She holds fellowships from Creative Capital and multiple residencies at Yaddo. [quintananawikswo.com]

DONNA WILLIAMS is a Deaf queer poet based in Bristol, U.K. She composes and performs poetry in English and British Sign Language on subjects ranging from identity to cats. In addition to poetry, she's written articles for *The Limping Chicken*, short plays, and a M.A. dissertation. A geek, she likes *Dr. Who, Discworld*, and anything written by Joss Whedon. [deaffirefly.com.]

KATHI WOLFE's *The Uppity Blind Girl Poems* (BrickHouse Books, 2015) was the winner of the 2014 Stonewall Chapbook Competition. Her other books include *The Green Light* (Finishing Line Press, 2013) and *Helen Takes The Stage: The Helen Keller Poems* (Pudding House, 2008). Wolfe is a contributor to the anthology *Beauty Is a Verb: The New Poetry of Disability*. In 2008, Wolfe was a Lambda Literary Foundation Emerging Writer Fellow.

ACKNOWLEDGMENTS

D. Allen's "A Collection of Thorns" first appeared in *cream city review*. The piece has been altered for publication in this anthology.

Jax Jacki Brown's "The Politics of Pashing" first appeared in *Archer Magazine*.

Lydia Brown's "How Not to Plan Disability Conferences" first appeared in their blog *Autistic Hoya*.

Meg Day's "On What I Didn't Hear You Say" first appeared in *Drunken Boat*.

Kenny Fries's "Disability Made Me Do It or Modeling for the Cause" is excerpted from his book *The History of My Shoes and the Evolution of Darwin's Theory* (Carroll and Graf, 2007). His poems ("Body Language," "Dressing the Wound," and "Beauty and Variations") come from his book *Anesthesia: Poems* (The Avocado Press, 1996).

John R. Killacky's "Necessary Action" comes from his video *Necessary Action* (2000); "Dreaming Awake," *Dreaming Awake* (2003); and "Night Swimming," *Night Swimming* (2004). All three were previously published online in *bent*, and an earlier version of "Dreaming Awake" appeared in Bob Guter and John R. Killacky's *Queer Crips: Disabled Gay Men and Their Stories* (Routledge, 2003).

Raymond Luczak's poems "My First Kill" first appeared in *Assaracus: A Journal of Gay Poetry*, and "Savages" first appeared in *RFD Magazine*.

Liv Mammone's "Vagina Resigning" first appeared in *Wordgathering*.

Donna Minkowitz's "How I Got Disabled" comes from her memoir *Growing Up Golem: How I Survived My Mother, Brooklyn, and Some Really Bad Dates* (Riverdale Avenue Books, 2013).

The Poet Spiel's "lapse" first appeared in *Poiesis*.

Quintan Ana Wikswo's "Charité" (originally entitled "Mercy Killing Aktion") first appeared in *Witness*.

Kathi Wolfe's poems ("Love at First Sight," "Mind's Eye," "Blind Porn," "A Pulp Fiction," and "If I Were a Boy") come from her book *The Uppity Blind Girl Poems* (BrickHouse Books, 2015).

ABOUT THE PUBLISHER

Established in 2007, Handtype Press is a company that showcases the finest literature and art created by signers, Deaf and hearing alike, or about the Deaf or signing experience the world over. Titles published include John Lee Clark's *Where I Stand: On the Signing Community and My DeafBlind Experience* and Kristen Ringman's Lambda Literary Award-nominated novel *Makara*. [handtype.com]

In 2012, Handtype created a new imprint called Squares & Rebels to bring out books initially about the LGBT experience in the Midwest. Titles included Kate Lynn Hibbard's *When We Become Weavers: Queer Female Poets on the Midwestern Experience* and Gregg Shapiro's *Lincoln Avenue: Chicago Stories*. With the publication of *QDA: A Queer Disability Anthology*, S&R has expanded its focus to include books that explore the queer and/or disability experience regardless of one's region of origin. [squaresandrebels.com]

Lightning Source UK Ltd.
Milton Keynes UK
UKHW011101231118
332829UK00006B/511/P